Hennen's Public Library Planner: A Manual and Interactive CD-ROM

Thomas J. Hennen, Jr.

Neal-Schuman Publishers, Inc.

New York London

Published by Neal-Schuman Publishers, Inc.
100 William Street, Suite 2004
New York, NY 10038

Printed and bound in the United States of America.

The paper used in this publication meets the minimum requirements of American National Standard for Information Sciences Permanence of Paper for Printed Library Materials, ANSI Z39.48-1992.

Library of Congress Cataloging-in-Publication Data

Hennen, Thomas J.
    Hennen's public library planner: a manual and interactive CD-ROM / by Thomas J. Hennen, Jr.
        p. cm.
    Includes bibliographical references and index.
    ISBN 1-55570-487-5 (alk. paper)
    1. Public libraries—Planning—Handbooks, manuals, etc. 2. Public libraries—United States—Planning—Handbooks, manuals, etc. I. Title: Public library planner. II. Title.

Z678.H46 2004
025.I'94—dc22
                                                                            2003071059

Dedication

To my Father,
who taught me that
thinking in rows and columns
won't stop your dreams.

Table of Contents

IV. Hennen's Handbook of Support Material

List of Figures

Chapter 1

Chapter 2

Chapter 3

Chapter 4

Chapter 5

Chapter 6

Chapter 7

Chapter 8

Chapter 9

Chapter 10

Appendix 1

Appendix 2

Preface

Successful library planners need a broad range of principles and data as well as vision and resolve. *Hennen's Public Library Planner: A Manual and Interactive CD-ROM* provides the tools and perspectives necessary to plan great library services. Its underlying philosophy is that, while every library and its plan should be unique to its community, no plan should be developed without comparison to other libraries. Plans should be developed based on principles and policies common to the grand ongoing experiment that is the American Public Library.

A winning library needs to go forward to basics, not back to basics. The basics include solid budgeting and finances, good policy development, and attention to what others have done well.

Purpose

Hennen's Public Library Planner recognizes that, while developing a library plan can be relatively easy, creating an *effective* plan is a true challenge. Effective planning does not start when an authority calls for a plan, nor does it stop when the planning committee presents its report; effective library planning is ongoing.

Audience

Hennen's Public Library Planner: A Manual and Interactive CD-ROM is intended for passionate people who want to make public libraries great. It is for library administrators, boards, and staff. It's specifically for the "library planner's" different stakeholders (the board, administration, council, planning committee, and so on) who have different responsibilities at different points in planning. It addresses the roles and responsibilities of each for the plan and for its implementation. Library Friends groups, elected officials, and library users will also find much information of value. The manual is for use with graduate school students in management and planning courses as well.

Perspective

The text differs from other public library planning books. It recommends that a library do comparisons with other libraries of comparable size and provides convenient methods for doing so. It insists that planners take inventories of current library policies and activities and address changes in written plans.

Hennen's Public Library Planner tackles nearly every aspect of effective public library planning. It deals with the substantial differences in governance, budgeting, and political structures of the 9,000 public libraries in the country. These differences matter for effective planning and all the planners need to bear them in mind.

This manual also examines many of the forces affecting today's American libraries. When planning, how do they learn how to think outside the box? More modestly, how do they simply reinvent the box that they are in? For example, changing the political or governance structure of a library is rare, of course, but planners should consider their options carefully in every planning cycle. The section on special planning issues addresses a number of these issues, including changing the form of organization of the library to a district or joint library and establishing alternative funding sources like impact fees or e-commerce.

Libraries with effective plans improve their funding, service profile, and their customer satisfaction ratings. Using the methods outlined in *Hennen's Public Library Planner*, I have worked with libraries to achieve a number of important things. Here are some planning success stories:

> The National Association of Counties presented a 2002 National Achievement Award to Wisconsin's Waukesha

County Federated Library System for planning efforts using the techniques presented in this book. A few examples involve libraries of various sizes with greatly differing needs.

In one small library, the written plan came up for approval by the city council the same night that they first got the news of the most major cut in state revenue in a generation. The mayor, a participant in the planning process, spoke eloquently of the need to restore the library to its rightful place in the municipal service profile. Notwithstanding the state budget cuts, the council endorsed the plan to continue seeking a new building and to implement its first ever automated circulation system.

A major report on the potential merger of two entire communities (not just the library operation) was being discussed for a suburban city of 7,000 and an adjacent city of 13,000. One city had an existing but cramped and substandard library. The other city had no library, relying instead on existing state and county provisions for library extension and funding. The communities requested a particularly challenging type of plan that looked at three alternatives: a stand-alone city library, a second stand-alone city library, and a joint library. Further challenges included mandatory county library standards, a devastating impact on county funding, and a city administrator's recommendation to close the existing library because of the state budget crisis noted above! Despite the complexity of the challenges, the plan outlined the options, and it is anticipated that the library will be in new quarters by the end of the year.

Another community of 6,000 built a new library in a rapidly expanding community just five years before, but found itself quickly running out of space. Its effective service territory was at least twice the population of the city and within ten years will easily be over four times its current size. The planning effort resulted in the development of an impact fee policy that generated a fee of about $400 for each new house built in the community. The funding will help pay for the needed expansion of the library and its collection.

A community of 40,000 with one of the best HAPLR ratings in the country, a new building, and a very high rate of local support developed a plan using these principles. The planners resolved to build on the current great service profile and, among other things, become, in the words of the board president, "the premier digital library in the Midwest, if not the nation."

Percentile Comparisons

Hennen's Public Library Planner touches on nearly every aspect of effective public library planning. In the cases where more in-depth discussion may be needed building planning, technology planning, budgeting, bonding, and referendum planning reliable sources are recommended in the text and in the bibliography.

I developed Hennen's American Public Library Ratings (HAPLR) to compare library performance on key measures. I believe HAPLR to be a useful tool, of course, but using this manual in no way requires library planners to use HAPLR ratings.

The comparisons in the percentile measures section allow planners to gauge where they are by comparison to other libraries their size. Not every library will choose to try to be in the top percentile for every library measure. An affluent suburban community with no problems with total municipal debt and tax loads will make different choices than will a struggling and impoverished one or an underfunded library in a rapidly growing community. The important thing is to look at how the library compares and then make informed choices.

Organization

The book deals with the three main parts of the planning process: Planning to Plan, Considering Essential Background Information, and Developing and Implementing the Plan.

Part I, "Planning to Plan," offers three chapters.

Chapter 1, "Setting the Stage," discusses assessing motivation, deciding on whether to use a consultant, determining the plan writer, accomplishing preliminary tasks, and establishing a budget.

Chapter 2, "Designing an Effective Long-Range Planning Document," examines getting initial impressions, asking overview questions, and establishing planning trends and outlines. It also looks at more than a dozen separate elements, including the executive summary, process description, mission and value statements, state standards, timelines, goals, and budgets.

Chapter 3, "Building Consensus for the Planning Elements," discusses setting rules, getting support, developing a vision, employing consensus-building tools, utilizing surveys and questionnaires, and communicating the planning process and the plan.

Part II, "Considering Essential Background Information," consists of the following chapters:

Chapter 4, "Using Comparative Data Effectively," contains a variety of information about data including data comparisons, demographics, federal and state data and statistics, and presentation of data graphically.

Chapter 5, "Defining Library Standards and Percentile Comparisons," gives not only a history of library standards, but also a list of current numerical and prescriptive standards, instructions and examples of staff certification, an explanation of how standards vary from state-to-state, and suggestions of how to use this data to set the standards for your own library.

Chapter 6, "Integrating Financial and Governance Issues into the Plan," talks about control and custody of funds, various types of taxation, audits and GASB 34, types of funds, library debt management, and everything else you need to know about proper fund handling for your library.

Part III, "Developing and Implementing the Plan," consists of four chapters.

Chapter 7, "Defining Major Planning Sections," covers electronic services, collection development, technology, access and facilities, staffing and personnel matters, and other service issues.

Chapter 8, "Planning for New Organizational Options," asks the question: "Are Wider Library Units Wiser?" and expands on other considerations for new forms of governance for your library.

Chapter 9, "be Using the Planning Checklist and Revising Policies," covers issues such as governance, funding, staffing, continuing education, special needs, reference services, and library policy revisions.

Chapter 10, "Writing and Implementing the Plan," includes all the practical material that's essential for the processes involved in writing and implementing your library's plan.

Part IV, "Hennen's Handbook of Support Material" includes a bibliography with over one hundred valuable sources including books in ten basic planning areas, as well as links to trustee manuals, outcome based measures, and outcome assessments.

This handbook also furnishes useful material that includes: HAPLR ratings information, recommended percentile measures for library comparisons, a sample impact fee statement, and two very different public library plans.

As the dedication indicates, I think in rows and columns. I provide numerous checklists and spreadsheets to help guide planners, but I have tried to remember throughout what my father taught me about not letting the rows and columns get in the way of the dreams. Without the details, dreams of greatness remain just dreams. Never let the dreamers ignore the rows, the columns, and the bottom line; but also never let the spreadsheet users obscure the vision.

Acknowledgments

In acknowledgements, the author's family often comes last, but not here. My wife Valerie has been the unacknowledged coauthor of *everything* I have ever published, including this book. No author could ask for a better editor or a better friend. My son Tom worked on much of the spreadsheet and Web site design for this book and the HAPLR ratings thanks. My loving daughter Rachel has taken a keen interest in my writing at all times, never fails to encourage me when I get down, and has become a key assistant in the process of preparing library reports so, thanks. Other members of my extended family, and there are many, dealt cheerfully with missed graduations, parties, and other responsibilities as I worked on the book. Thanks especially to my mother, who has been encouraging me to write a book since the third grade, and to my father, who, to our great sadness, did not live to see the book.

Thanks must go to the many library boards that allowed me to help them plan. Each of them taught me much. The Brookfield Public Library Plan is reprinted with permission. The Barbara Sanborn Library in Pewaukee, Wisconsin, and the libraries in Big Bend, Butler, Eagle, Menomonee Falls, Mukwonago, and Town Hall joined the Waukesha County Federated Library System in planning endeavors.

Dave Polodna of Winding Rivers Library System graciously allowed the printing of the Planning Issues Checklist in Chapter 2. A great staff helped with these plans as part of their library system duties. Thanks to Claudia Backus, Diane Barwinski, Nancy

Fletcher, Laurie Freund, Nancy Hause, Sandy Jaeger, and Mellanie Mercier.

Thanks must also go to the excellent editorial staff at *American Libraries* magazine, including Leonard Kniffel, Beverly Goldberg, Karen G. Schneider, and Gordon Flagg. All have edited articles I have written on HAPLR ratings, library standards, library districts, and budgets in the red. Substantial portions of those articles, much improved by their editorial assistance, are included in this book.

John Carlo Bertot, Charles McClure, Joe Ryan, and ALA publications deserve credit for permission to reprint the networked environment tables (Figures 7–1 and 7–2). The PUBLIB listserv, co-moderated by Karen Schneider and Sara Weissman, provides over 5,000 public librarians a unique sounding board for the discussion of public library issues. I greatly appreciate the advice and suggestions on this book, HAPLR ratings, and other issues that members have provided to me as "DatCalmGuy" over the years since I started subscribing in 1998.

It is no wonder that public library professionals so highly value Neal-Schuman books. They have an extraordinary editorial staff. Charles Harmon provided prompt and efficient editorial direction and forgave ill-considered e-mails from the author thanks. Michael Kelley provided expert guidance and support throughout the production process.

Did I mention that my wife is a great editor and my best friend? Oh, yeah, that's where the acknowledgements began. What better place to end? Except for this: She thinks I look sexy in the kitchen with a mop in hand. Is that effective planning for clean floors, or what?

What's On the CD-ROM?

All 104 figures (including the two sample plans, and the sample impact fee statement) are included on the CD-ROM as either Microsoft Excel spreadsheets or as Microsoft Word documents (see the complete list on pages vii–xi.).

The Interactive Element of the CD-ROM—the Capital Cost Calculator

The attached CD includes a handy tool that the author has developed for projecting capital costs. Planners will need to collect the needed data population, tax base, square feet needed, interest rate for funds borrowed, term of the loan, and so forth. Once the data are available, the spreadsheet allows planners to experiment with an infinite number of "what if" scenarios. (Note that the CD also has instructions for how to change the parameters for each slider bar if they do not meet your needs.)

Library planners often find themselves asked to estimate the costs of building a new library. The answer to the question depends on many factors and can be highly controversial, so be very careful.

The *Capital Cost Calculator* can be very effective for planners when used with a computer and projected on a screen for the library board or a community group. It is then easy to demonstrate that there is no one "answer" to the "how much will it cost" question. There are several uncertain variables affecting the cost how the bids for various components come in, how large the building is (something that is usually not known for certain in the early stages of a program), the size and term of the loan, and the prevailing interest rates.

How to use the Interactive "Capital Cost Calculator" on the CD-ROM

Enter your library's name in cell C1. Enter the population served in cell C2, and the total property tax base in cell C3. (Note that property value assessments vary quite widely in the U.S. Some jurisdictions require property to be assessed at or near full market value while others allow assessment for tax purposes to be as little as 5 or 10 percent of market value.) In cell E23, the national "average" is listed at $60,000 using full market value, but if your jurisdiction assesses at, say, 33% of market value, you will want to reset this value to 33 percent of $60,000 or $20,000 to get a proper comparison.

Do not change any other values directly in their cells; move the horizontal slider bars back and forth to change the values.

This is what a slider bar looks like:

On the spreadsheet, you can either pull the tab along horizontally or press one of the left or right arrows to move it. Moving it will change the values in the cells in column D. If you want the value to be zero, move it all the way to the left.

By moving the slider bar in column C from left to right, you can adjust building costs, equipment costs, site costs, and other costs in lines 6 to 9; column D, the combined cost per square foot, will total automatically. The national averages in Column E will remain the same and your new rate compared to the national average will be automatically calculated as a percentage in Column F.

By moving the slider bar in column C from left to right, you can change the number of square feet you need in line 11, column D. The total cost for buildings and furnishings will be calculated in column D, line 12.

If you are adding volumes, use the slider bars to specify the number and estimated cost in lines 13 and 14. Combined building and volume costs will be calculated in line 16.

Next, specify the percent of the costs in line 16 to be financed by borrowing.

Now select the bond interest rate in line 18 and the amortization period for the loan in line 19. The annual payments, as well as total principle and interest are calculated in lines 20 and 21.

The last four calculations provide context.

Tax capacity is a measure used by planners. More affluent communities have higher tax capacities. A tax capacity of $60,000 per person is cited as "average." That would mean that the typical home with about three residents is worth a market value rate of about $180,000.

The building size is indicated in square feet per capita.

Payments per capita and per $1000 of market value are provided because these are the most commonly used measures for evaluating taxes.

Introduction

Library Planning in the U.S.

In 1950 L. R. McColvin[1] made an observation that is all the more true today:

> "Library services that are not based on high standards are probably not worth bothering about at all. Many of the public libraries operating throughout the world are an extravagant waste of public money because they are too bad to do anything that is worth doing. *A good library is never an extravagance, a bad one always is.*"

The long-range planning advice provided to libraries by library leaders has evolved over the years. For over a hundred years, public librarians have debated about whether librarians should *lead* or *follow* public tastes in the materials they select.

Over a half century ago social scientist Robert D. Leigh challenged the library community to examine its "Library Faith" and consider the tension between quality selection and public demand for materials.[2] He defined six fields of knowledge and interest to which the public library should devote its resources that are echoed by the roles set in 1987 by the Public Library Association (PLA) for the first edition of its *Planning and Role Setting for Public Libraries.*

In 1977 Vernon E. Palmour, former director of Baltimore County Library, became the chief investigator of a research project funded by the U.S. Office of Education to prepare a manual for community libraries engaged in long-range planning. In earlier decades at Baltimore County Library System, he and others had pushed the "give them what they want theory" of book selection and services. That put him "beyond the pale" in the eyes of many of the "we select for quality" librarians of the time.

In 1980 the American Library Association (ALA) published Vernon Palmour's *A Planning Process for Public Libraries*, a volume that marked the abandonment of standards in favor of planning for outputs. The decade-long endeavor of the PLA to revise the 1966 public library standards came to a close.

In 1987 ALA published *Planning and Role Setting for Public Libraries*, by Charles R. McClure, Amy Owen, Douglas L. Zweizig, Mary Jo Lynch, and Nancy A. Van House, a revision and simplification of the 1980 document intended primarily for use by small- and medium-sized public libraries. The document identified eight distinctive roles for library service roles.

The old standards published by ALA from the 1940s through 1966, judged inputs only: books owned, magazines subscribed to, hours open, staff available, and spending per capita.

Palmour and others of the "new school," emphasized outputs: circulation, visits, in-library use data, collection turnover, user satisfaction rates (did they find what they wanted or go away empty-handed?), use of materials in the library, and so forth.

For many years in the library community there was something of a civil war over planning and library assessment. On one side were those who wanted to "give the public what it wants," and pump up circulation numbers. On the other side stood those who wanted to maintain input standards and then let the librarians choose materials tastefully, regardless of the circulation numbers. This civil war ended in an armistice rather than a victory for either side. ALA opted for a "Planning Process" that let library planners choose the type of library services they wanted for the community regardless of input standards (or indeed, it seemed, output measures).

Individual states were left with the task of setting standards. ALA pursued planning processes and output measures, while the states dealt with inputs. In my HAPLR ratings, I have tried to reunite the input and output threads. I believe that both are important and that a library must tailor its services to the community served.

We need thoughtful planning at the local level in reasonably sized units, and wider units may be wiser. We must measure outputs and be willing to compare them to one another. We must also specify minimum standards for libraries. Otherwise a collection of cast off books and *National Geographic* magazines can be called a library and demean the very name "library" for all adequate and excellent libraries everywhere.

Of course, having created the HAPLR ratings, I am very partial to them, but let this be said clearly from the outset: the HAPLR ratings, numbers, and methodology do not need to be used in order to use the planning process indicated in this book.

Our Business Plan

What has kept libraries going through the years is that we have a business plan inspired by and fueled by passionate beliefs. Not only do libraries keep their promise to share knowledge and seek wisdom whether through print or nonprint (now electronic) sources, and we do so at bargain prices. The longevity of libraries is society's reward.

For most businesses, it is an axiom that if an agency consistently meets or exceeds all expectations, soon enough the customer expectations will change. The result is a never-ending treadmill of higher quality and higher expectations. The axiom's converse is not deemed to be true in a competitive environment customers usually change businesses when a firm consistently disappoints them. The exception to that rule is in a monopoly setting. Libraries may have felt we had a near monopoly in the past, but with the Internet barking in the foreground and cybercafes and mega bookstores baying in the background, few public librarians feel immune any longer.

Fundamentals Matter

All too often libraries get caught up in the data gathering, mission development, and role selection and ignore the fundamentals. Any library needs some fundamental standards to be minimally effective. After these fundamentals, library planners should choose roles, set objectives, and do the other elements of the planning process, but *first* they should go "forward to basics" by having the necessary policies and procedures on hand and up to date. Going forward to basics also means comparing the library to other libraries in a comprehensive and consistent manner. This book will provide the tools to supply those basics now and in the future.

Many libraries are already doing planning, of course. All too often, a library finishes an entire planning process and still lacks such fundamental things as a personnel policy, a selection policy, an Internet acceptable use policy, a comprehensible budget, or a host of other essentials! A library could avoid comparing itself to any other libraries in the state or nation and not realize that it has not even begun to live up to its potential. These things should not happen if you follow the advice in this book.

It is not just about the planning process; it is about implementing the plan. Different stakeholders (the board, administration, council, planning committee, and so on) have different responsibilities at different points in planning. Some of the issues and suggestions in this book should *not* be dealt with by the planning committee. The administration or the board will need to deal directly with issues such as the Comprehensive Annual Financial Review, the bylaws of the board, or policies for staff.

This book challenges library planners to assure that their library has the fundamental policies and budgets in place, but it goes further. It provides checklists for planners that can help assure that basic accounting, legal, and management issues have been covered. It also challenges library planners to compare their library's profile with other comparable libraries in the country and to ask hard questions about the library's past, present, and future performance.

Notes

1. L. R. McColvin, (Paris: UNESCO, 1950), 103.
2. *The Public Library in the United States* (New York: Columbia University Press, 1950), sponsored by the American Library Association and supported with funds from the Carnegie Corporation of New York.

Part I. Planning to Plan

Chapter 1
Setting the Stage

Overview

This chapter deals with the context in which library planning takes place. It looks at who should be involved in the writing of a plan, who should do the writing, how the staff and other stakeholders should be involved, and other aspects of what is often called "planning to plan." "The Recipe for a Successful Planning Process" provides an overview of the chapters to come in this book. Note also that Chapter 10 provides two table summaries on the steps needed in a planning process and the ingredients for a written plan.

The chapter urges planners to:

- Remember that the reason for their planning may affect the outcome.

- Decide on who should be involved, the stakeholders, and how to get them involved.

- Assign a single editor or author for the actual writing of the plan.

- Establish a budget for the planning process.

- Use the provided checklist for activities at this stage of planning.

- Use the library planning self-assessment checklist to gauge what needs to be done.

- Assign activities using a planning matrix.

- Estimate the expected levels of participation at various stages of the planning process.

RECIPE FOR A SUCCESSFUL PLANNING PROCESS

1. *Set the stage.* This step requires the administration and board to assess the issues, set a budget, and get the critical pieces into place. Use the planning matrix and self assessment checklist to help assure that the process goes smoothly. Consensus-building is a continuous part of the

planning process, and stakeholders, staff, board, and governing officials all need to reach agreement on the elements of the library's plan. See Chapter 1 for assistance.

2. *Design an effective plan.* The structure of the printed plan is important to its success, but more important is establishing a process so the stakeholders can get the work done. Chapter 2 provides guidance on these structural and process matters. The chapter provides the outline of a recommended plan, as well as hints on what needs to be done to bring each section of the plan to life.

3. *Build consensus for the planning elements.* Producing a plan is no good unless it can and will be implemented. Library board approval is not enough; it takes city council funding support, staff agreement, public interest, and much more. Building consensus for the plan is an ongoing responsibility, as Chapter 3 makes clear. The public relations section of the bibliography will help on this topic as well.

4. *Use comparative data effectively.* Effective planners must approach the data-gathering and presentation step with great care. Demographic data, library statistics, and financial information are critical for good decision making; however, it is important to keep the data gathering targeted to what is needed and to present it effectively. The director or other lead person should become familiar with the data sources indicated in Chapter 4 and be ready to present the assembled data.

5. *Define standards and percentile comparisons.* Effective planning means looking closely at comparable libraries by examining the current measures on these factors of all libraries of a similar size in the country. Chapter 5 provides directions on how to do these comparisons. The appendix provides percentile comparisons on 39 measures for 10 population categories in the country. Many states have library standards, but the standards vary in their degree of specificity. Every planning process should track the numerical and prescriptive standards for the library's

own state and Chapter 5 provides the tools to do so. It is also helpful to refer to standards in other states or to the percentile measures in Chapter 4. Library planners will find the bibliography a valuable source of further references to standards and trustee manuals.

6. *Integrate financial and governance issues into the plan.* It is an often-quoted truism that the budget is the primary policy statement of any agency. In that case, effective planners cannot ignore critical budget and financial issues as they develop their plans. Chapter 6 provides strategic guidance on budget and financial issues. For further detail and advice, planners can look to the Budgeting and Financial, as well as the Fund Raising sections of the bibliography. Library planners plan in a context of state laws that constrain their activities to a large degree. Chapter 6 provides a framework for asking relevant questions about library governance in each specific circumstance. The Governance and Administration section of the bibliography allows for further reading on the topic.

7. *Define major planning sections.* Chapter 7 provides specific recommendations for the development of goals, objectives, and tasks in six main areas: electronic services, collection development, technology, access and facilities, staffing and personnel issues, and other service issues. The recommendations in this book differ from the method used in the PLA Planning Process documents where the goals and objectives—rather than being listed by functional area—are listed under the various roles or service responses that the library has chosen. The two plans found in Appendices 4 and 5 each use one of the methods: St. Joseph organizes goals and objectives by service response, while Brookfield's plan uses the functional area approach. Consult the bibliography for further detail on each section.

8. *Plan for new organizational options.* The group should always ask whether the current type of organization is the most appropriate for this library and its current population. Changes are rare, of course, but the questions should

4

be asked in every planning cycle. It is possible that a new form of governance and taxation may be preferable, and strategic plans should consider these new forms. Chapter 8 provides food for thought on important issues relating to organizational structure, and asks effective library planners to consider multi-jurisdictional, joint library and library district structures.

9. *Use the planning checklist and revise policies.* Effective planners must assure that the library has all the current bases covered before embarking on new endeavors, and the extensive checklists provided in Chapter 9 provide powerful tools for doing so. Only a very few libraries will be able to check yes on each item in these checklists, but negative and partial answers will provide excellent starting points for the development of goals and objectives. A library's policy manual should reflect its mission and plan, so a plan revision requires a review of policies.

Among other things, Chapter 9 provides a comprehensive checklist of the types of policies a library should have. The chapter also provides information on key policy issues, such as Internet access and privacy that all libraries need to consider.

10. *Write and implement the plan.* This chapter provides two key tables. The first is a summary of all the steps in the planning process with short tips on what planners should expect and references to appropriate chapters and tables or figures. The second is an outline of the plan suggested in Chapter 2 with commentary from the various chapters of the book and references to key tables and figures. Effective planning does not start when an authority calls for a plan, nor does it stop when the planning committee presents its report. This chapter considers some of the strategies and questions that can be used to assure that the plan is properly implemented.

11. *Assemble the tools: bibliography and appendix.* The director will often be the lead person in any library planning process. He or she should become familiar with the

language, techniques, and processes of library planning by consulting items in the bibliography, which is arranged by broad topic. The section on the ALA Planning Process documents will be especially helpful. Appendix 1 includes information on Hennen's American Public Library Ratings (HAPLR), and Appendix 2 contains Percentile tables for all 9,000 libraries in the country on 38 data elements for 10 population categories.

Assessing Motivation for the Planning Process

At the beginning of any planning project, the planners should take time to discuss the motivation for making a plan. The reasons may vary widely by participant, of course, but the perceived need often affects the outcome. The level of effort and dedication will be far different if the planners are committed to meeting the demands of the future than if they are preparing a plan merely to meet the requirements of a state or regional library authority.

Because the list of possible motivations is seemingly endless, everyone involved should understand the background of the planning process. The library board, administration, staff and, especially, the planning committee, should all understand why the planning is taking place. Failure to do so invites frustration and failure.

Sometimes libraries undertake a major planning effort because of a recent scandal or a failed referendum; at other times it is because a city council member has questioned library activities. Counties and cities frequently demand long range plans from all departments and on a regular basis, and many libraries have found a three to five year planning cycle most useful.

Many public libraries are part of public library systems that are usually state funded, but sometimes include membership dues or fees. State library agencies usually have long-range plans as well, and effective planners will want to place the library's activities and plans within the context of these wider plans. Often states or regional systems require that local libraries establish wider plans as a condition for grants.

USING A CONSULTANT

At the beginning of the process, the library board—typically in conjuction with the director—will need to decide whether to continue the process with existing staff or to engage a consultant or consultants to lead the project. The director must decide whether or not existing staff resources can handle the additional burden of a planning project. If the library has not conducted a previous planning process, or if a previous process was found wanting, serious consideration should be given to hiring a consulting firm for the process. Funding is a key issue here as well.

Consider what type of consultant and consulting you need, and be careful what you ask for. For example, if the board really wants a new circulation system or a new building, but simply asks for a comprehensive long range plan, they will be disappointed if the consultant delivers that comprehensive plan, but gives short shrift to the building plan.

Carefully consider the outcome expectations of the board, staff, and the governing authority. If the board wants Sunday hours that staff are resisting, the staff want a new building, and the governing body wants a reduced staffing complement, it may be tough to use existing staff for the project.

Experience and ability to communicate about library issues is important. There are many consulting firms that specialize in strategic planning but that have no specific library experience. The library board will need to weigh the issues carefully and decide if the consultant should be a librarian with planning skills or a more general strategic planner.

The board and administrator should determine whether the potential consultant has previous experience locally and nationally. Local experience can be both a plus and a minus; it can keep the consultant too focused on local ways of doing things and cause him or her to ignore the broader vision often needed for long range planning. But local experience can allow the consultant to devise strategies that work that a consultant from another area would have missed. If you are thinking of hiring a consultant from far away, you may want to find out if they are willing to work with a local consultants as a team. It is important to know if the consultants being considered will train local staff on the skills and techniques used in the planning process.

Keep in mind that many libraries across the country, libraries of all size, do a superb job of long range planning without a consultant. This book should help make that process and outcome even easier. But if the library board decides to hire a consultant for the project, the table below indicates the types of items that should be included in the Request for Proposal.

DEFINING THE LEVEL OF EFFORT

All participants should agree on the level of planning effort involved. Staff resources can be rapidly eaten up with requests for additional information on specific issues—information that may not result in any useful elements for the final plan. Clarify, and clarify yet again, the level of effort expected. Clarify—and clarify yet again—*who* will do the heavy lifting when it comes to finding the data and doing the research requested. Clarify—and clarify yet again—the projected target dates for publication and approval of major elements of the plan.

The director and board determine the level of effort involved with the project: Intensive, moderate, or basic.

1. An *intensive* process

- involves a broad-based planning committee representing all stakeholders.

- can result in extensive data collection, surveying, and development of data for patron outcomes (with substantial funding and support of staff, clerical help, and consultants).

- is needed if the library has recently weathered a crisis, if the outcome of the previous plan was disappointing, or if there are substantial challenges in the community.

2. A *moderate* process

- involves far less collection of survey data and typically utilizes focus groups, demographic data, and library statistics.

- may restrict the planning committee to the board or the board with a few staff and community members.

- requires additional consulting or clerical help, especially if the inventories cited indicate substantial needs.

- is indicated when a library already has a good long range plan but feels an internal or external pressure (budget cuts, community growth or decline, etc.) to change.

3. A *basic* process

- involves the planning of the board and the director with perhaps some assistance from staff.

- relies primarily on existing demographic and library statistical data rather than added information from surveys, focus groups, or similar activities and is less likely to require consulting or clerical assistance (unless the director is inexperienced in planning or is too busy).

- may be sufficient if the library already has a satisfactory plan, has not experienced any major crises lately, and if the internal and external pressures on the library are relatively moderate.

DEFINING THE STAKEHOLDERS

A library planning effort usually begins when a library board member or an administrator suggests it, because of a perceived need, or because the previous multiyear plan has run its course. All of the library's major stakeholders should be involved:

9

- the library board,

- administration,

- library staff,

- city council (or other governing board),

- the friends of the library group and library foundation,

- area businesses,

- civic and social groups, and

- the public at large.

The library director or a designated library representative should contact each of these groups to explain the need for the planning effort, expected outcomes, and how much of the participant's their time and effort will be required in the planning process.

All the stakeholders need to be substantially committed to any library plan. Without staff commitment, new objectives for service will not be carried out with vigor. Without city council support, the needed resources will not be there. Without the Friends, support for special programs may falter, and so on. The greater the support for the plan, the more likely it is to succeed.

Contact the local media. Explain what the planning process is about, and invite reporters to the meetings. Press releases will often work for newspaper and local TV and radio, but a followup phone call will have better results. Good coverage of the process and the final plan can be good publicity for the library.

ESTABLISHING THE PLANNING COMMITTEE

Often the library board will be the planning committee, but consider other options as well. A broader based committee, including representatives from the municipal governing board, the library staff, and the public at large is usually the most beneficial. A subcommittee of the board is also an option. Keep in mind that, while a larger group will be harder to schedule and communicate with, the results will usually be worth the extra effort.

The composition of the committee will depend on local circumstances, but several things should be clear to all planning committee participants:

- the plan deadline,

- the authority possessed by the planning committee,

- to whom the planning committee is reporting, and

- what level of effort and staff participation can be expected.

At times planning committees go off the deep end, developing grandiose plans with no chance of approval by the library board or governing council. If approved, such plans stand no chance of implementation because of staff or library user resistance, and committee members have wasted their time. The library will continue, rudderless and adrift.

A plan that stands no chance of approval or implementation is worse than no plan at all. A plan without vision or excitement may be nearly as bad, as it will neither inspire nor excite anyone enough to do anything very worthwhile.

Developing a plan is not just a matter of getting all the people on a planning committee to agree on things; there must also be political and economic reality checks built into the process. Nonetheless, those reality checks must not stand in the way of the dreamers and visionaries among the planners. Strive for a mix of participants on the planning committee, and remember, reaching agreement on exciting plans is an art, not a science.

CHOOSING THE PLAN WRITER

There are many signatures on the Declaration of Independence and all the signers had a hand in its development; but luckily for posterity, they left the final wording to Jefferson. Committees can develop ideas and plans, but a committee should not even try to put the final plan into words; that job should go to a single individual—either the project consultant or someone on the staff or board with good writing skills. Sections of the plan may be written by others, but final editorial control should rest with a prime author. The committee can review the draft for clarity and completeness after it is drafted, but the person chairing the committee should make it clear that the committee is responsible for content, not form.

LEADING THE PROCESS

There are several choices for facilitating the plan, and each option has its pros and cons. The library director is very often the most logical leadership choice, but he or she may be too committed to the status quo to take a fresh look at the operation. Other groups choose a board member with expertise in planning, but he or she may be more used to private sector than public sector planning. In some circumstances, libraries call on state or regional consultants to assist in the planning process, or it may be necessary or preferable to hire an outside consultant, usually a firm with a proven record of accomplishment in library planning. While outside consultants may be more objective, they also may overlook the difficulties the planning committee may encounter in implementing the plan. Sometimes the city or county has a planning office that can assist in the process, but they may be more accustomed to land use planning than library issues.

ASSURING STAFF PARTICIPATION

Involving the entire staff in all stages of plan development is not usually possible, but try to keep the staff involved in the formulation process, since the implementation of any plan will depend on their willingness and ability to help it succeed. Willing volunteers will do a better job than draftees will. Libraries with unions will want to work out arrangements for selecting and compensating staff before the meetings begin.

LIBRARY PLANNING SELF ASSESSMENT

Figure 1–1 Library Planning Self-Assessment Checklist

Plan element	Response			Comments
	Y	N	Some	
Vision Statement				
The library has an exciting, compelling vision that looks to the future.				
It has been updated recently.				
The entire staff, governing body, the public, and all major stakeholders can tell you what it is.				
Mission Statement				
The library has a meaningful mission statement that reflects its fundamental purpose in a clear set of statements.				
It has been updated recently.				
The entire staff, governing body, the public, and all major stakeholders can tell you what it is.				
Role Statements				
The library has adopted one or more roles (or service definitions) that broadly indicate the type of library that users can expect.				
The entire staff, governing body, the public, and all major stakeholders can tell you what these roles are.				
Core Values				
The current library plan indicates the core values by which the library operates.				
The entire staff, governing body, the public, and all major stakeholders can tell you what it is.				
Goals and Objectives				
Goals and objectives are clear and support the vision and mission of the library.				
Progress towards goals and objectives is measurable and time specific.				
If conditions change, the plan allows for necessary changes in the goals and objectives.				
Budget				
The budget allocation process supports the goals and objectives established.				
A consistent and continuous review process assures that resources are allocated to achieve the stated objectives.				
Major costs for plan implementation have been clearly identified and included in the plan.				

Plan Element	Response			Comments
	Y	N	Some	
Stakeholders				
The library has developed a complete list of stakeholders.				
The list of stakeholders includes a broad range of groups with divergent opinions.				
The plan was developed with stakeholder input.				
Consistency of Plan and Actual Activities				
All current programs and activities of the library support the vision, mission, core values, and strategic goals laid out in the plan.				
Accountabliity				
Those responsible for carrying out the objectives of the library have the motivation, the capability, and the means to do so.				

PRELIMINARY TASKS

Figure 1–2 Preliminary Tasks for Planning Committee

Task	Comments	Assigned to:
Get board approval, endorsement by city council (or governing body), agreement by staff association.	This should be the first step in the process.	
Establish timeline	Depending on circumstances and resources, usually three months to a year.	
Budget for the funding and staff resources needed.	Even with a consultant, there will be additional planning costs for meetings, staff release time, printing, staff research, and related activities.	
Select Facilitator(s)	library director, staff member, library board member, municipal planner, consultant, volunteer from community.	
Determine authority of committee and method of gaining adoption of plan.	Put the charge to the committee, timeline, and proper reporting process into written form.	
Determine participants. Assign library representative to make appropriate contacts.	library board, administration, library staff, city council (or other governing board)	

Task	Comments	Assigned to:
	• friends of the library group and library foundation • area businesses • civic and social groups • public at large	
Choose lead writer for the plan and any additional authors for sections of the planning reports.	The lead author must be thoroughly familiar with the library, relevant state laws, and the local community and should have both writing and speaking skills. Additional authors can be enlisted for specific sections of the report.	
Set up publicity and public relations activities schedule.	Depending on local media outlets, contact newspapers, radio, TV, etc. with press releases and media kits on planning efforts.	
Other appropriate preparations.		

ESTABLISHING A BUDGET

Make sure the library board knows up front that it can take substantial resources to plan well. The budget below lists in-kind, as well as direct costs, for the library. In-kind costs include items that are already a part of the ongoing library budget, such as salaries and office materials. Direct costs include things like contracts for consultants, postage, printing and meeting refreshments.

The sample budget in Figure 1–3 will help planners to draw up a budget for a planning process. The items listed will not apply to every planning process, so be sure to tailor it to your own circumstances. Depending on the size of the project, you may want to include additional subbudgets for some of the listed categories to better illustrate the components going into the salary costs or the mailing costs, for instance.

Figure 1–3 Sample Budget for a Planning Process

Item	Description of activity	In-kind	Direct
1. Personnel	___ hours of director's time___ hours for various other staff	$_____ $_____	
2. Personnel	____ temporary clerical		$_____
3. Contract services	Consultant for project based on bid		$___
4. Contract services	Staff assistance from state or regional system	$___	
5. Contract services	Survey design and printing	$___	
6. Contract services	Survey execution - telephone, mail, other @ $___ per respondent		$___
7. Postage	For ___ separate mailings @ $.____ each.		$___
8. Paper and envelopes	For ___ separate mailings @ $.____ each.	$___	
9. Mailing labels	Purchased from municipality voting records or private vendor @ $____ each		$___
10. Mailing labels	Developed in-house with existing staff @ $___ each	$___	
11. Mail distribution			$___
12. Travel	By staff and board to ___ meetings @ $___ per mile	$___	
13. Printing	In house printing of ___ separate reports of ___ pages each @ $___ per page.	$___	
14. Outside printing	Contract printing of interim and final reports and plans @ $ _____ per page for ___ copies of reports		$___
15. Advertising	Paid notices for meetings		$___
16. Refreshments	___ meetings with an average of ___ participants @ $___ per participant.		$___
17. Other			$___
18. Totals		$___	$___

LIBRARY PLANNING MATRIX

Consider the following matrix. The stakeholders in any public library will have various levels of response to library planning. The levels of activity indicated below are typical in this author's judgment. Consider your own circumstances and plan accordingly.

Figure 1–4 Library Planning Matrix Worksheet
Key: H = High; M = Medium; L= Low; N = None.

Activity	Director	Outside consult- ant (if any)	Board	Planning commit- tee	Staff	Other stake- holders
Planning to plan	H	H	M	L	L	L
Research and measures	L	H	L	M	L	L
Environmental assess- ment	H	H	L	M	M	L
Develop mission	H	H	H	H	M	L
Developvision	H	H	H	H	M	M
Develop core values	H	H	M	M	M	M
Develop Goals	H	M	M	M	H	L
Assess current program	M	M	M	M	H	L
Approving planning elements	M	N	H	N	N	N
Approving new goals and objectives	M	N	H	N	N	N
Developing plan budget	M	M	M	M	L	N
Communication of plan	M	N	M	H	M	L
Implementation of plan	H	N	M	M	H	N

Figure 1–5 Typical Request for Proposal for Library Consultant

Library Background

Include short history and current circumstances of the library with circulation and use data.

Financial Circumstances

Indicate budget circumstances for the past several years and anticipated future prospects. If there are major problems or opportunities, highlight them here.

Current Planning Issues

Indicate the library's current planning status. If there is an existing plan, indicate when it was developed, by whom, and its current status.

Need for the Project

The board and administration should have developed a list of reasons for requiring the assistance of a consulting firm. Those reasons should be spelled out here.

Budget

A preliminary budget for this project has been approved and vendor bids may not exceed $_____. (Optional)

Project Description

As succinctly as possible, provide a description of the project and the outcome that the library is expecting. This will be expanded upon in later paragraphs under Scope of the Work.

Scope of the Work

1. Tasks—lay out the specific tasks envisioned for the consultant, including the type of meetings, surveys, and other activities expected. If there are special requirements, such as a budget review or building assessment, these should be noted.

2. Reports—specify the types of reports needed; for example, if a building assessment is required in addition to a long range plan, that fact should be specified. If a number of drafts are being required for review by the planning committee and/or board, that should be noted as well.

3. Meetings—inform consultants regarding the number and location of meetings they are expected to attend, especially if they are coming from out of town.

4. Presentations—note if interim or final reports will need to be made to the library board and/or other agencies, and indicate the time frame and type of presentation required.

5. Work not required—list specific things that are not expected of the consultant, such as local research on demographics or the conducting of surveys.

6. Stakeholders—indicate the key groups and individuals that have a major stake in the success of the operation (this group may expand during the project).

7. Timeline—determine the length of time allotted for the project and any significant interim steps or milestones.

8. Costs—require the consultant to indicate travel, communication and other costs as part of the entire bid. The bid should indicate the hourly (or daily) consultant costs for visits, as well as for background work.

Required Proposal Format

1. Overview of the Project—consultants provide their understanding of the project, its purposes, and expected outcomes.

2. Statement of Work—consultants provide the specific details of the project and how it will be carried out for this library. Tasks should be listed with details on deadlines and benchmarks along the way. There should be a summary of the timeline for the entire project with additional schedules and timelines for more extensive projects.

3. Experience, Credentials and Qualifications—consultants provide their professional background information. If the library has specific requirements, such as having at least one person in the consulting firm with a Masters Degree in Library Science and library administrative experience, this is the place to indicate it. Consultants should be asked to provide information on all individuals who will be working on the project, not just the main members of the firm.

4. References—consultants provide the names of other libraries for whom they have done work, along with contact persons at these organizations.

19

5. Exclusions or Exceptions—consultants indicate any parts of the proposal that they feel are beyond the scope of the project, beyond their expertise, or better handled by local library staff.

6. Additional Documentation (optional)—consultants present additional documentation to help the library in its decision.

Assumptions and Agreements

The contract between the library and the consultant is expected to include the following items:

1. The project must be completed by _____. [Indicate penalty for noncompletion.]

2. The library will appoint one person with decision making authority to serve as a project coordinator/manager.

3. The library will provide appropriate support documentation for the successful completion of the project.

4. There will be no significant changes to the project during the project, unless they are mutually agreeable to the library and vendor.

5. At the conclusion of the project, all materials developed will become the exclusive property of the library. In addition, any and all work sheets and other working documentation will also become the property of library.

6. When applicable, travel and lodging will be billed at cost. Ground travel will be billed at the standard rate used by the library. Air travel will be by coach with a major U.S. airline. Lodging and meals will not exceed $____ per day. All postage, UPS ground, overnight delivery, and shipping charges will be billed at cost. All telephone and data transmission charges will be billed at cost.

7. The basis for billing for services and products completed will be submitted at the end of each month (or at the end of the project).

8. Billing for travel, lodging, meals, postage, shipping, etc. will be invoiced separately at the end of each month (or at the end of the project).

CONTACT FOR QUESTIONS

1. Contact person—indicate name and preferred contact method (e-mail, fax, phone, mail, etc.) for all consultant questions.

2. Questions—indicate deadline date for all questions. (Relevant questions and answers will be distributed to all who have confirmed their intentions to submit a proposal.)

3. Available library documents—indicate which current library documents are available for distribution to bidders. Examples are: previous long range plans, annual reports, etc.

CONTRACT AWARD

1. Basis for award of contract—indicate the method of bid award. Use current board or municipal guidelines. The basis could be the lowest bid or the most appropriate bid for the project. The library should probably reserve the right to reject any and all bids.

2. Interview dates (if any)—indicate when the board will be interviewing selected candidates.

3. Award date—indicate when the contract will be awarded.

Conclusion

This chapter provided:

- the context in which library planning takes place;
- ideas for involving the staff and other stakeholders;

- advice about the effect intentions have on plan outcomes. Readers are urged to carefully consider the reasons for their planning effortsand to assign a single editor or author for the actual writing of the plan;

- a preplanning checklist, a library planning self-assessment checklist, and a table indicating expected levels of participation at various stages of the planning process. The Request for Proposal form is available on the CD.

Chapter 2
Designing an Effective Long-Range Planning Document

Chapter Contents

Overview
Getting Initial Impressions
Overview Questions for Planners
Planning Trends
Plan Outline
Plan Sections
  Executive Summary
  Process Description
  Stakeholders
  SWOT: Strengths, Weaknesses, Opportunities, Threats
  Vision Statements
  Mission Statements
  Core Values
  Role Selection
  State Standards and Data Comparisons.
  Timeline for Key Activities
  Goals, Objectives and Tasks
  Sample Form for Goals, Objectives, Tasks and Timeline.
  Demographics and Statistics
  Budget Data
  Appendix and other
Planning Issues Checklist
Conclusion

List of Figures

Overview

This chapter provides an overview of the elements of a plan with descriptions and recommendations. Later chapters provide greater detail on each section outlined here. In this chapter you will learn about the following plan elements:

- Executive summary
- Stakeholders
- Strengths, Weaknesses, Opportunities, and Threats (SWOT)
- Vision statement
- Mission statement
- Core values
- Service roles for the library
- State standards (if any)
- Goals and objectives
- Demographics and statistical comparisons
- Budget data
- Relevant Appendix materials

Getting Initial Impressions

This chapter provides sample forms designed to elicit input on current library operations and needed improvements. Early in the process, a designated individual or group will collect and condense the focus group information for the entire committee and revise the information as needed. The information gathered here will be valuable in the final drafting stages.

The planning committee does not need to use the specific forms provided here; the important point is to get information from all the different stakeholders on how they perceive the library and the community it serves. The intent is to illuminate areas of broad agreement or disagreement on current and projected library needs, issues, and plans. Consider any divergence in the opinions expressed by the major stakeholders. If library board issues differ from those of library staff, municipal representatives, or public members, make efforts to resolve the differences early in the process.

You might want to have your planning team members each write a 500-word essay describing the library, its services, values, mission, strengths and weaknesses. Chances are very good that if you have a dozen planners, you will get a dozen *different* descriptions of the library. The object of the planning effort is to get the planning team to all agree on some fundamental points about the library, and that is why it is important to develop a set of core values and a simple, straightforward mission statement.

Overview Questions for Planners

Figure 2–1 Overview Questions for Planners

Imagine that you are writing an article for an encyclopedia about the library and the community that it serves. Write an essay describing what you see.
Indicate what is bad about the current library and the services it provides
Indicate what you believe is good about the current library and the services it provides.
Tell us where you want the library to go in the future and what will keep us from getting there.

Planning Trends

Library planners need to consider the trends and latest developments in library planning and evaluation. Over the past half-century, librarians saw the planning trends go from input measures to output measures; in recent years, there has been an increasing emphasis on outcome measures.

Input measures include those things that a community or a library provides for the library, such items as number of staff, collection size, hours open, and spending levels—and these measures are usually the easiest to generate and compare. Output measures provide a way of counting some of the tangible items or services that a library produces, such as the number of visits, reference queries and, especially, circulation. Starting in the mid 1970s library researchers and planners searched for more extensive output measures; a major result of that search was the publication of *Output Measures for Public Libraries* in 1982.[1]

In late 2002, the federal agency for library services, the federal agency overseeing library development in the U.S., the Institute of Museum and Library Services (IMLS), announced a new resource for libraries called "Putting Outcome Evaluation in Context." The press release noted "73% of librarians in a recent survey said that they are unsatisfied and frustrated with current evaluation tools." The research team, led by Professor Joan C. Durrance (School of Information, University of Michigan) and Professor Karen E. Fisher (The Information School, University of Washington), launched the "Outcome-Based Evaluation Toolkit," which can be found at www.si.umich.edu/libhelp.

Planners should remember that, for the most part, it is hardest to define and evaluate outcomes, easier to assess outputs, and easiest of all to plan for input measures.

Consider the distinctions between inputs, outputs and outcomes: missions, vision statements, and goals usually have *outcomes*, and objectives and tasks are usually stated in terms of *inputs or outputs*.

- Spending a given amount per person for books is an *input*.

- Producing a given level of visits per capita is an *output*.

- A literate society is an *outcome*.

Planning Timetable

Establish a timetable at the beginning of the planning process so you can target activities, set budgets, and assure participants and governing bodies of the expected deadlines. An example follows. Copies of this work form are available on the CD and can be customized to your library's specific needs. The grayed areas below indicate when the activities are scheduled to begin and end.

Figure 2–2 Planning Timetable Sample

Activity	Ja	Fe	Ma	Ap	My	Jn	Ag	Se	Oc	No	De	Notes
Secure library board and city council approval.	█											
Provide budget for planning process.		█										
Pepare RFP for consultant.	█											
Choose consultant or project leader.			█									
Involve all stakeholders in plan development.			█	█	█	█	█	█	█	█		
Prepare press and media releases on the plan process.			█	█	█	█	█	█	█	█		
Compare and evaluate library demographic data.		█	█									
Gather staff, board, and public input on library needs.		█	█									
Write or rewrite the mission statement.			█									
Complete the standards checklist.			█									
Write or rewrite the policy manual.			█	█								
Write or rewrite the major item budget.				█								
Write or rewrite the long-range plan document.					█							
Develop a building program statement.			█	█	█	█						
Develop a capital budget.						█						
Prepare both a short and long form of the plan.												
Hold public hearings on the plan.							█					
Revise plan as necessary based on public input.								█				
Submit plan to library board for approval.									█			
Submit plan to city council.										█		
Publish and communicate the results.											█	
Schedule next planning cycle.											█	

Plan Outline

Include the following elements in the library's planning process. While not every item will appear in the final written document, the planners will have dealt with them, discussed them thoroughly, and planned accordingly. The next portion of this chapter considers each of these element in turn.

A. Executive Summary

B. Planning Framework

- Process description
- Stakeholders
- Problems and opportunities
- Vision statement
- Mission statement
- Core values
- Role selection
- State standards (if any)
- Timeline for key activities

C. Goals and Objectives

- Collection development
- Electronic services
- Access and facilities
- Staffing and personnel
- Technical and automation services
- Other services

D. Demographics and Statistical Comparisons

- Population and tax base comparisons and projections
- Circulation and library use comparisons

- Comparison to state standards
- Other comparative data

E. Budget data

- Include past three to five years
- Project into future as appropriate
- Use narrative section of GASB 34[2]
- Indicate capital improvement plan (if any)

F. Relevant Appendix materials

- Survey results
- Focus group results
- Publicity items
- Other items

Plan Sections

EXECUTIVE SUMMARY

Every library plan should have an executive summary. Although it appears first in the document, it should be the last section written. Tell the reader about the high points of the new plan—if the plan calls for a new building, a change in roles for the library, or an initiative to change how the library does business—and indicate who was involved in developing the plan.

A long-range plan for a library should be a living document that tells a reader in clear, simple terms where the library is and where the planners intend to take it in the future. Since no organization can reasonably do everything at once, a good plan must set priorities and indicate timelines.

The plan should identify shortcomings of the library—no matter how painful for the staff and board—and indicate needed improvements. If the library is missing a materials selection policy or if it is woefully out of date, it can be difficult for some library planners. If the library has inadequate materials or staff, it can be both disheartening to the planners and threatening to municipal budget authorities. However, those who cherish the library will be willing to list its shortcomings in the hope of making it better.

Planning never takes place in a political vacuum. Libraries, by definition, operate in the political arena. Most of us are aware of this, but we often forget as we are caught up in data-gathering and discussions with the primary planners. However, just as the three most important things in real estate are location, location, and location, the three most important things in planning are communication, communication, communication. The communication must be with the city council, public groups, library staff or trustees not on the primary planning committee, library Friends groups, and other important "stakeholders" for the library. Public hearings, written progress reports, and oral briefings by library planners to other groups will be critical before, during, and after the formal planning process by the designated planning team.

PROCESS DESCRIPTION

This section of the plan document provides the reader with the context and background of the plan. Remember that not all readers will be familiar with the many meetings, planning activities, and surveys that you as a planning committee member remember so well. Record the number and type of planning committee meetings that took place, and make reference to surveys, questionnaires, focus groups and other data gathering activities. Indicate how consensus was achieved on important issues, note when and where public hearings and discussions took place, and indicate endorsements of the document by the library board, governing boards, and so forth. Note the scheduled revision date and what process will be used to modify or amend the current plan.

STAKEHOLDERS

A sample listing of stakeholders—those who have a stake in the library and its activities—is included in Figure 2–3 below. A good planner identifies the stakeholders and allows them to shape the plan at all stages of development. However, since all stakeholders cannot be involved in all stages of planning, it is necessary to use surveys, polls, and other sampling techniques.

In the classic film *Casablanca*, Claude Raines, the police inspector in a Vichy French territory is informed that he is to find a Free French Partisan. "Round up the usual suspects," he commands, appearing to collaborate with the Nazis while, in fact, aiding the partisan. Rounding up the usual suspects can mean purposely ignoring the obvious. There are several groups that the library planners may try to avoid consulting as stakeholders: The folks who worked to defeat the last referendum, people who don't use the library, the local taxpayer's alliance, or the group that has been harassing the library board to remove objectionable materials. Avoid the impulse to round up the usual suspects, such as the Friends group, the literacy council, and the library board. Get all the stakeholders involved.

Contact the local and state Friends of the Library group along with the national Friends of Libraries U.S.A. (www.folusa .org), a membership organization of more than two thousand individual and group members whose mission is to motivate and support local Friends groups across the country in their efforts to preserve and strengthen libraries. Friends groups are critically important when it comes to lobbying, capital campaigns, and referenda.

Figure 2–3 Involving Stakeholders in the Planning Process

Stakeholders	Method of involvement
Library board of trustees	Board meeting, retreats, focus group activities, written questionnaires
Residents of the local service area	Focus groups, public hearings, demographic data, library data, surveys
Library staff	Staff meetings, focus groups, joint meetings with the board, surveys
Volunteers (if any)	Focus groups and surveys
Library foundation (if any)	Formal meetings, focus groups, surveys
Library Friends group (if any)	Formal meetings, focus groups, surveys
Municipal or county governing council(s)	Formal meetings, surveys
Other municipal departments	Surveys, networking meetings
Community service agencies	Surveys, networking meetings
Regional library system (if any)	Existing Library System planning documents, meetings with regional staff or board, system staff involvement in planning process
The state library agency	Existing state long-range plans, correspondence on key issues, state library staff involvement in planning process
Local media	Press releases from planning committee, meeting with the editorial board, invitation to press to attend planning sessions
A partial listing of groups to consider: • Civic and social groups • Taxpayer's alliance • Chamber of commerce • Other business organizations • Labor organizations • Literacy and related, • Home schoolers • Museums • Education groups	Speeches at group meetings by planners, surveys, focus groups, initiations to officers to attend public hearings

SWOT: STRENGTHS, WEAKNESSES, OPPORTUNITIES, THREATS

This section of the plan, which indicates the key problems and opportunities, as well as the strengths and weaknesses of the library, may be one of the harder ones to gain consensus on, since it requires planners to say potentially negative things about their community and their library. It is standard practice for planners to use what is called a SWOT (Strengths, Weaknesses, Opportunities and Threats) analysis. The method itself is described in the next chapter.

Using a SWOT analysis helps keep planners from planning in a vacuum by encouraging planners to look at the broader context in which they are planning for library services. The technique works best in a group setting so that members can reinforce one another in determining the key factors to consider.

Participants often fill out a form such as the one in Figure 2–4 below before beginning group discussions; then the discussion leader asks for items to list in each of the SWOT areas. Most planners start with the strengths of the library and opportunities before going on to its weaknesses and the threats to the community and the library. Using a SWOT analysis with a number of groups such as the library staff, board, city council, and library Friends will help complete the analysis. Don't worry too much about grammatical issues at this point; in the end, the plan writer will describe each element in sufficient detail so that the reader can grasp it.

Figure 2–4 Sample SWOT Analysis Worksheet

SWOT Analysis Worksheet	
Strengths	Weaknesses
Opportunities	Threats

VISION STATEMENTS

How the planners see the library and community greatly affects their defininition of the library's vision, mission, and goals. Consider how the vision, mission statements, and goals of a public library might change if the planning process were by two historical individuals magically transported in time and place. Suppose Benito Mussolini had not become Il Duce in World War II Italy and had instead become a library consultant called to do library planning in Delhi India in 1948. Imagine the library plan of a sublimated fascist for a library in postcolonial India. Then imagine that Mahatma Gandhi had taken a different career path and become an international library consultant for a library in Milan in 1943. Consider that pacifist library plan in war-torn Italy. Vision matters.

If the prior Gandhi and Mussolini examples seem too extreme, consider how the vision, mission and goals of any given public library would have been altered by the perspectives of two library leaders of the last fifty years in the U.S. Let us consider the perspectives of Robert D. Leigh and Kathleen de la Peña McCook.

In 1950, Robert D. Leigh challenged the library community to consider what he called the "Library Faith."[3] He noted that only one in four adults used libraries in 1950, despite librarians' belief that they provided a universal service. Leigh recommended against being all things to all people; instead, he urged, that libraries carefully define their roles and missions while staying mindful of the fact that "opinion leaders"—a group of educated patron elite who used the library—were critical to its success. Leigh believed that there would be a trickle-down effect to the rest of society from the benefits that opinion leaders derived from public library use.

Fifty-one years later, in 2001, Kathleen de la Peña McCook stated: "For librarians democracy is our arsenal, our cornerstone, our beacon, our strongest value. And a commitment to democracy leads us without a doubt to be committed to serving poor people."[4] McCook believes that unless special efforts are made, the poor will get nothing of value from libraries.

A long-range plan by Leigh in 1950 or by McCook in 2001 would reflect the underlying beliefs of the authors. Is the library

35

an arsenal of democracy? Do we replenish the arsenal by attention to the elite or to the poor? Differing answers to such questions will mean differing visions, missions, and objectives. Acknowledging the bias of the planners is critical.

Sample Vision Statements

Included here are vision statements from a number of public libraries. Each of them are compelling in their own ways and worth considering as models.

- "*Brooklyn Public Library* (NY) will be a vital center of knowledge for all, accessible 24 hours a day, and will be a leader in traditional and innovative library services, which reflect the diverse and dynamic spirit of the people of Brooklyn."

- "*The Columbus Public Library* (OH) will provide a variety of resources to meet the community's informational, self-directed personal growth, recreational, and cultural needs. Policies, procedures and services will be designed to promote use of the library. A caring, innovative, quality-minded and professional staff will be provided to serve the community."

- "*The Crystal Lake Public Library* (IL) will be the primary gateway to the universe of information to meet the lifelong needs of the citizens of our community."

- *Glen Ellyn Public Library* (IL) pledges that "[e]ach resident will enjoy satisfying lifelong learning and leisure experiences as a result of their contact with the library, provided by a knowledgeable staff and a sophisticated array of current materials, in sufficient quantity to satisfy local demand, complementing the offerings of other local recreational and educational institutions. Glen Ellyn residents, from preschoolers to seniors, will be introduced to information technology in a manner appropriate to individual learning styles, enhancing their ability to utilize electronic resources for their individual benefit."

- *"The Saskatoon Public Library* (Canada) is an essential, innovative community service and an accessible resource for people of all ages and backgrounds, enhancing our quality of life and affirming our sense of community and our spirit of optimism and discovery."

- *"The Topeka and Shawnee County Public Library* (KS), a vital community resource, will become one of the finest public library facilities in the nation. The library will serve an increasingly diverse population, and it is committed to becoming the community gateway for information access in the 21st century."

- *"The [Washington] DC Public Library* will be a recognized force in the community for engaging the mind, expanding opportunities, and elevating the quality of life. We believe equitable access to information, tailored to customer needs, equips people to learn all their lives, embrace diversity, and build a thriving city."

MISSION STATEMENTS

A brief and concentrated mission statement that speaks to the purpose of the library should be part of any plan. Most often libraries end up with bland statements that have the library, for example, "promoting informational, educational, and recreational uses of library materials." The best mission statements are short and memorable. Put some spark in your language.

Do not despair that working by committee will cause the mission statement to become bland and meaningless. A well constructed mission statement, even one crafted by committee, can stand the test of time. Consider one of the most famous mission statements of all time:

> "We the people of the United States, in order to form a more perfect union, establish justice, insure domestic tranquility, provide for the common defense, promote the general welfare, and secure the blessings of liberty to ourselves and our posterity, do ordain and establish this Constitution for the United States of America."

Note that the preamble to the U.S. Constitution provides a mission statement in one sentence of fifty-two words. Effective planners will aim for similar results.

Of course, many libraries will already have mission statements. If your mission statement is too long, planners may wish to shorten it. Remind them of the word count of the preamble to the Constitution and compare your library's word count. It is possible to say who we are, why we exist, and what we hope to accomplish in just a few words.

Here is a test for your mission statement:

1. What library is this a mission statement for?

2. Why does the library exist?

3. What does it hope to accomplish?

4. How many sentences are in it?

5. If it contains more than 50 words, is there a compelling reason?

Sample Mission Statements

Here are some particularly succinct and useful mission statements.

- *Salt Lake City Public Library* (UT): "The Salt Lake City Public Library is a dynamic civic resource that provides free access to information, materials, and services to all members of the community to stimulate ideas, advance knowledge, and enhance the quality of life."

- *Evanston Public Library* (IL): "The mission of the Evanston Public Library is to promote the development of independent, self-confident, and literate citizens through the provision of open access to cultural, intellectual, and informational resources."

- *San Francisco Public Library* (CA): "The San Francisco Public Library is dedicated to free and equal access to information, knowledge, independent learning, and the joys of reading for our diverse community."

- *Dayton and Montgomery County Public Library* (OH): "The mission of the Dayton and Montgomery County Public Library is to respond to the interests and needs of its community by providing recorded information and thought."

Core Values

Star Trek fans will be familiar with the "prime directive," which states that starship crews must never interfere in the natural development of other civilizations. Other organizations have prime directives. For example: for physicians the prime directive is "first, do no harm"; for carpenters, it is "measure twice, cut once." The military knows, or at least has best expressed the fact, that without a prime directive, mission creep sets in.

Library planners will want to phrase the directives in terms of core values, and the author has two favorites:

- Share knowledge, seek wisdom.
- Balance the books and bytes.

What better outcome could there be for library users than seeking and finding wisdom? Libraries exist to share knowledge, not information or data, although data is certainly part of it all. It is important to remind city councils, library boards, library staff, and even users that we need to balance books and bytes. Some would have the library be solely digital and virtual; others cherish the print legacy. Plan with balance and perspective.

In the 1930s, Indian library philosopher Shiyali Ramamrita Ranganathan taught five library laws that librarians still quote and use today.

- Books (and now bytes, of course) are for use.
- For every reader, his or her book.
- For every book, its reader.
- Save the time of the reader.
- A library is a growing organism.

As the planning committee considers core values, it will want to examine those values through the prism that Ranganathan provided with these five laws. Do the values shine when seen through the prism of these laws?

Core values should be expressible in short phrases such as:

- Sharing knowledge

- Promoting teamwork

In 1999, the American Library Association (ALA) appointed a task force to consider the core values of the library profession. The much-debated "Core Values Statement" was defeated at the ALA annual conference in 2000 and a second committee was charged with revising them by 2004.

According to the ALA's Core Values Task Force, a textual analysis of ALA documents indicates a set of ten value domains—ideas that are referred to consistently in key policy documents. They are:

- Access

- Collaboration

- Diversity

- Education

- Intellectual Freedom

- Preservation

- Privacy

- Professionalism

- Public Good

- Service

Similar core values can be seen in several libraries' "prime directives."

VALUES

Queensborough Public Library (Jamaica, NY) has established the following values:

1. *Service.* We believe that library and information service is essential to a learning society because information and knowledge are indispensable to the development of human potential, the advancement of civilization, and the continuance of enlightened self-government.

2. *Customers.* We believe that meeting the needs of our diverse customer base is first and foremost.

3. *Quality.* We value the importance of providing rapid and comprehensive access to knowledge and information and strive to constantly improve the services we provide to our customers.

4. *Technology.* We believe the Queens Library must be an active partner in the development and implementation of technology to ensure that access to knowledge and information will be equitably available to all.

5. *Individuality.* We respect the individuality and integrity of each customer and each employee, and foster an environment in which creativity, productivity and individual responsibility are encouraged, recognized and rewarded.

6. *Teamwork.* We believe that each individual is a member of the team, working together to serve our customers.

ROLE SELECTION

For half a century and more, library practitioners have urged us to carefully select roles for our public libraries. A library that targets its audience and limits its role will be will be more effective than a library that tries to be all things to all people. Selecting from a list of commonly used library roles allows planners to focus their activities and consider the role their library will play in the community.

There is ample information elsewhere on role selection, so this work will not dwell excessively on the issues; nor should planning committees dwell excessively on this element of the process, as sometimes happens. It is probably only necessary to briefly review the roles, especially if a prior plan has selected roles for the library. Changing roles frequently would be a tremendous disservice to the public.

Library planners usually pick more than one of the roles (or service responses) for their library. Choosing three roles is common; some libraries have included five or more, but that is extreme. Library planners frequently try to organize their planning documents so that the goals, objectives, outcomes, and so forth cluster around these different service responses; such an attempt can be frustrating, since many of the potential goals and objectives overlap or cut across several of the service responses. Instead, arrange your planning documents by broad function (collection development, access and facilities, and so forth).

In his classic 1950 work, *The Public Library Inquiry*,[5] Robert D. Leigh recommended six potential roles for libraries. By 1987 the list had grown to eight roles in the first ALA Planning document[6] authored by Charles McClure and others. Figure 2–5 lists the thirteen potential service responses suggested in Sandra Wilson's 2001 work *The New Planning For Results*.[7]

Public Library Association Library Service Responses

Figure 2–5 Public Library Association Library Service Responses
Reprinted by permission of the American Library Association.

1.	BASIC LITERACY: A library that offers BASIC LITERACY service addresses the need to read and to perform other essential daily tasks.
2.	BUSINESS AND CAREER INFORMATION: A library that offers BUSINESS AND CAREER INFORMATION service addresses a need for information related to business, careers, work, entrepreneurship, personal finances, and obtaining employment.
3.	COMMONS: A library that provides a COMMONS environment helps address the need of people to meet and interact with others in their community and to participate in public discourse about community issues.
4.	COMMUNITY REFERRAL: A library that provides COMMUNITY REFERRAL addresses the need for information related to services provided by community agencies and organizations.
5.	CONSUMER INFORMATION: A library that provides CONSUMER INFORMATION service helps to satisfy the need for information that impacts the ability of community residents to make informed consumer decisions and to help them become more self-sufficient.
6.	CULTURAL AWARENESS: A library that offers CULTURAL AWARENESS service helps satisfy the desire of community residents to gain an understanding of their own cultural heritage and the cultural heritage of others.
7.	CURRENT TOPICS AND TITLES: A library that provides CURRENT TOPICS AND TITLES helps to fulfill community residents' appetite for information about popular cultural and social trends and their desire for satisfying recreational experiences.
8.	FORMAL LEARNING SUPPORT: A library that offers FORMAL LEARNING SUPPORT helps students who are enrolled in a formal program of education or who are pursuing their education through a program of home-schooling to attain their educational goals.
9.	GENERAL INFORMATION: A library that offers GENERAL INFORMATION helps meet the need for information and answers to question on a broad array of topics related to work, school, and personal life.
10.	GOVERNMENT INFORMATION: The library that offers GOVERNMENT INFORMATION service helps satisfy the need for information about elected officials and governmental agencies that enable people to participate in the democratic process.
11.	INFORMATION LITERACY: A library that provides INFORMATION LITERACY service helps address the need for skills related to finding, evaluating, and using information effectively.
12.	LIFELONG LEARNING: A library that provides LIFELONG LEARNING service helps address the desire for self-directed personal growth and development opportunities.
13.	LOCAL HISTORY AND GENEALOGY: A library that offers LOCAL HISTORY AND GENEALOGY service addresses the desire of community residents to know and better understand personal or community heritage.

STATE STANDARDS AND DATA COMPARISONS

Many states have public library standards, and effective library planners will note how the library compares to them and indicate any actions needed to meet or maintain compliance with these standards. There are two types of issues relating to standards: 1) using numerical data for comparisons, and 2) completing prescriptive checklists. Chapter 5 deals with these issues and problems associated with state library standards and provides guidance on how to use nationally consistent data to measure your library's current profile.

Most often when we think of standards, we immediately jump to the numerical standards such as the number of books per capita, the hours of operation, or the computer workstations a library of a given size should have. Equally important are prescriptive action standards—does the library have policies in place for challenged materials, Internet acceptable use, and the like? Are there bylaws for the board? There are no numbers here, simply an answer of yes or no to things that *every* library should be doing.

TIMELINE FOR KEY ACTIVITIES

Most plans do not need time management charts. Usually a simple listing of critical activities for the time period of the plan will suffice. However, larger libraries with extensive activities to plan for the future sometimes use Gannt charts.

A Gannt chart is a bit like a combination of a calendar and a database. Building a Gannt chart takes time and some expertise; you need to focus on what critical things must happen first, not just when something needs to be done or is scheduled to be done. Details on building a Gannt chart are beyond the scope of this book; planners may want to consult a book like *Project Management for Dummies,* by Stanley E. Portny for guidance on project management. Most library planners today will opt for a software product like MS Project™ to help them through the process.

For most plans, a a simple chronological listing of the key objectives and events for the planning period will be sufficient, for example:

- Install new library automation system in all library branches by the third quarter of 2007.

- Assuming city council approval and union agreement, initiate expanded Sunday hours schedule in all branches by the 1st quarter of 2006.

- Revise entire policy and procedure manual for the library and make it available in HTML format so staff have easy access to it from any staff workstation in the library by the 2nd quarter of 2006.

Remember that more detailed descriptions of the entire plan's goals and objectives will be presented later in the plan. At this stage, you are just hitting the highlights.

GOALS, OBJECTIVES, AND TASKS

A goal is a broad, qualitative statement. An objective is a specific, measurable activity that can be accomplished within a given time period. There may be a number of specific tasks to undertake to meet any given objective—buy the books for the summer reading program, hire performers, count attendance, and so forth.

Many library planners group their goals and objectives under service responses as indicated in the section on role setting. This book groups recommended goals and objectives into six main areas. This grouping is, of course, not the only possible one.

- Collection development

- Electronic services

- Access and facilities

- Staffing and personnel

- Technical and automation services

- Other services

Tests for Goals and Objectives

Figure 2–6 provides key questions to ask about each goal and objective in a library's plan.

Figure 2–6 Test for Good Goals

The goals are:	Yes	No
1. Written in clear, concise, and jargon free language		
2. Part of a plan formally endorsed by the library board		
3. Assigned to a department or an individual for completion		
4. Supported by objectives and tasks that will allow for achievement of the goals.		
5. Compatable with the **CARE** test:		
• Consistent with the roles, vision, and mission of the library, and the community supporting it		
• Attainable by the library in this community		
• Realistic and supported by objectives with budgets		
• Evaluated based on specific objectives set forth in the plan		

Figure 2–7 Test for Good Objectives

The goals are:	Yes	No
1. Written in clear, concise, and jargon free language		
2. Part of a plan formally endorsed by the library board		
3. Subject to review by the board and revision as necessary		
4. Assigned to a department or an individual for completion		
5. Ranked in order of importance		
6. Assigned a budgeted cost		
7. Compatable with the **SMART** test:		
• Specific		
• Measurable		
• Attainable		
• Realistic		
• Timely (there is a deadline)		

Note that the first three statements are the same as for the test for goals.

SAMPLE FORM FOR GOALS, OBJECTIVES, TASKS, AND TIMELINE

Putting the goals, objectives and tasks into a format that includes a timeline will encourage managers to report back on progress throughout the planning period. The sample in Figure 2–8 indicates quarters within a single year, but the format can be extended for multiple years. The CD-ROM accompanying this book includes a template for the form displayed here.

Form for Goals, Objectives, and Tasks

Figure 2–8 Sample Form for Goals, Objectives, and Tasks

Goal	Obj	Task	Task	2004				2005				2006			
				Q1	Q2	Q3	Q4	Q1	Q2	Q3	Q4	Q1	Q2	Q3	Q4
Goal Four: Collection Development. To develop and maintain a diverse and dynamic collection (regardless of format) that meets the library's mission and service roles.															
Objective 4.1: Maintain collection standards and benchmarks.															
Call	4.1	1	Meet or exceed a total collection size at the moderate level by state standards.	x				x				x			
Call	4.1	2	Maintain the base materials budget at the excellent level by state standards.				x				x				x
Call	4.1	3	Meet or exceed an annual book addition rate of about 11,000 volumes. This is a book replenishment rate allowing for a complete replacement of the collection in just under 13 years.	x				x				x			
Call	4.1	4	Meet or exceed an annual book-weeding rate of 10,000 volumes. This rate would allow for an increase in book collection size of 1,000 volumes per year.	x				x				x			
Call	4.1	5	Plan to maintain the periodical collection between the enhanced and excellent rate by state standards.	x				x				x			
Call	4.1	6	Maintain audio collection at between the moderate and enhanced rate by state standards.	x				x				x			
Call	4.1	7	Maintain video & DVD collection at the moderate to enhanced rate.	x				x				x			
Call	4.1	8	Evaluate the collection development plan annually based on usage in each Dewey Decimal category.	x				x				x			

DEMOGRAPHICS AND STATISTICS

The planning committee will almost certainly need a broad range of data to assist in decision-making. Demographic data such as population projections and educational levels can be obtained from local planning councils or the library's own reference collection. Your municipality's budget office can offer tax base information and projections, and the library's own reporting structure or the state library agency can provide circulation and other library statistics.

In the course of planning, it may be useful to examine the library's scores on the HAPLR rating system to help place performance data for the library into a national context. Chapters 5 and 6 contain further information about using demographic and statistical data for the plan.

BUDGET DATA

All too often plans gather dust on shelves, rather than accolades from the public; that is why the budget is the single most important policy document for any agency. Library planners must have the resolve not only to plan, but also to budget for and implement the plans. Projecting costs three to five years into the future may seem difficult or even impossible, but difficult or not, it should be done. A plan without a budget is, all too often, no plan at all.

New accounting rules codified as GASB 34 (Government Accounting Standards Board rule 34) require that the annual audit for an organization include a management analysis and review. Since this statement is a component of the library or its parent municipality's bond rating, it is important to review the current statement and determine what it can and should look like in the future.

BUILDING AND CAPITAL IMPROVEMENTS

A building program statement should clearly articulate the library's vision to an architect by discussing the types of library service envisioned and how they relate to one another in the building. The statement does not usually include either a budget or drawings, but provides a conceptual plan in simple words that help an architect to design the building that library planners want and the public needs. In addition to the building statement, indicate in the plan how the funding for the building or remodeling will be raised.

If the library building is relatively new and up to date, the building program statement is unnecessary, but it will still be important to assess the strengths and weaknesses of the building. Is the lighting and wiring adequate? Are all aisles and accessories handicapped accessible? The staff and the public should help in the assessment of the current building or buildings through surveys, focus groups, or some other method.

Figure 2–9 presents a recommended budget layout for purposes of the plan. Note that using this balance sheet format may be inappropriate if a library is not allowed by law or practice to retain unexpended funds from one year to the next; in that case the library would drop the last two lines and indicate that unexpended funds revert to the municipality (and that overspending is the municipality's responsibility). In Figure 2–9 the next three years are not yet filled; the planning committee, with the cooperation of the board and administration, should calculate at least three years into the future for the budget. Assumptions made in the planning process that will change the budget significantly should be noted in the narrative for the budget. Note that this figure is a summary—the actual library budget is likely to be longer, but for purposes of the plan a summary will usually be sufficient.

Figure 2–9 Sample Operating Budget Summary

Library	Last yr.	This yr.	Yr. 1	Yr. 2	Yr. 3
Municipal	$700,000	$735,000			
County	$300,000	$315,000			
State	$100,000	$50,000			
Federal	$10,000	$10,500			
Fines and fees	$100,000	$105,000			
Other	$150,000	$157,500			
Operating revenue total	**$1,360,000**	**$1,373,000**	**$0**	**$0**	**$0**
Salaries	$710,000	$739,024			
Benefits	$155,000	$161,242			
Materials	$199,000	$207,792			
Other operating costs	$232,000	$255,816			
Operating expend. total	**$1,298,000**	**$1,363,874**	**$0**	**$0**	**$0**
Revenue over (under) expend.	$62,000	$9,126	$0	$0	$0
Beginning oper. balance	$200,000	$200,000	$200,000	$200,000	$200,000
Ending balance	**$262,000**	**$209,126**	**$200,000**	**$200,000**	**$200,000**

The sample capital budget in Figure 2–10 assumes that the library is part of a municipality with an ongoing capital budget plan and that the municipal revenue has been approved for the next several years as is the usual practice for municipal budgeting. The sample also assumes that the library has reserves or fund balance from its operating fund that can be used for capital and that the library has a foundation which has (or will) agreed to fund specific projects.

Figure 2–10 Sample Capital Budget

Category	Last yr.	This yr.	Yr. 1	Yr. 2	Yr. 3
Debt retirement	$35,000	$35,000	$35,000	$35,000	$35,000
Roof replacement			$100,000		
Server upgrade	$15,000				$15,000
Capital expenditures total	$50,000	$35,000	$135,000	$35,000	$50,000
Foundation revenue			$50,000		$15,000
Library reserves	$15,000		$35,000		
Municipal revenue	$35,000	$35,000	$50,000	$35,000	$35,000
Capital revenue totals	$50,000	$35,000	$135,000	$35,000	$50,000

The budget in Figure 2–11 is provided as an example of how to budget for added initiatives proposed in the long-range plan. The sample assumes that the plan recommends three options or new initiatives for year one of the plan (the first year of the new plan). It starts with the first column indicating the status quo budget anticipated for year one. Three options are indicated; the first assumes that the library has determined that it has a sub-standard materials collection and that another $53,000 should be spent to beef it up. The library has a pledge from its Foundation to cover $40,000 of the cost, but at present is still short of the goal by the $13,000 in the last line of the worksheet. The second option—the hours open goal—can be partially funded by a $25,000 state grant anticipated, but that still leaves $24,000 to be covered. In option 3, the library has sufficient reserves to cover the $35,000 cost for a server upgrade. Overall, the library will be $37,000 short of its funding needs unless it can convince the municipality or some other funding agency to cover the difference. Lacking that, one of the options may need to be delayed and the planners, working closely with the library board and administration, will need to develop a fiscally sound solution.

Figure 2–11 Sample Decision Package Budget Summary

Category	Estimated Status Quo Budget: Year 1	Option 1: Add to Meet Materials Goal	Option 2: Add to Meet Open Hours Goal	Option 3: Upgrade Circulation Computer Server	Total with Options
Salaries	$710,600		$40,000		$750,600
Benefits	$155,040		$8,000		$163,040
Materials	$199,800	$50,000			$249,800
Other operating costs	$232,560	$3,000	$1,000		$236,560
Operating expend. total	$1,298,000	$53,000	$49,000	$0	$1,400,000
Capital account	$50,000			$35,000	$85,000
Operating and capital expend.	$1,348,000	$53,000	$49,000	$35,000	$1,485,000
Current municipal revenue	$1,100,000				$1,100,000
Foundation operating revenue	$18,000	$40,000			$58,000
State, federal and other revenue	$180,000		$25,000		$205,000
Total operating revenue	$1,298,000	$40,000	$25,000	$0	$1,363,000
Municipal capital revenue	$50,000				$50,000
Library reserves				$35,000	$35,000
Foundation capital revenue					$0
Total Capital Revenue	$50,000	$0	$0	$35,000	$85,000
Total operating and capital revenue	$1,348,000	$40,000	$25,000	$35,000	$1,448,000
Revenue over (under) expend.	$0	($13,000)	($24,000)	$0	($37,000)

APPENDIX AND OTHER

Every library needs a collected, board-endorsed set of policies that the to give the staff and the public a clear set of rules for library use. The existence of well-written and timely policies can usually avoid conflicts that might otherwise turn into bitter battles with the staff or the public.

Planning Issues Checklist

All too often standard planning books and processes focus on developing visions, missions, goals and the like but neglect the basics that allow a library to operate effectively. In the course of a planning process, it is important to take an inventory of these fundamentals and assure that the library has them in place. Figure 2–12 provides a sample checklist for most libraries and boards. It is likely that even the best run library will discover a few shortcomings when using this checklist.

Effective planners will examine the answers to the listed questions and recommend that the board or administration correct any deficiencies. Consider the checklist responses very early in the planning process so that goals and objectives in the plan can reflect any shortcomings.

This table combines yes and no answers with specific questions. For your convenience, when certain answers are irrelevant, they have been shaded out. Also, there is room for comments for each question.

Figure 2–12 Planning Issues Checklist

Question	Yes	No	Answer	Comments
How many trustees are there on the board?				
Are the trustees appointed and reappointed according to state law?				
Does the board or director notify the governing body or bodies about the need for new appointments or reappointments?				
Does the board make recommendations to the governing body for new board appointments (if appropriate)?				
Have term limits been established?				
If there are term limits, what is the limit?				
If permitted by state law, is there a representative on the library board from the municipal governing body or bodies?				
If permitted by state law, are there representatives on the library board from outside the municipal boundaries?				
Has the board established bylaws?				
When were the bylaws last revised?				
Do trustees regularly attend training sessions sponsored by the state library, library association, or regional library?				

Question	Yes	No	Answer	Comments
Is there a budget for trustee attendance at training sessions?				
If appropriate by state law, are trustees and the board as a whole bonded?				
Is the board covered by errors and omissions insurance?				
Does the board recruit, hire, and evaluate the director?				
How often are director evaluations conducted?				
Does the board properly delegate the administration and personnel supervision to the library director?				
Does the board regularly review and revise policies?				
Is there a compiled policy manual?				
What is the review schedule for the policy manual?				
Does the director recruit, hire, and evaluate all staff?				
If not who does?				
Does this comply with state or local law?				
Does the director prepare job descriptions for board approval?				
If yes, are they up to date and revised frequently?				
Does the director provide orientation opportunities for new staff and trustees?				
Does the director provide continuing education opportunities for staff?				
Are staff continuing education activities paid for by the library?				
Does the director prepare and present background reports on important issues before the board?				
Does the director implement adopted plans and policies and report to the board on progress?				
Does the director participate in regional, state and national planning efforts?				
Does the director cooperate with other community agencies to address the needs of library users?				
Does the director attend all board meetings?				
Doest the director collect and report all required statistics and information for the board?				
Does the director collect and report all required statistics for state and regional reports?				

Question	Yes	No	Answer	Comments
Does the director collect and report all financial and budget reports needed by the board to conduct business?				
If not who does?				
Is this in compliance with state and local laws?				
Does the director prepare preliminary budgets for the consideration of the board and the governing body?				
Does the director participate in the presentation of the budget to the municipal governing body?				
How many square feet are there in the library?				
When was the building built?				
When was it last remodeled?				
Is there adequate space for all library activities?				
List areas of concern about space needs (list details on separate page)				
Does the building meet all Americans with Disabilities Act (ADA) requirements?				
List areas of concern about ADA compliance.				
Is there adequate electrical service?				
Is the lighting in all public access and staff areas of the library adequate?				
Are the collection stacks open and accessible?				
Is there adequate interior signage?				
Are there adequate interior emergency and accessibility signs?				
Is there a sufficient number of ADA restroom facilities available?				
Do external signs clearly indicate where the library is?				
Are directional signs placed strategically throughout the community to direct patrons to the library?				
Is there an adequate book drop for return of library materials?				
If the bookrop is directly into the building is it adequately fireproofed?				
How many parking spaces are available?				
Are there enough parking spaces available?				
If no, how many more are needed?				
Are there marked spaces for individuals with disabilities?				
Is there adequate exterior lighting?				
Are there public meeting room(s)?				

Question	Yes	No	Answer	Comments
What are the dimensions of the meeting room(s)? Attach details on separate page.				
Are the meeting facilities adequate?				
If not, what is needed?				
Is the wiring adequate for all the computer and other workstations in the library?				
Are there an adequate number of photocopiers, telephones, fax machines, and audiovisual players for use in the library?				
If not, what is needed?				
List the other shortcomings or needs of the building.				

Conclusion

This chapter provided:

- an outline of what a written long-range plan should look like, along with the main sections that should be included a plan;

- a plan outline and descriptions of each element of the plan;

- a checklist of fundamental things that all libraries engaged in planning need to consider. If there are shortcomings not covered by this checklist, goals and objectives should be written to correct them.

Notes

1. Zweizig, Douglas, and Eleanor Jo Rodger. 1982. *Output Measures for Public Libraries: A Manual of Standardized Procedures*. Chicago: American Library Association.

2. GASB 34 is a set of rules published by the Government Accounting Standards Board. These new rules require that financial audits include a narrative section by the audit firm that states the condition of the agency being audited in plain, non-technical language.

3. Leigh, Robert D. 1950. *The Public Library in the United States*. New York: Columbia University Press.

4. McCook, Kathleen de La Peña. 2001. "Poverty, Democracy and Public Libraries," in *Libraries and Democracy: The Cornerstones of Liberty*, ed. Nancy Kranich. Chicago: American Library Association.

5. Leigh, Robert D. 1950. *The Public Library in the United States*. New York: Columbia University Press.

6. McClure, Charles R., et al. 1987. *Planning and Role Setting for Public Libraries: A Manual of Options and Procedures*. Chicago: American Library Association.

7. Wilson, Sandra, for the Public Library Association. 2001. *The New Planning for Results: A Streamlined Approach*. Chicago: American Library Association.

Chapter 3

Building Consensus for the Planning Elements

Chapter Contents

Overview
  Setting Rules for the Planning Committee
  Getting Support of Key Influencers
  Developing Vision
  Employ Some Consensus Building Tools
  Surveys and Questionnaires
  American Library Association @ your Library Survey
  Communicating the Planning Process and Plan
Conclusion

List of Figures

Overview

Producing a plan will not be useful unless there is substantial agreement that it should be implemented. Library board approval will not be enough; it also takes city council funding support, staff agreement, public interest, and much more. Building consensus for the plan is an ongoing responsibility of the library planning group and the library administration. Effective library planners will:

- Understand the methods for helping diverse groups come to a consensus on planning elements.
- Assess the groups with which they will be working to estimate the degree of divergence of opinion for each.
- Consider eight different methods for getting agreement on planning elements.

SETTING RULES FOR THE PLANNING COMMITTEE

The major decision on the composition of the planning committee was described in Chapter 2. The composition of the committee must be decided early in the process. As soon as the committee meetings begin, provide participants with some ground rules.

If the planning group is the library board, it will usually have an established meeting process and culture. While that process and culture may work for board meetings, it may not be the most effective for long range planning. Especially in the early stages of long range planning, the group needs to be more free-flowing. Board members may be used to parliamentary procedure and precise wording for resolutions, but long-range planning requires more attention to the wider picture and less to details. The process should provide for brainstorming and consensus building rather than parliamentary votes.

If the planning group is a committee representing a range of stakeholders, setting the meeting rules will be even more crucial. The ad hoc group will have no history or meeting culture, and group members are likely to bring different expectations and behaviors to the table. Establishing at least some clear rules early in the process will make all participants more comfortable.

Some Basic Rules for a Successful Planning Group Meeting

- Get people to take meeting seriously by starting and ending on time.

- Value the time of the participants.

- Have an agenda and stick to it. Consider having someone be the "we're off topic" cop.

- Explain how the results will be used and communicated back to participants.

- Have the necessary data and get it to people ahead of time. Reward them for reading it by asking questions about the document and praising those who can answer them.

GETTING SUPPORT OF KEY INFLUENCERS

While the key elected or business officials in a community may be far too busy to attend public hearings and focus groups, effective planners will want to assure that their voices are heard nonetheless. Without their input, the entire plan is likely to fail. The planning committee may need to arrange for individual interviews with these key officials. Usually one or two committee members or the project consultant will do the interviewing, but the entire committee should talk about the kinds of questions that will be asked. It is not easy to make time for individual interviews, but it may be the only way to get responses from these stakeholders—responses that will tell the planners, board, and administration much about the prospects for approval and funding of important items in the plan.

Some sample questions for key stakeholders are:

- Does the library play an important and vital role in the community? How?

- What does the library need to do to become more effective in serving the community? What should it stop doing?

- Does the stakeholder support some of the following initiatives being discussed (examples only, develop the initiatives based on your library's needs):

  - A new or expanded building

  - Expansion of hours.

  - A business center.

  - Closure and consolidation of branches.

The committee should be sure the questions are unambiguous and clear; the questions should provide for explicit alternatives but not lead to a preferred answer.

Avoid generalized expressions of support for libraries. Few elected officials or community leaders are likely to indicate their opposition to libraries in general, but they are more likely to indicate opposition to building plans or tax increases.

If you plan to publish the results of these interviews in the proceedings of the group or in the final report, make this completely clear to each interviewee *before* you start the interview. It will probably be a good idea to include a statement to this effect in a written note given to each interviewee after the meeting. Send a thank you note, and consider including a few words about how you expect to use their input for your planning.

DEVELOPING VISION

The planning group needs to state the vision of the library. A vision statement differs from a mission statement by offering an inspirational vision for the future. For example, one of the most famous vision statements of all time is Dr. Martin Luther King Jr.'s "I Have a Dream" speech. Dr. King was speaking of his vision for the world he wanted his children to live in; the speech was not about his plans to get there or the purpose of his organization. Vision statements are about how the future looks when the planners are feeling positive.

Here are two interesting exercises to use if the planning group is having trouble with "the vision thing." Geiske's book on "scenario planning" asks planners to look at alternative futures and to plan accordingly.[1] The first scenario is that of the Pottersville Public Library; the second is that of the Bedford Falls Public Library.

The Two Visions scenario below will help planners focus on both the sunniest and the darkest visions and how they are affected not only by the skill of the planners, but also by circumstances beyond their control. The contrasting scenarios help planners realize that they are not planning in a vacuum, that the wider societal forces in their community will have an important impact on their plan. All the goodwill and citizen support in the world probably cannot save an ambitious library program if the community's main employer closes up shop and moves to another community, putting the entire community in financial jeopardy.

Two Visions for "It's a Wonderful Library"

Most planners will be familiar with the classic Christmas film, *It's a Wonderful Life*. The only library in Capra's Classic film is the one in Pottersville. What was the Bedford Falls Public Library like? In the film, we never get to see.

George Bailey is a reluctant once and future Building and Loan Manager. His angel Clarence shows him many of the horrors of a world into which he has never been born.

Overwhelmed by what he has seen, George turns in terror to his angel Clarence and asks of his wife: "Where's Mary?" Terrified in his turn, Clarence replies, "She's closing up the library!"

When George finds Mary, she does not recognize him and runs away, adding to George's despair. George wakes from his nightmare, (or miraculously returns to the world, depending on your interpretation) when he touches his daughter Zuzu's flower petals from her school project.

The Challenge to Library Planners

Now, suppose that you, as library planners, were the writers for the film. Suppose further that the touch point is not Zuzu's petals but rather her library card. Compare and contrast the Bedford Falls Public Library to the Pottersville Memorial Library, and pay particular attention to the funding, legal, and policy aspects of each library's profile.

Since our audience is more interested in the future than 1947, frame your answer for today's libraries.

- More than two generations later, how would library service in Pottersville differ from that in Bedford Falls?

- What does Zuzu's library card get her in each library?

Leave aside the logical inconsistency of this question—that if George and Mary never meet they cannot have the child named Zuzu in Pottersville, so she can only have a library card in Bedford Falls and not in Pottersville. There are always Zuzus. Will they always have library cards?

Community leaders in Bedford Falls had one vision of community, but in Pottersville there was another darker vision. Planning for the best you can hope for in bad circumstances is sometimes all a planning committee can do.

Scenario planning is an experiment that allows library planners to prepare for various contingencies in an unknown future. Look at the services and costs of the respective libraries from the vantage point of library users, as well as nonusers. Effective planners will understand that, while a library is a public good, not every member of the public benefits equally from that good. The Bedford Falls Library, one imagines, would be supported by a community that valued the benefits that an excellent library has to offer the community at large. The Pottersville Library, however, would be far less effective because it would be starved for financial resources—resources that have been allocated to other, more self-centered purposes.

All this is a way of saying that it is important to develop a vision for the community, as well as for the library. Often the wider community will already have developed a vision statement for the community at large. Find out if that is the case and incorporate that wider vision into the library planning effort. You can apply the consensus building techniques to the Pottersville/Bedford Falls scenarios, as well as tyour own situation. The Pareto Analysis and the Force Field Analysis, descibed in the next section, will be particularly useful for such an exercise. The important thing is to get the committee to think in terms of developing the plan in the broader context of your community rather than focusing simply on the needs of the library and the desires of those most devoted to it.

Employ Some Consensus Building Tools

It can be difficult to acheive substantial agreement on a written plan; the document must reflect the will and consensus of the group. Getting to consensus can be harder with some groups than with others; that is why several consensus building tools are presented here. Pick the technique that you are most comfortable with as an individual and that appears to be best suited to the type of group or groups with which you will be working.

A small focus group comprised of library users expects a different level of agreement on issues than a city council. If your plan includes potentially controversial statements such as allocating resources to branches or member libraries in a consortium, expect that group of administrators to need a more formal method of achieving consensus than will be necessary for less controversial meetings. It will be important for the planners to determine what methods will be most effective with each group; even the planning committee itself is likely to approach some issues with more dissension than others.

This section describes tools that planners can use to gain consensus for all types of diverse groups; following sections explain how to use each consensus tool in turn. Figures 1 and 2 will help planners anticipate the levels of divergent opinion to be expected for each of the stakeholder groups engaged in planning. Consider each of the following eight methods for gaining consensus; your method will depend on the degree of diversity of opinion expected.

Figure 3–1 Consensus Building Planning Grid

Consensus Building planning grid	Anticipated degree of divergent opinion			
Group	High	Medium	Low	Comments
Overall planning group				
Focus groups				
Friends of the Library groups				
Civic, social, commercial groups				
Library staff groups				
Library administrative staff groups				
Library board groups				
Municipal/County elected officials				
Municipal/County appointed officials				
Other				

The Consensus Building Planning Grid will help planners anticipate the degree of divergent opinion for each of the groups considered. Consider each group, anticipate the level of divergent opinion that each will have when confronted with planning options, and anticipate the consensus building tools needed in Figure 3–2.

Figure 3–2 Tools for Consensus Building

High	Medium	Low
• Formal vote on each item in plan • Formal vote on entire plan or document • Forced choice questionnaire or "paired comparison"	• Informal votes by section • Colored dot voting • PMI table • Grid analysis • Surveys or questionnaire • Focus groups	• Leader calls for consensus on total plan • Leader calls for consensus on each section of planning • Force field analysisÆ • Pareto analysis

Tools for Consensus Building helps effective planners use the appropriate type of consensus building tool based on the anticipated or actual level of divergent opinion found with each group.

The following are descriptions of the tools listed in Figure 3–2.

Formal Votes

This method is fairly self-explanatory—a member seconds a motion, there is debate, amendments are made if necessary, and there is a vote on the motion. It is important, however, that the group doing the voting understands the limits of its authority. For most of the planning process, various ad hoc groups will be giving advice to the planning committee that will, in turn, advise the library board. The vote can be on either an entire document or on elements of a plan. The formal voting process can tie up a committee or group in far more detail and dissension than necessary, but sometimes groups will insist on voting—not a surprising outcome in a democracy, after all!

Leader Calls for Consensus

For most ad hoc groups and in most circumstances, having the leader call for a consensus on each section of a document or a set of proposals will be sufficient. Again, the group must be reminded of the limits of their power. The plans and proposals are advice to the library board and the board may or may not accept all the proposals forwarded. Group leaders need to be patient when using this technique because calling for a group consensus too early is almost a certain method to get at least one person to object that there has not been sufficient time for group discussion and reflection.

Colored Dot Voting

Colored dot voting is an interesting and interactive approach to establishing priorities and building consensus that also allows for a bit of exercise and interaction. The leader hands out adhesive colored stickers, dots, squares, or even magic markers to each participant, and each color has a different point value. The group brainstorms a list of options such as establishing new branches, expanding hours, developing a new teen service program, or building a new headquarters library. These lists are posted on the walls by the group leaders, and the group approaches the lists and affixes stickers to their favored options.

The rules should be clear to start. Make it clear to participants whether or not they can use all of their stickers on a single favored issue (the answer is usually yes). Assign the colored stickers with different values—a red sticker is worth 10, a blue one 5, and a yellow sticker worth one, for instance. Using this process several times to progressively winnow the field of options to a manageable number can be very effective in building consensus among the group.

Paired Comparison Tool—Forced Choice

Paired Comparison Analysis is a good way of ranking the relative importance of a list of different options, especially when priorities are not clear or are competing in importance. Use this tool to set priorities when there are limited resources and conflicting demands. First list your options, then draw up a grid with each option as both a row and a column header. Use the grid to compare each option with each other option, one at a time.

For instance, say that the group is trying to narrow down the possible Public Library Association Library Service Responses (see Figure 2–5) from a total of six to three. The current service responses that the library has established are:

1. Commons
2. Community referral
3. Current Topics and titles
4. General information
5. Information literacy
6. Consumer information

Using Figure 3–3, follow these steps:

1. List the options. Assign a number to each option.
2. Set up a table with these options and compare the options to one another.

3. Ask the responder to compare cell A1 to B1, choose and record a preference in Column C, Cell 1, then compare the Commons with Current Topics and titles (A2, B2) and record his or her preference in C2.

4. Note that the table has darkened out sections that run diagonally from the top left to the bottom right because with each set of comparisons, the needed number of comparisons is narrowed.

5. Add up the values for each of the options. The one most frequently chosen is the top choice, and the choices will fall into ranked order after that.

6. Add the scores together for all the committee members to provide a consensus of how the committee sees the priorities for each.

Figure 3–3 Sample Paired Comparison Tool 1

	A	B	C	D	E	F	G
1	1. Commons	2. Community referral					
2	1. Commons	3. Current topics & titles		2. Community referral	3. Current topics & titles		
3	1. Commons	4. General Information		2. Community referral	4. General Information		3. Current topics & titles
4	1. Commons	5. Information Literacy		2. Community referral	5. Information Literacy		3. Current topics & titles
5	1. Commons	6. Consumer information		2. Community referral	6. Consumer information		3. Current topics & titles

	H	I	J	K	L	M	N	O
1								
2								
3	4. General Information							
4	5. Information Literacy		4. General Information	5. Information Literacy				
5	6. Consumer information		4. General Information	6. Consumer information		5. Information Literacy	6. Consumer information	

As an alternate, you can lay out the forced choice comparisons as indicated in Figure 3–4. It can be easier to set it up this way because it takes less room for the grid, but scoring is more difficult.

Figure 3–4 Sample Paired Comparison Tool 2

Role Selection	a. Commons	b. Community referral	c. Current topics and titles	d. General information	e. Information literacy	f. Consumer information
a. Commons		b	a	a	a	a
b. Community referral			c	b	e	c
c. Current topics and titles				c	d	d
d. General information					e	e
e. Information literacy						e
f. Consumer information						

Pareto Analysis

Pareto Analysis helps identify the most important problems to solve. Vilfredo Pareto, an Italian economist, studied the distribution of wealth in different countries around 1900, and his observation about economics eventually became known as the "80:20 rule" or "Pareto's Principle." The rule reflects the idea that most results (of a life, of a program, of a financial campaign) come from a minority of effort (or people, or input). It usually works best with two individuals who are the team leaders—one will solicit comments from the group while the other writes them down on a whiteboard or large sheet of paper.

1. Have the group brainstorm a list of the problems faced or the options available. You might start with each participant taking five to ten minutes to write down problems faced by the library.

2. Combine problems or options that appear to be part of a larger problem (i.e, poor internal communication or inefficient allocation of staff hours)

3. Ask the group to agree on a scoring method so they may apply an appropriate score to each problem or option group that has been identified.

   a. Scoring can be by acclamation if there is a great deal of consensus on the problems indicated.

   b. Individuals can write down their scores on a piece of paper and the interviewer can list them one at a time for each section. The recorder will keep a running tally of the results.

   c. You can use the colored dot voting method suggested earlier in this chapter to come up with scores for each problem.

4. Work on the problem or option group with the highest scores and brainstorm solutions to the problems indicated.

5. Repeat steps one through four for each of the problems you have identified.

   The results of a Pareto Analysis will help the group narrow down a list of options or factors to a more manageable listand allows a group to identify the critical issues to consider.

PMI Tables

PMI, developed by Edward de Bono in his book *Serious Creativity*, stands for "Plus/Minus/Implications." The technique can be used either by individuals or by a group for assessing options and weighing pros and cons. It works well in a group setting because it is easy to follow but focuses the group on thinking about the issues involved.

   Draw up a table with three headings: Plus, Minus, and Implications. Write down something on the plus side of the equation and have the group give it a weighted score. Add up the score. A strongly positive score shows that an action should be taken; a strongly negative score shows that it should be avoided.

Figure 3–5 is an example of a PMI table used for comments on implementing Virtual Reference in a medium-sized library.

Figure 3–5 Sample PMI (Plus, Minus, Implications) Table

Plus	Minus	Implications
Good visibility for the library (+5)	Union issues involved (-5)	Good publicity options (+5)
Fits well within the current mission (+5)	Heavy training needs (-3)	Public will see us as cutting edge (+4)
Staff are enthusiastic about it (+3)	May require added equipment (-2)	Hard to evaluate impact on existing services (-3)
		Uncertain response from city council. (-2)
+13	**-10**	**+5**

Force Field Analysis

Force Field Analysis allows a group to look at the pros and cons of a given plan of action. The chart is simple to construct and use in a group setting: simply write down the "Driving Forces" or pros on one side and the "Restraining Forces" or cons on the other. The group can start by writing down their points individually; a round robin approach can be used to write the issues on a whiteboard or poster.

Figure 3–6 Example of Force Field Analysis Table

Driving Forces (the pros)	Restraining Forces (the cons)
• Interest in the problem has recently been expressed by advocacy groups. • The reference service staff support the plan. • The City Council supports the plan.	• Finances are limited, allowing only a test run of the program. • Repeated attempts to get grants have failed.

Grid Analysis

Grid Analysis is a useful technique to use when there are a number of good alternatives and many factors to take into account.

1. List your options and the factors that are important for making the decision. Lay these out in a table with options as the row labels and factors as the column headings.

2. Work out the relative importance of the factors in your decision. This can be either predetermined or part of the group exercise. Weight your preferences by the importance of the factor. These values may be obvious, but if they are not, use a technique such as Paired Comparison Analysis to estimate them.

3. Fill out the table, scoring each option for each of the important factors on a scale. The number need not be different; you could score several as one, "easily done" and none as a five, "extremely tough to do."

4. Multiply each of your scores by the values for the relative importance. This will give you the correct overall weight in your decision. Finally, add up these weighted scores for your options. The option that scores the lowest wins.

   In the example below, we compare four options: Sunday hours, evening story times, 24/7 reference and a one-book reading program for the community at large. The first section of the chart is the unweighted score assigned. The weight is separately determined either by the group or by the leader and each is compared again with the weighted importance. Note that in the example below Sunday hours fell to the bottom when weighting was applied.

Figure 3–7 Sample Grid Analysis Table

Factors:	High cost	User resistance	Staff resistance	Publicity problems	User education	Total	Rank
Sunday hours	5	1	5	1	1	13	3
Evening storytime	1	3	2	2	2	10	1
24/7 reference	3	4	4	4	5	20	4
One-book reading program	2	2	1	3	4	12	2
Weights:	15	5	10	1	5	36	
Sunday hours	75	5	50	1	5	136	4
Evening storytime	15	15	20	2	10	62	1
24/7 reference	45	20	40	4	25	134	3
One-book reading program	30	10	10	3	20	73	2

Scale

1= Easily done

2= Less easily done

3= Moderately easy

4= Hard to do

5 = Extremely tough to do

Focus Groups

Focus groups are a form of group interview that work well for evaluating current services, as well as getting feedback on potential changes.

1. Establish objectives. Determine the major objectives of your focus group sessions. Do you want to assess current services, test possible new services, or evaluate unmet user needs?

2. Identify potential participants. Identify participants by considering the stakeholders you identified in Chapter 2 (For instance, if you are evaluating business services, you may want to get a listing of the members of the local

Chamber of Commerce and invite a sample group for the focus group sessions).

3. Send invitations. Include the sponsors of the meeting, the time, place, purpose, duration, and expected outcomes of the meeting. Mailings with a self-addressed stamped envelope and follow-up calls a few days before the meeting will be effective.

4. Determine the number of sessions. Determine the number of sessions you will have and where they will take place. The ideal group size is 6 to 10 participants, but you will probably need to invite many more individuals to get that many to each session.

5. Select interviewers. Determine interviewers and note takers. Interviewers should be as neutral as possible and capable of keeping the group on the task and question at hand; they will also provide clear transitions from one set of questions to the next. Good interviewers make constant eye contact with all participants and encourage responses with head-nodding and affirmative comments.

6. Choose appropriate meeting rooms. Focus group sessions will work best in a conference room with adequate airflow and lighting. Chairs should be set up so that all members can see each other and nametags should be provided. It may be a good idea to provide refreshments, especially box lunches if the session is held over lunch. Be careful of dietary concerns.

7. Develop key questions. Develop at least three but usually no more than ten key questions to ask the focus group. Arrange questions so that questions of fact, behavior, and participant demographics come before questions about attitudes or feelings. Save the most controversial questions for the end of the session so that participants start talking and sharing before you get to tough issues. It usually works best to ask about the present before asking about the future. Questions should be open-ended, as neutrally worded as possible. Stick to one topic at a time if possible.

8. Issue an agenda and rules. A written, short agenda will help participants feel more at ease. The focus group interviewer should tell the group that it is important that all members participate as much as possible. Have a few, short ground rules that sustain participation. Ground rules might include: a) stay focused, b) maintain momentum, c) don't interrupt speakers (the interviewer will discourage individuals who monopolize the conversation) and d) getting concise answers is more important than getting complete answers.

9. Record the session. If the meeting will be tape recorded or videotaped, all participants should be informed before the session begins—preferably in the invitation, but at least at the beginning of the meeting. It is usually hard for the interviewer to ask questions and take notes, so a separate notetaker is a good idea.

10. Monitor the session. At the beginning, introduce yourself and the co-facilitator, if there is one. Announce the sponsors of the meeting (usually the planning group, possibly in conjunction with another group, like the Chamber of Commerce or PTA). Explain the means you will use to record the session. Distribute the agenda. Carefully word each question before that question is addressed by the group. It is sometimes useful to allow a few minutes for each member to write down their answers (If you do this, provide pencil and paper). After each question is answered, give a summary of what you (or the notetaker) heard. Ensure even participation; a round table approach may keep one or two individuals from dominating the conversation.

11. Closing the session. Provide participants with a method for communicating further with the planning group after the session. Offer to provide participants with copies of the focus group results. Be sure to thank them for participating.

12. Write up the session. The results of the session, including the time, date, place, and number of participants should

be recorded immediately after the session. The sooner you write down your observations and expand on the notes you took, the more complete and accurate the report will be.

SURVEYS AND QUESTIONNAIRES

It may be necessary to find additional information that is not available from either the library's current data sources or from demographic and statistical sources.

Libraries frequently use surveys to gauge public sentiment about library issues. Unless someone on the planning committee, staff, or board is well trained in survey construction, it may be preferable to get assistance from a consultant or from your local municipal planning department, the university extension office, or a nearby academic institution. Ambiguous or poorly constructed surveys usually result in misleading results, and such surveys can be just the ammunition that library plan detractors need to invalidate the survey results, and by implication, the entire planning process. If you are going to use questionnaires, use them wisely.

Libraries are increasingly turning to the World Wide Web for survey information. A useful source for such survey information is *Instant Web Forms and Surveys for Public Libraries* by Gail Junion-Metz and Derrek L. Metz (see "Outcome Assessment" section in the bibliography). The CD that accompanies Instant Web Forms has a number of predesigned Web forms and includes PERL scripts that enable you to gather surveys online and direct them to a specific e-mail address for review, tally, or other action. There is a tutorial on how to apply and use the forms on a library's Web site.

There are a variety of potential types of questionnaires to use:

1. Individual questionnaire. Individual questionnaires are usually conducted by an interviewer with a single individual. Either the interviewer or the person being interviewed writes down the responses to a set list of questions. This setting allows for interaction and questions about the questionnaire so the interviewer can get to difficult issues. This type of interview is expensive and time consuming.

77

2. Group questionnaire. In a group questionnaire there are one or two interviewers and a group of participants being asked the same questions. This form is more efficient in terms of interviewer time than the individual method, so it can be done for less cost; however, it is still an expensive method.

3. Focus group. A focus group is a type of group interview that allows for more group interaction and is less structured than the group questionnaire. Leading a focus group can take considerable skill. This method tends to be expensive but yield good results. The previous section of this chapter indicated rules for running focus groups.

4. Mail interview. Mail interviews offer participants anonymity that group or individual interviews do not. They are relatively inexpensive to administer when compared to other types considered here, but the response rate is usually quite low. Library planners will want to take care that the sample is not biased by mailing to only known library users. Because this type of interview produces such a genuinely random sample, planners might not get the kind of information they are seeking.

5. Personal interview. Because of its high cost, this method ordinarily will be restricted in its use to questions for the key stakeholders. Without a personal visit, it may not be possible to get answers to the questions that planners have for elected officials, business and community leaders, and other key influencers.

6. Phone interview. Phone interviews are less expensive than many of the other options here, with the exception of mail interviews, but it is important that the sample size and distribution be appropriate for the library service area. Volunteers with no experience are not likely to come up with valid, useable, and reliable responses.

Questions about Survey Construction

Figure 3–8 Issues for Survey Questions

Question	Comments
Is the question unambiguous?	If you ask for marital status, does that include just "yes" or "no" or do you want to specify "divorced," "separated," etc.
Are there assumptions in the question?	If you are asking about reference questions, consider that not all members of the public understand the concept. You may have to explain the topic before asking the question.
Does the question include a clear time frame?	It is better to ask "should the city build a new library within the next two years?" than to simply ask if a new building should be built.
Does the question lead the responder to your preferred answer?	Asking "Is the library budget totally inadequate?" leads to an affirmative answer. If the respondent says "no," did he or she mean that its not totally inadequate or did he or she mean that it is adequate?
How personal is the wording of each question?	Asking if the quality of service is satisfactory is different from asking if you personally are satisfied with all elements of library service. All questions should be parallel in their degree of personal nature.
Does the question make each alternative explicit?	If you ask how often someone uses the library, all possible answers need to be considered, from "never" to "less than once a year" all the way to "over 10 times a year."
Do the questions provide for demographic comparisons?	To be valid, a sample should reflect the demographics of the actual population. For instance, the sample should reflect the male/female ratio, the age ranges, and other demographic characteristics of the population. If you don't ask such questions, you can't compare to your population. If you do ask, be sure the comparable demographic data is readily available from census data or local statistics.
Is the sample size sufficiently large to reflect the entire population?	A sample of 1,000 is sufficient on a national basis, but the number doesn't fall with the size of the population. Even for a city of 5,000 you need a sample size of at least 400.

AMERICAN LIBRARY ASSOCIATION @ YOUR LIBRARY SURVEY

The survey questions indicated here are from "@ your library: Attitudes Toward Public Libraries," a national survey commissioned by the American Library Association and conducted by KRC Research and Consulting. This random study of attitudes and beliefs about libraries found that most that most Americans are highly satisfied with their current library services, would be happy to pay more than they currently pay for library service, and few believe that the Internet will substitute for library services anytime soon. It polled about 1,000 adult Americans in a national random-sample telephone survey conducted March 8–11, 2002. The estimated margin of error was 3 percent.

Waukesha County Federated Library System (the author's library system) replicated the study to determine if county residents reflected the library use patterns and attitudes found nationally and had very similar results.

The questions on the survey are easily replicable by any library, although the cost to do a statistically significant telephone survey can be quite high because of the high number of calls that must be made to get a reasonable number of responses. A random sample of 1,000 is statistically likely to be representative of the U.S. as a whole, but even for moderately sized communities the sample will usually need to be around 400. To get 400 answers on a phone survey, your callers will probably need to call ten times that many individuals. Mail surveys receive an even lower rate of return, usually less than 15 percent of the number sent out.

Replicating an existing survey has a number of advantages. The survey questions have already been designed and have produced valid and reliable results so you don't have to worry on that score. Also, you can compare your local responses to the entire U.S. as a baseline, providing you and others with further context on the survey results.

Before you decide to have volunteers conduct this or any survey, take the time to contact the local extension office, municipal planning department, or a local academic institution for imformation on conducting surveys. They should be able to provide guidance and assistance on how much time it will take and on how likely you are to get valid results by using volunteers.

The questions below are the precise questions asked in the ALA survey. Asking the same questions to users of your library allows you to have a national basis of comparison to the responses in your library area.

Figure 3–9 American Library Association Survey on Library Use

1. Do you have a library card?

Answer	U.S. percent	This library
Yes		
No		
Refused		

2. During the last 12 months, how often were you in your local public library?

Answer	U.S. percent	This library
Not sure/not at all	35%	
1 to 5 times	31%	
6 to 10	9%	
11 to 15	11%	
Over 20 times	14%	

3. Which libraries did you visit in the last 12 months? (More than one response possible.)

> [Open ended question; answers are likely to reflect the range of libraries in your area]

4. When you used your local library during the last 12 months, which of the following did you use? (More than one response possible.)

Answer	U.S. percent	This library
Take out books (e-books or book on paper or tape)	67%	
Use reference materials, like the encyclopedia	47%	
Consult the librarian	47%	
Read newspapers or magazines	31%	
Connect to the internet	26%	
Take out CDs, videos, or computer software	25%	
Hear a speaker, see a movie, or attend a special program	14%	
Take a class or workshop	7%	
Other	5%	

5. Did you contact your public library by phone during the last 12 months? By computer?

(Both responses possible)

Answer	U.S. percent	This library
Phone	12%	
Computer	18%	

6. If you used your library by phone or computer, which of the following did you use? (More than one response was possible.)

Answer	U.S. percent	This library
Computerized catalog	46%	
Library staff consulting	35%	
Resources on web	31%	
Book renewal	26%	
Other	18%	

7. Listed below are several reasons a person could use a library. After I read each one, please tell me if you used that item in the last 12 months. (More than one response was possible.)

Answer	U.S. percent	This library
Educational	46%	
Entertainment	41%	
Travel information	12%	
Health issues	10%	
U.S. or local news	9%	
International news	7%	
Financial/investment	7%	
Job search	6%	
Start business	5%	
Other or don't know	20%	

8. Do you ever use a computer in the library?

Answer	U.S. percent	This library
Yes	31%	
No	68%	
Refused/don't know	1%	

9. How do you use the computer? (Multiple answers possible).

Answer	U.S. percent	This library
See what library has available	58%	
Use Internet	45%	
Consult on-line databases	24%	
Check e-mail	24%	
Use computer programs	20%	
Other	5%	

10. Do you ever visit the library with your child?

Answer	U.S. percent	This library
Yes	69%	
No	30%	
Refused/don't know	1%	

11. Thinking of your public library, based on what you know or have heard or read, how satisfied are you with your public library?

Answer	U.S. percent	This library
Extremely satisfied	20%	
Very satisfied	40%	
Somewhat satisfied	24%	
Somewhat dissatisfied	4%	
Extremely dissatisfied	3%	
No answer	9%	

12. Listed below are several terms that can be used to rate a library. After I read each one, please tell me how you would rate your library regarding that term.

Answer	U.S. percent	This library
Modern	82%	
Friendly	87%	
Up to date	81%	
Dynamic	67%	
Comfortable	88%	
Constantly changing	63%	
Convenient	87%	
Offers world wide information	78%	
Meets people's needs	87%	
Highly skilled staff	82%	
Good activities.	74%	

13. Tax Money is used to support any public library. Please rate how good a job your library is doing considering the amount of taxes you pay for its support.

Answer	U.S. percent	This library
Excellent	30%	
Good	58%	
Fair/poor	8%	
No response	3%	

14. How much tax support per person, per year, do you feel should be spent to support your public library?

Answer	U.S. percent	This library
$0	4%	
$1 to $25	30%	
$26 to $40	16%	
$40 to $99	29%	
$100 or more	6%	

15. Please rate the library staff at your public library.

Answer	U.S. percent	This library
Excellent	22%	
Good	63%	
Poor	10%	
No response/ not sure	5%	

16. Some people think libraries will be replaced by the Internet in the future. Others think libraries will still be needed despite the growth of the Internet. Do you think public libraries will no longer exist in the future, or do you think there will still be a need for them?

Answer	U.S. percent	This library
Libraries will continue to exist	91%	
Libraries will cease to exist	7%	
No response	2%	

Demographic Section

GENDER RESPONSES FOR THE SURVEY

Answer	U.S. percent	Population served by this library	Respondents to this library survey
Male	45%		
Female	55%		

AGE RANGES FOR THE SURVEY

Answer	U.S. percent	Population served by this library	Respondents to this library survey
18 to 24 years	14%		
25 to 34	19%		
35 to 44	23%		
45 to 54	17%		
55 to 64	8%		
Over 65	13%		

MARITAL STATUS

Answer	U.S. percent	Population served by this library	Respondents to this library survey
Married	54%		
Divorced, separated, single, other	46%		

HOUSEHOLD INCOME

Answer	U.S. percent	Population served by this library	Respondents to this library survey
Under $25,000	16%		
$25,000 to 49,999	25%		
$50,000 to $74,999	14%		
$75,000 to 99,999	14%		
Over $100,000	8%		
No answer/ refused	23%		

EDUCATION LEVEL

Answer	U.S. percent	Population served by this library	Respondents to this library survey
Less than High School	5%		
High School Graduate	25%		
Some College	27%		
College Graduate	25%		
Post Graduate Work	15%		
Professional/Technical Degree	3%		

COMMUNICATING THE PLANNING PROCESS AND PLAN

Effective library planning is not just a question of getting the planning committee to agree on the plan, the vision, and the process. The city council, the public, and even the library's worst enemies, must understand (if not agree upon) where the library is going.

If the library has a newsletter, use it to communicate with all the stakeholders about the progress of the planning process; if not, perhaps it is time to launch that newsletter. In addition, the library director, board members or members of the planning committee should be designated to contact the governing body, members of the staff, and representatives from key stakeholder organizations about the ongoing activities in the library planning process. The planning committee should ask the designated liaisons to report periodically to the committee on feedback from their assigned groups.

The news media can help a lot in getting the word out about the library's planning activities. Assign someone on the staff to assure that press releases go to the local media on a regular basis throughout the course of the planning process.

The director and the library board chair, along with the chair of the planning committee, should consider making contact with the editorial committee of the local paper. Schedule a meeting to discuss the library's long range planning efforts and the challenges it faces for the future; if the editorial board is convinced of the value of the planning being done, there may be several results. First, the paper may run an editorial on the planning process, an obvious advantage. Second, the paper is more likely to assign reporters to cover future meetings of the library planning committee. Finally, it may help reporters and editors put the entire planning process into perspective so that the reporting does not become centered on controversial items discussed in the planning process. There is no guarantee on this point; some media outlets search out controversy because it makes good headlines and sells papers.

It may not be possible to avoid controversy, and in many cases it may not even be a good idea to do so. Good planning requires that planners look at tough issues and make hard choices. For example, should a branch be closed for lack of use, should videos be dropped entirely in favor of DVDs, or should the library start providing homework help to students? Communicating the tough issues to the public by way of the media can generate interest in the planning process that can be most helpful. Board members or committee members who belong to civic and social clubs should be enlisted to arrange speeches and make progress reports about the plan and its current progress to their individual organizations. In addition, include the planning documents, data reports, committee minutes and related material on the library's Web site.

Conclusion

This chapter provided:

- examples of what effective planners can do to ensure that there is substantial community support for the implementation of the plan that they have developed;

- examples of what effective planners can do to assure that the governing and financial body (county, city, city, etc) supports and will fund the plan;

- methods of building consensus for the plan. The staff, administration, the board, and other stakeholders must be in substantial agreement to make the plan work;

- methods for helping diverse groups come to a consensus on planning elements. It provided tools for assessing the groups with which they will be working to estimate the degree of divergence of opinion for each;

- variety of different methods for gaining agreement on planning elements;

- a description of an ALA survey tool and discussion of how to communicate the plan to the public.

Note

1. Geiske, Joan. 1998. *Scenario Planning for Libraries*. Chicago: American Library Association.

Chapter 4

Using Comparative Data Effectively

List of Figures

Overview

Effective planning requires the use of data to measure where we have been, where we are, and where we are going. This chapter points to specific data sources and methods, briefly describes them, and warns of potential problems. This chapter contains:

- An explanation of the role of comparative data

- A data relevancy test

- Sources of comparative data, including state, fedeal and private sources

- A summary table of sources for demographic and library data

- Tips on how to use graphs effectively in your reports

THE NEED FOR DATA COMPARISONS

I believe that numbers are important; just examine the HAPLR Scorecard system to see the truth of that statement. But numbers are neither everything nor the only thing. Use the data supplied by your own circulation system and routine data gathering efforts. If time and circumstances permit, do additional surveys of user needs and demographic characteristics as recommended in the various books cited in the bibliography section on data gathering. Remember, however, the numbers tail should never wag the planning dog. Be selective—gather the data you will use. And if your planning team is becoming too tied up with numerical data, remember to take the simple four-point Data Relevancy Test in Figure 4–1.

Figure 4–1 Data Relevancy Test

Question	Your answer
Why do we need to know? If you are looking for or planning to collect a set of data, can you explain why you need to know? Too often planners go in search of data that is interesting to them personally but adds nothing to the library planning effort.	
Who can do the data collection? Usually the data collection tasks fall to library staff who already have other duties at the library and who may or may not be comfortable with data collection and presentation. Consider whether the regional system in your area or the state library can assist in data collection. Consultants or local community planners are also good sources of assistance.	
How will the answers affect our plans? Often planners begin the process by demanding huge amounts of data, both internal and external. Internal examples are the number of books processed or loaned. External data include such things as the number of housing permits issued in the last ten years or comparative education statistics from the federal census. The list can be endless and often very interesting, but if it won't affect the planning effort, don't do it.	
Will collecting the data unduly slow down the process? Even using readily available data such as census data, HAPLR scorecards, or state library agency reports will take time and effort. The data must be assembled and distributed to planners and it must be discussed and assessed for its relevance to the library, its needs, and its future. Be sure the data will answer important questions rather than just delay the process.	

SERVICE POPULATION CONSIDERATIONS

Calculating the population served by the library is a critical component of library planning; give it the careful consideration it deserves.

Many—indeed most—of the data measures used for standards or other comparisons are based on the population served. For many libraries, the population served extends beyond the population of the community that established it and provides its initial support. Determining the appropriate population size to use for any given library is difficult and imprecise.

Libraries are often urban institutions, founded and maintained financially by cities and villages. Often there are nearby rural or suburban townships, counties, or even entire cities that have no direct library service of their own. These communities may obtain their library services in a variety of ways depending on the state; some are taxed by counties or legally established library districts and others contract directly with nearby library communities.

Left to their own devices, libraries could claim service territories that, when added together, would far exceed the total population of the country; hence, for national library data purposes, the Federal State Cooperative System (FSCS) has made assignments of population that can appear to be arbitrary. In these times of electronic access to library sites, the population allocation an be even more confused and confusing

The FSCS data report two different population numbers, the Legal Service Population and the Unduplicated Population. Depending on the state circumstances, the Legal Service Population of all the libraries in a state, when added together, can exceed the total population of the state. That is because some residents have been assigned to more than one library in overlapping jurisdictions.

It is important to remember that claiming a wider population for the library service area will diminish the per capita measures. For example, a $100,000 budget for 5,000 residents yields a per capita spending rate of $20. If the library instead has 10,000 residents in its "service area," the rate falls to $10 per capita. Claiming more to look more needy may not be the wisest course of action. Conversely, if your library really serves that wider population, it is erroneous to leave them out of the equation for planning purposes.

Carefully investigate the assignment of the service population for the library and who does the assigning. The state library agency usually has a consistent methodology for assigning service population, but this may be far from the population that the library typically uses for planning.

Planners should either agree to use the state-assigned population method or clearly identify and define what assumptions they are using instead. Whatever population number is used, it should be noted on all charts, graphs, and tables that compare the library's per capita performance.

In many cases, it may be best to plan based on only the direct municipal population rather than the wider service population. These population numbers and projections are more readily available from census sources and elsewhere. More important, from a political point of view, may be the presentation of the plan to the city council. An argument to increase the number of books per capita is more likely to be persuasive to the city council if the population considered is only the direct population.

Some state library agencies accommodate this distinction between service and primary population in their library standards. This allows a library the flexibility to plan its service profile in either the primary or service population.

DEMOGRAPHIC DATA

Library planners will, of course, be interested in more than just population data. However, remind the planning team that there really is such a thing as information overload when it comes to demographic data. Sources for demographic data include the regional library system, state library agency, the state's population data service, and the federal government.

Consider the following factors when planning and developing library services:
- education levels
- income levels
- population density

The demographic factors of the population you are serving will have an impact on the library plan. Experience indicates that all other things being equal (though admittedly they rarely are) the higher the education level, income level, and population density of the community served, the higher the library usage rate.

NATIONAL INFORMATION STANDARDS ORGANIZATION DEFINITIONS

In July of 2002 the National Information Standards Organization (NISO) issued its fourth revision of recommended library statistics first defined in 1968. According to NISO:

> The 2002 revision diverges from the former process of developing a print-only standard, and takes the path of developing an interactive web-based utility for identifying standard definitions, methods and practices relevant to library statistics activities in the United States (US).
>
> Not unlike the previous versions, the aim of the 2002 revision remains: "to assist librarians and researchers [now defined as the information community] by indicating and defining useful quantifiable information to measure the resources and performance of libraries and to provide a body of valid and comparable data on American libraries."

The above is NISO's way of saying that the Web is a better place for developing and revising current definitions of the activities of a modern public library because the Web allows those definitions to be presented in ways that can be readily identified and quantified.

The NISO site (www.niso.org/emetrics/index.cfm) is an excellent place to check definitions for the myriad of data collection items that libraries use. The site provides standardized definitions for a branch, reference transaction, and so forth. In 2003, there were forty-six standardized definitions for the public library survey conducted annually by the National Center for Educational Statistics and the Federal State Cooperative System; there were another 168 general definitions for all libraries, including everything from Abstracting Databases to Volunteers and Workstations.

The following is a selected list of the definition to be found on the NISO Web site.

Attendance at Library Events
Attendance at User Training
Audio-Visual Materials
Audio-Visual Materials Additions—Physical Units
Audio-Visual Materials Additions—Titles
Available Internet Workstations
Bookmobile
Books and Serials (print materials)
Books and Serials Additions—Physical Units
Branch Library
Capital Expenditures
Capital Revenue
Compact Disc Read-Only Memory (CD-ROM)
Current Serial Expenditures
Current Serial Titles—Electronic
Current Serial Titles—Print or Microform
Databases
E-books
Electronic Access Expenditures
Electronic Serials
Employee Benefit Expenditures
Federal Government Income
Furnishing and Equipment Expenditures
Government Documents
Gross Measured Area
Hours Open
Hours Open in Branch Libraries
Hours Open in Main/Central Library
In House Use
Interlibrary Loan
Internet Access
Library Cooperative
Library Events/Programs
Library User
Local Government Income

Measuring Public Library Networked Services: Preparing
    Your Library to Collect Network Statistics
Measuring the Use of Electronic Library Services
Microform Material Expenditures
Microforms
Mobile Facilities
Multimedia Documents
Network and Cooperative Target Population
Newspapers
Number of Public Access Workstation Users
Number of Public Access Workstations
Operating Expenditures by Type of Expenditure
Operating Income by Source
Other Digital Documents
Other Library Documents
Other Materials
Other Operating Expenditures
Other Sources of Income
Other Staff
Primary Target Population
Professional Staff
Professional Staff Salaries and Wages
Public Access Workstations
Public Library
Public Library Target Population
Seating Capacity
Staff Hours of Training
State Government Income
Support Staff Salaries and Wages
User Training
Virtual Reference Transactions
Volunteers
Workstations

FEDERAL STATE COOPERATIVE SYSTEM (FSCS) DATASET

The National Center for Education Statistics, through the Federal State Cooperative System (FSCS), collects library statistics for the entire country and publishes the results on an annual basis. Figure 4–2 lists the current data collected by the FSCS on library service measures. Note that many states collect data beyond the minimum listed here. Other data elements include the size of the building, electronic use measures, further detail on salary, and further output measures like in-library use or satisfaction ratios. Chapter 5 recommends which of the data elements in Figure 4–2 to use and provides a convenient and consistent method for using them to measure and evaluate your library's performance.

Figure 4–2 Federal State Cooperative System Data Element Definitions

FSCS name	Translation
LIBNAME	Address of the main library
ADDRESS	City in which library is located
CITY	City in which library is located
STABR	State
ZIP	Five digit zip code
ZIP4	Extended zip code
ADDRES_M	Address of the main library
PHONE	Phone number of main library
CENTLIB	Central Library
BRANLIB	Branch library
BKMOB	Bookmobile
MASTER	Librarians with masters degree
LIBRARIA	Librarians without masters degree
OTHPAID	Other paid staff
TOTSTAFF	Total staff
LOCGVT	Local government revenues
STGVT	State government revenue
FEDGVT	Federal government revenue
OTHINCM	Other income
TOTINCM	Total income
SALARIES	Salary costs
BENEFIT	Benefit costs
STAFFEXP	Total salaries and benefits expenditures
TOTEXPCO	Total expenditures on library materials
OTHOPEXP	Expenditures on other
TOTOPEXP	Total operating expenditures
CAPITAL	Capital expenditures

FSCS name	Translation
BKVOL	Book volumes owned
AUDIO	Audio items owned
VIDEO	Video items owned
SUBSCRIP	Subscriptions to periodicals
HRS_OPEN	Hours open at all service outlets
VISITS	Annual visits to the library
REFERENC	Reference questions answered
TOTCIR	Total circulation
LOANTO	Interlibrary loans to the library
LOANFM	Interlibrary loans from the library
KIDCIRCL	Children's circulation
KIDATTEN	Attendance at children's programs
ELMATEXP	Electronic materials expenditure
ELACCEXP	Electronic access expenditure
ELMATS	Electronic materials available
ELSVCACC	Electronic Services access available
INETACC	Internet access
INETUSE	Internet access for the public
YR_SUB	Year the data was submitted

STATE LIBRARY AGENCY DATA

For many years, statistical compilations have been published by each state library agency. A print version of the statistical compilation is often distributed annually to all public libraries in the state, and many states now publish the data on the Web. The data is usually in a spreadsheet format that can be easily downloaded and manipulated for comparisons. Check with your state library agency on the availability of the data. Even if it is not available on the Web, it may be possible to get the data in spreadsheet form on a disk from your state data coordinator.

PUBLIC LIBRARY DATA SERVICE STATISTICAL REPORT

The Public Library Association annually publishes a statistical report called the Public Library Data Service (PLDS) Statistical Report. The data are collected from more than 1,000 public libraries that are identified by name, and categories include financial information, library resources and output measures, annual use figures, and technology in public libraries. This report is not as comprehensive as the FSCS data, but it is published sooner in the year, which may be useful for libraries that want the latest data even if it is not as comprehensive.

The current edition can help library managers identify top performing libraries, compare service levels and technology usage, and provide documentation for funding requests. Also included are the results of a special survey on public library facilities.

BIBLIOSTAT

Bibliostat is a commercial service that provides a convenient source of library statistics, albeit at a hefty price for many. It is based on Dynix Automation data, but the vendor plans to make it available to other vendors as well. The customizable database of specially prepared library statistics drawn from information in the PLDS report, the FSCS, and each state's own annual statistical report, is available from library product vendor Baker and Taylor. Bibliostat includes computed output measures along with statistics such as rank, percentile, and standard deviation.

U.S. CENSUS DATA

The U.S. Census has always presented a wealth of demographic and statistical information for library planners to use for evaluating their service territory and its characteristics; but the advent of the Internet has had a major and very positive impact on how that data can be located and used.

The American Factfinder Web site (http://factfinder.census.gov/home/saff/main.html) is especially useful. It allows planners, with the help of staff reference librarians, to quickly and easily generate tailor-made demographic data about their community far more efficiently than the old print census data allowed.

Maps provide a quick way to communicate demographic information to planning groups, and they often tell a surprising story about the library's service area. The FactFinder site is relatively easy to use for developing maps, as well as tables and charts. Census data can be presented at a wide variety of levels from national, to state, to county, to municipality, and the data can also be sorted by zip code, Standard Metropolitan Statistical Areas, and more.

Chances are good that someone on the library reference staff already knows how to use this resource. If not, assign someone on the team to come up with relevant data. In either case, caution the searcher to be very selective—the site is so easy to use that searchers can end up with an overwhelming amount of data.

The Census Data File Descriptions in Figure 4–3 provide a brief example of the wealth of data available on the FactFinder site. The data provided by numbers, charts and maps draw a statistical picture of the community served by the library that can help planners put the community into context as compared to the rest of the county, state, and nation. A community with a high level of educational and economic statistics will have a different set of expectations from its library than one with high poverty and low education rates. But often the census data will reveal surprises—a higher than anticipated level of non-English speakers or a lower than expected rate of single parent households, for instance. Such data can be used to plan for new services.

Figure 4–3 Census Data File Descriptions

SUMMARY DATA	
Census File	**Description**
2000 Summary File 1	Complete *geographic* detail to the block level
1990 Summary Tape File 1	Similar subjects from the 1990 Census
2000 Summary File 2	Subjects for up to 249 *race* or *ethnic* groups
SOCIAL, ECONOMIC, AND HOUSING DATA TO THE BLOCK GROUP LEVEL	
Census File	**Description**
2000 Summary File 3	Social, economic, and housing data to the block group level
2000 Summary File 4	Social, economic and housing data for up to 335 race, ethnic and ancestry groups
1990 Summary Tape File 3	Similar subjects from the 1990 Census
108th Congressional District Summary Files	• Subjects as in Summary Files 1 and 3 to the census tract level • Data from Census 2000 have been retabulated for the 108th Congressional District boundaries

ANNUAL RELEASES	
Census File	Description
American Community Surveys	Annual surveys that provide estimates of detailed subjects for all states, most areas with a population of 250,000 or more, and selected areas of 65,000 or more
Annual Population Estimates	Estimates of total population based on birth, death, and migration records. Available for the U.S., states, cities and towns, and more
1997 ECONOMIC CENSUS	
Census File	Description
Number of establishments, employment, payroll, and receipts by industry and area: • Industry Quick Reports • Geography Quick Reports	Detailed statistics for all economic sectors: more characteristics of industries, product detail, and other options

METROPOLITAN AREA RESEARCH CORPORATION

For the nation's twenty-five largest metropolitan areas, an excellent source of ready-made demographic data is the Metropolitan Area Research Corporation (MARC). MARC is a nonprofit research and geographic information systems (GIS) firm with a history of service to the public, government, philanthropic organizations, academia, and private research institutions. It provides demographic research through spatial display of data.

**Figure 4–4 Sample Census Bureau GIS Map
(Key: This map indicates the percent of residents below poverty level in the
area.)**

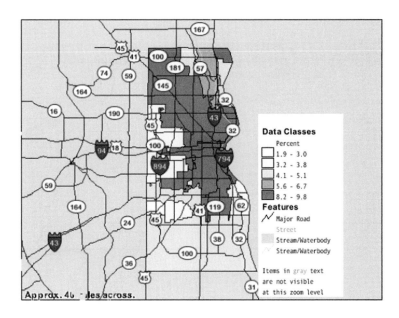

Figure 4–5 Sample GIS Depiction of Tax Capacity

Tax Capacity per Household by Municipality—Denver Metropolitan Area

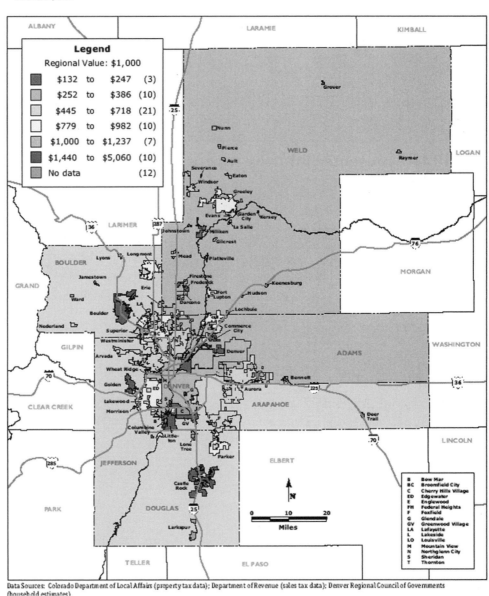

Data Sources: Colorado Department of Local Affairs (property tax data); Department of Revenue (sales tax data); Denver Regional Council of Governments (household estimates)

GeoLib, National Public Library Geographic Database

Florida State University's GeoLib Program (www.geolib.org) launched the National Public Library Geographic Database (NPLGD), which includes the locations of 16,000 public libraries, data sets from the U.S. Census, and library use statistics from the National Center for Educational Statistics in an effort to provide consolidated information on public libraries nationwide that is easily accessible over the Internet. The project is sponsored by the Institute of Museum and Library Services (www.imls.gov) in partnership with FSU's Information Institute (www.ii.fsu.edu), and is a research program of the Florida Resources and Environmental Analysis Center (FREAC), which is within FSU's Institute of Science and Public Affairs (ISPA).

NPLGD presents libraries with a great opportunity to use GIS data quickly and cheaply. Many stakeholders find that the use of map data greatly enhances their understanding of the library's demographic and statistical data that they need for good decision making.

Figure 4–6 National Public Library Geographic Database Sample

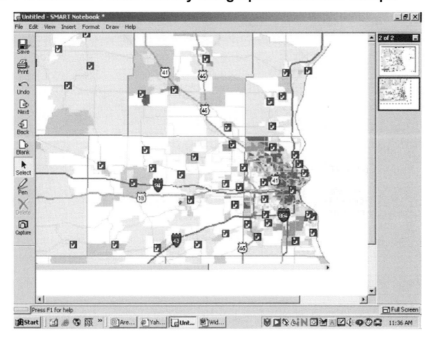

Figure 4–6 presents a sample of the type of map that the NPLGD can provide. The interactive maps are available over the Web so that planners can tailor them to their area and their specific information needs.

RYAN INFORMATION MANAGEMENT

Since 1995, Joe Ryan has been the sole proprietor of Ryan Information Management, a consulting and publishing company specializing in information management, network-based information resource evaluation and services, and information policy development and evaluation. The company occasionally publishes guides and manuals as a byproduct of research activities. Ryan, an Adjunct Professor and Research Associate at the Syracuse University School of Information Studies, maintains a very useful Web site on "Library Statistics and Measures," the official publication of the American Library Association.

HAPLR RATINGS

The HAPLR ratings (http://haplr-index.com/) create comparative rankings in broad population categories by using data provided by nearly 9,000 public libraries in the United States. The HAPLR ratings have received newspaper, magazine, and television coverage all over the country.

The HAPLR Index includes fifteen factors with a focus on circulation, staffing, materials, reference services, and funding levels. The index does not include data on audio and video collections, interlibrary loan, and other items that can be calculated from FSCS data. The top ten libraries in each population category are featured annually in American Libraries. For more information on HAPLR ratings, see Appendix 1.

SUMMARY LISTING OF SOURCES FOR DEMOGRAPHIC DATA AND LIBRARY STATISTICS

Figure 4–7 List of Sources for Demographic and Library Data

Data source	URL (if available)
NISO Z39.7 definition of library terms	www.niso.org/emetrics/index.cfm
Federal State Cooperative System (FSCS) statistics	http://nces.ed.gov/surveys/libraries/public.asp
Metropolitan Area Research Corporation	www.metroresearch.org/index.asp
Bibliostat	www.informata.com/eserv.cfm
U.S. Census Data	Follow link to American Factfinder: www.census.gov
GeoLib	www.geolib.org
Library Statistics and Measures by Joe Ryan	http://web.syr.edu/~jryan/infopro/stats.html
HAPLR Public Library Ratings	www.haplr-index.com
Office for Research and Statistics-Statistics About Libraries	www.ala.org/Content/NavigationMenu/Our_Association/Offices/Research_and_Statistics/Statistics_About_Libraries/Statistics_About_Libraries.htm
Public Library Association— Public Library Data Service Statistical Report	Not available on the Web, but order information is at: www.ala.org/Content/NavigationMenu/Our_Association/Divisions/PLA/Publications_and_Reports/PLDS_Statistical_Report/PLDS_Statistical_Report.htm
State Library Agency Data	Check with your state library agency

PRESENTING DATA GRAPHICALLY

Each of us absorbs numerical data in different ways. Some of us see things best visually with either graphs or maps; others need numeric depictions of data, and still others need narrative descriptions. Knowing this, effective library planners should present data to appeal to these different modes of understanding by providing graphs and/or maps, narrative descriptions, and tables.

Figure 4–8 illustrates this principle. The same information is displayed as a narrative, a table, a graph, and a map. Each of the four ways communicates the same basic information, that the average spending per capita varies in the Great Lakes region ranges from a high of $51.58 in Ohio; to $39.97 in Indiana; $37.80 in Illinois; $29.86 in Wisconsin; and a low of $28.68 in Michigan.

Figure 4–8 Four Ways to Illustrate the Same Information

Narrative form for data:

> The average spending per capita varies in the Great Lakes region ranges from a high of $51.58 in Ohio; to $39.97 in Indiana; $37.80 in Illinois; $29.86 in Wisconsin; and a low of $28.68 in Michigan.

Table form for same data:

State	Operating Expenses	Population	Spending per Capita
OH	$585,593,197	11,353,140	51.58
IN	$231,701,102	5,796,333	39.97
IL	$427,866,693	11,319,616	37.80
WI	$161,260,479	5,400,449	29.86
MI	$285,442,692	9,952,761	28.68

Bar graph for same data:

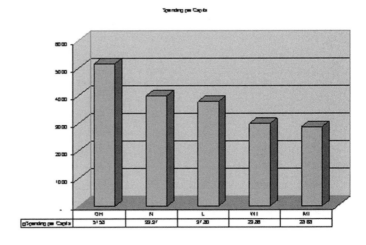

Map for same data:

Using Graphs

Graphs help us to tell stories about numerical relations. Using a spreadsheet program such as Microsoft Excel makes the production of graphs fairly easy.

Here are some rules for the effective use of graphs in any report:

- Make graphs big enough to read.

- Have someone else proofread to be sure that you included all the information that will communicate your points to readers—a missing scale, time series, or even a dollar sign can leave your reader confused.

- Indicate the source and the date of your data.

- Title the graph.

- Number graphs sequentially.

Line graphs

Line graphs are usually used to demonstrate trends in one or more pieces of data over a period of days, months, or years. For example, line graphs are used to illustrate circulation trends by type of material or decimal category over time. The chart in Figure 4–9 could be used to illustrate the relative circulation trends for three libraries. Library A's circulation has been growing quickly, Library B's circulation has been falling gradually, and Library C's circulation, while growing, is not growing as quickly as Library A's. The source data is included at the bottom of the graph to illustrate the factors involved.

Figure 4–9 Sample Line Graph for Circulation at Three Libraries

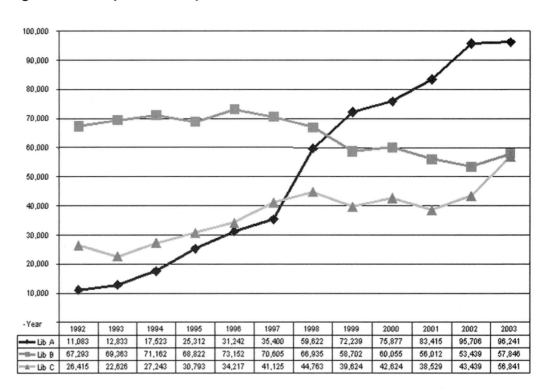

-Year	1992	1993	1994	1995	1996	1997	1998	1999	2000	2001	2002	2003
Lib A	11,083	12,833	17,523	25,312	31,242	35,400	59,622	72,239	75,877	83,415	95,706	96,241
Lib B	67,293	69,363	71,162	68,822	73,152	70,605	66,935	58,702	60,055	56,012	53,439	57,846
Lib C	26,415	22,626	27,243	30,793	34,217	41,125	44,763	39,624	42,624	38,529	43,439	56,841

Bar Graphs

Bar graphs work well for illustrating comparative levels for a number of items. Suppose you wanted to illustrate the relative number of visits in three nearby libraries in the last year. The graph in Figure 4–10 would quickly and easily communicate the high level of visits at Library B.

Figure 4–10 Sample Bar Graph for Library Visits at Three Libraries

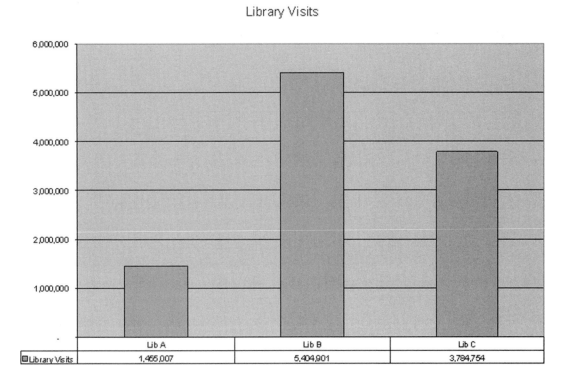

100% Bar Graph

100% bar graphs can be used to indicate relative changes over time. This type of graph works better than trying to put a series of pie graphs next to one another to illustrate market share trends over time. In Figure 4–11 it is easy to see that Branch A has experienced a sharp increased of visitors when compared to the other branches.

Figure 4–11 Sample 100 Percent Bar Graph for Library Visitors at Four Different Branches

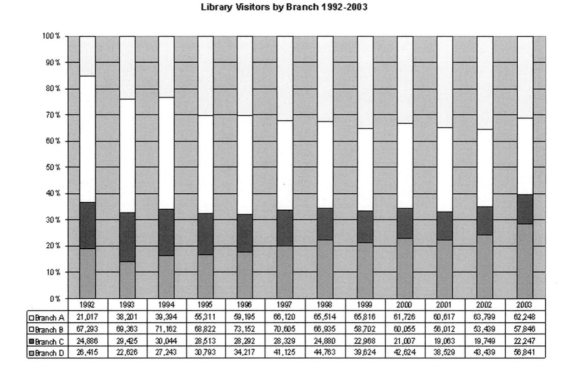

Library Visitors by Branch 1992-2003

	1992	1993	1994	1995	1996	1997	1998	1999	2000	2001	2002	2003
□ Branch A	21,017	38,201	39,394	55,311	59,195	66,120	65,514	65,816	61,726	60,617	63,799	62,248
□ Branch B	67,293	69,363	71,162	68,822	73,152	70,605	66,935	58,702	60,055	56,012	53,439	57,846
■ Branch C	24,886	29,425	30,044	28,513	28,292	28,329	24,880	22,968	21,007	19,063	19,749	22,247
▨ Branch D	26,415	22,626	27,243	30,793	34,217	41,125	44,763	39,624	42,624	38,529	43,439	56,841

Pie Graphs

Most people can look at a pie graph and get a quick idea of what proportion a given element contributes to the whole. Pie graphs work particularly well for budget presentations. The graph in Figure 4–12 indicates spending by category for a library with a $2.8 million budget, but it could just as easily depict a budget of $28,000, since both graphs would have a similar amount of their "pie" devoted to each category.

Figure 4–12 Sample Pie Graph for Library Operating Expenditures

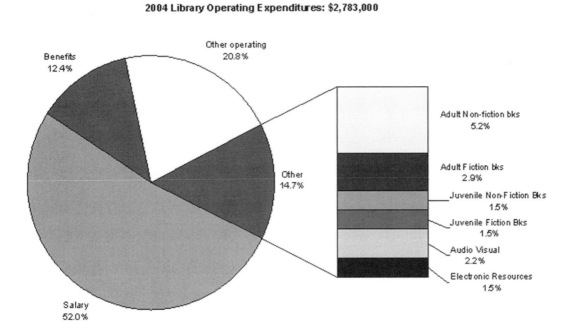

Area Graphs (or Stacked Bar Graphs)

Area graphs (or stacked bar graphs) can illustrate the relative weights of categories over a period of time. For instance the area graph in Figure 4–13 indicates the declining share of periodicals and the rising share of videos in the circulation total that includes book circulation. Compare that to the line graph below it, which uses the same numbers. The stacked bar graph makes it clear that although periodical circulation is declining, the total circulation is up. The line graph shows the switch between videos and periodicals very clearly, but it is not as clear what is happening to the total circulation data.

Figure 4–13 Sample Stacked Area Graph Compared to Sample Line Graph

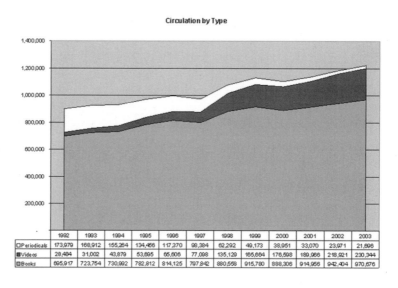

Circulation by Type

	1992	1993	1994	1995	1996	1997	1998	1999	2000	2001	2002	2003
Periodicals	173,979	168,912	155,264	134,456	117,370	98,384	62,292	49,173	38,951	33,070	23,971	21,696
Videos	28,484	31,002	43,879	53,695	65,606	77,098	135,129	165,664	176,598	189,966	218,921	230,344
Books	695,917	723,754	730,992	782,812	814,125	797,842	880,558	915,780	888,306	914,956	942,404	970,576

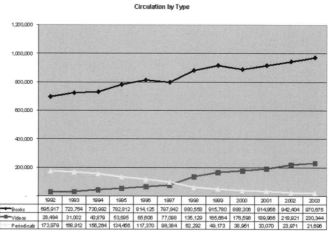

Circulation by Type

	1992	1993	1994	1995	1996	1997	1998	1999	2000	2001	2002	2003
Books	695,917	723,754	730,992	782,812	814,125	797,842	880,558	915,780	888,306	914,956	942,404	970,576
Videos	28,484	31,002	43,879	53,695	65,606	77,098	135,129	165,664	176,598	189,966	218,921	230,344
Periodicals	173,979	168,912	155,264	134,456	117,370	98,384	62,292	49,173	38,951	33,070	23,971	21,696

116

Bar and Line Graph on Two Scales

The bar and line graph on two scales can be very effective for illustrating the relationship of two very differently sized numbers. For example, the chart in Figure 4–14 demonstrates that even though the library's spending has grown considerably in recent years, the expenditure per item circulated has remained stable. This kind of graph can be used to good effect with budget committees of city councils looking at rapid increases in library budgets. One can argue that yes, the budget is up substantially, but the stability of the amount spent per item circulated during the entire growth period is a testimony to the library's efficient allocation of resources.

Figure 4–14 Sample Bar and Line Graph on Two Scales

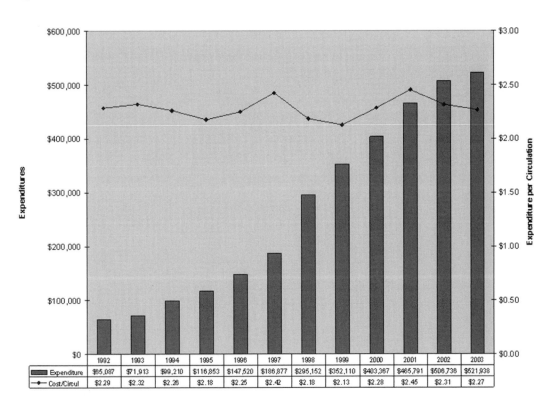

	1992	1993	1994	1995	1996	1997	1998	1999	2000	2001	2002	2003
Expenditure	$65,087	$71,913	$99,210	$116,853	$147,520	$186,877	$295,152	$352,110	$403,367	$465,791	$506,736	$521,938
Cost/Circul	$2.29	$2.32	$2.26	$2.18	$2.25	$2.42	$2.18	$2.13	$2.28	$2.45	$2.31	$2.27

Conclusion

Planners may or may not use graphs, maps, or other such data in their final plan, but when they do it is usually in the form of a demographics and statistics section at the end of a plan. They are more likely to use such comparative data during the planning process when communicating to planning groups about library activities. Comparative data help planners begin to formulate appropriate goals and objectives that are based on the present and aimed at the future.

This chapter provided:

- a variety of data sources and methods to help stakeholders understand the issues. Don't get caught up in data gathering at the expense of planning or data analysis, however;

- a list of sources for comparative data, including state, federal and private sources;

- tips on how to use graphs effectively in planning reports.

Chapter 5
Defining Library Standards and Percentile Comparisons

Overview

This chapter discusses the need for and the uses of standards and benchmarking in public library planning. It defines and explains the differences between various kinds of standards and points library planners to methods and resources to use in developing their own plans. A standard is specific and measurable benchmark for achievement. The two major types of library standards are numeric, which measures by counting, and prescriptive, which prescribes an action. An example of a numeric standard is the common state library standard for a given number of books or staffing per capita. Prescriptive standards include statements that a library should have a collection development policy, follow open meeting laws, or employ a properly certified director.

Most states have library standards, but these standards are usually advisory only. There is usually no penalty for failing to meet the standards set by a state, although there are exceptions. Effective library planners will carefully consider library standards in their state., especially if there are any mandatory standards, of course. Voluntary standards can and usually should be fundamental to the plan developed. Effective planners will also consider the percentile comparisons in the prior chapter.

This chapter provides information on:

- The history of library standards

- Standards and excellence

- Numerical standards

- Prescriptive standards

- Personnel certification

- Standards in each state

- A public library standards database

- A listing by state of available standards

Setting specific numerical targets for key input and output measures makes most of the key objectives in your plan easily measurable. You can set specific numerical targets for your library by examining the current measures on these factors of all similarly sized libraries in the country. This chapter provides a mechanism for making those comparisons. Tables with specific data for each size of library are found in the appendix. Updated information, when available, will be posted at http://haplr-index.com.

The Metrics Worksheet featured in this chapter (Figure 5–4, also available as an Excel spreadsheet on the CD) allows you to compare your library to all other libraries in its population category on each of the thirty-eight measures listed in Appendix 2.

BRIEF HISTORY OF STANDARDS

Until 1966 the American Library Association (ALA) took an active role in setting standards. Since then, they have concentrated on variations on planning and have encouraged libraries to set their own standards. Individual state library agencies assisted by state library associations have taken on the job os setting standards. I believe that ALA should develop new standards for the twenty-first century based on the models set by England and a number of U.S. states, including Iowa and Wisconsin; however, it is highly unlikely that ALA will heed that advice.

Starting in the 1930s, Carnegie Corporation spurred the push for standards and wider units of service. Carnegie was disappointed by the failure of individual libraries built with Carnegie grants to garner sufficient support to thrive. Standards that the Carnegie Coprporation hoped would help. The University of Chicago and Carlton Joeckl, among others, began to push the American Library Association in the direction of national standards.

In 1956—the year that Congress enacted federal aid for public libraries—the ALA published a compendium of standards for public libraries designed to be used by local boards and governmental officials. The document stated this dictum unequivocally: "Libraries working together, sharing their services and materials, can meet the full needs of their users. This cooperative approach on the part of libraries is the most important single recommendation of this document." The 1966 revision of the public library standards reiterated this premise and was entitled more precisely "Minimum Standards for Public Library Systems, 1966."

By 1980 ALA had abandoned standards in favor of locally defined planning processes. There are library standards for at least forty-two states. At last count, forty-one of the states' library standards were available on the World Wide Web. Note the state-by-state listing at the end of this chapter.

Libraries in states without numerical comparisons for various input measures such as books or staffing per capita may want to refer to the percentile comparisons in this chapter for possible target numbers. Consult the planning checklist in Chapter 9 for the prescriptive measures needed to keep the library running effectively, especially if your state does not have such prescriptive standards.

Some states do not have library standards, and for most of the states that do, they are voluntary or advisory rather than mandatory. In a few states, however, receipt of state aid is contingent upon meeting the minimum standards outlined by the state. A few other states have authorized standards at the county or regional level as well.

STANDARDS AND EXCELLENCE

Perhaps one of the fundamental reasons for the abandonment of national standards by the ALA was the fear that minimum standards would come to be seen as maximums and hold back quality libraries. The output measures focus epitomized by the 1980 edition of the ALA Planning Process document worried many who feared that catering to the circulation and numbers game diluted and potentially destroyed the public library's responsibility for building quality collections and achieving solid educational objectives. In response to this fear, many states have established varying levels of standards. Minimum standards are established to mean just that—minimums. Beyond these minimums are standards that set the bar at moderate, advanced, and excellent.

Library planners must address this issue head on and decide what they want their library to be—basic, moderate, enhanced, or excellent. That decision will drive the objectives established for collection development, staffing levels, hours, and all other elements of library services. If the state has no established definitions for these categories, planners should strongly consider using the national comparison measures and percentiles in this chapter.

NUMERICAL STANDARDS

Mandatory minimum standards get some attention, but only a few states have implemented such standards for any but the narrowest of measures such as certification of library staff and hours of service. At times state aid or eligibility for grants are tied to meeting these minimum standards, so it is important for library planners to review them carefully where they exist.

Many states have target standards. These involve moving target standards pegged to some proportion of the median measures for a given library population. For example, a state may choose to peg the recommended standard for books per capita to the median for all libraries in the state. This standard will move over time as libraries change collections and the median shifts. Many libraries cannot meet these types of standards because half of all libraries will, by definition, always fall below the median. Such standards are advisory. Libraries seeking improvements often lament the lack of target standards, particularly the numerical standards for collection size, expenditures per capita, and the like; however, those libraries well above the targets fear such targets will hold them back and they push for community-based planning instead of hard standards.

NUMERICAL VERSUS PRESCRIPTIVE LIBRARY STANDARDS

When we think of standards, what most often comes to mind is numerical standards such as the number of books per capita. Equally important are prescriptive standards that enquire about the existence of a challenged materials policy, bylaws for the board, and Internet acceptable use policies. These standards represent items or processes that are necessary in all public libraries of every size, and effective planners will use such standards to determine if their library has all the necessary items in a plan.

PERSONNEL CERTIFICATION

Quite a number of states have requirements for library staff that usually include the types of initial and continuing education required for directors or other paid staff. Sometimes, as in the case of New York, these requirements are written into state statute. More often they are published in state library documents that are easily obtainable from the state library agency. Find out whether there are such requirements in your state and if your library meets them.

LIBRARY CERTIFICATION

A few states, including Iowa and Nebraska, certify libraries. Certification may mean merely the prestige of meeting the grade, or it may include eligibility for state funds or federal grants controlled by the state library agency. In any case, it is important to be aware of these requirements and to know whether or not the library meets the certification criteria.

STANDARDS IN VARIOUS STATES

A total of forty-one states have public library standards and all but a handful of these standards are available on the Web. Carefully consider your library in relation to your state's standards, if any. Illinois, Kansas, Oklahoma, Texas, Virginia, and Wisconsin include very specific quantitative or numerical formulas for staffing ratios, collection size, budget levels, recommended technology, and other elements in their standards that might prove helpful if your state lacks standards. State standards are often voluntary documents developed by the state library agency or the state library association and some are included in state law or administrative rules with the force of law.

Review the current state statutes whenever a planning process is undertaken. States constantly revise laws that affect libraries, and it is easy to drift away from both the letter and spirit of the law unless there are periodic reviews.

Consult the regional library system or state library agency staff on the issues. Often there is a simple checklist that has been developed for use by individual libraries to assure statutory compliance.

Libraries must also follow all legal requirements for public entities in addition to those aimed specifically at libraries. For example, there are open meeting laws, fair labor standards requirements, and proper bidding procedures for large spending projects. The size and composition of the board and its meeting frequency are usually laid out in statutes, and the legal relationship between the library board and its parent municipality (city, town, city, county, parish, etc.) is most often outlined with some degree of specificity. State laws also deal with the sometimes-contentious issues of whether the library board or city council is in charge of hiring and firing, the line items in the budget, or building a library or branch.

States vary in the latitude they allow. When reviewing plans and policies, ask the library's usual legal counsel to review statutes aimed at libraries and public organizations.

PUBLIC LIBRARY STANDARDS DATABASE

Central Colorado Library System (www.cclsweb.org/plsp/view .php) has an easy-to-use database of Public Library Standards that includes all known standards for every state. The database can be searched by state, major topic, and date and even allows full-text Boolean searching. Each state's standards are assessed within a consistent matrix that allows for quick comparisons.

The database allows for very useful searches. If you search for all the state standards that include the items "facilities," "collections," "staffing levels," and "hours of operation," the database quickly indicates that nineteen states include sections on all four items. This database will be especially useful when the planners find that some of the standards for their own state are lacking.

Figure 5–1 State by State Standards List

State	URL
AK	None
AL	www.apls.state.al.us/webpages/pubs/standardsdraft.pdf
AR	None
AZ	None
CA	None
CO	www.cde.state.co.us/cdelib/slpdfdocs.htm
CT	www.cslib.org/stand.htm
DE	www.flalib.org/library/fla/flplstan.htm
FL	http://dlis.dos.state.fl.us/standards/
GA	www.public.lib.ga.us/pls/publibs/standards-final.pdf
HI	None
IA	www.silo.lib.ia.us/thirded.html
ID	http://spidaweb.eils.lib.id.us/standards/
IL	www.cyberdriveillinois.com/library/isl/ref/readyref/serving/index.htm
IN	www.statelib.lib.in.us/WWW/LDO/PUBSTAN17.HTML
KS	http://skyways.lib.ks.us/KSL/development/standard.html
KY	www.kdla.state.ky.us/intro/lstaata.htm
LA	www.state.lib.la.us/Publications/lla/standards.PDF
MA	http://mlin.lib.ma.us/mblc/sadac/stananrp.shtml
MD	None
ME	http://mainelibraries.org/standards/
MI	http://tln.lib.mi.us/~plfig-committees/qsac-committee.htm
MN	http://cfl.state.mn.us/library/stand.html
MO	http://mosl.sos.state.mo.us/lib-ser/libser.html
MS	None
MT	http://msl.state.mt.us/admin/libstandards.html
NC	http://statelibrary.dcr.state.nc.us/ld/ncplda/guidelines.htm
ND	Not available online. In process.
NE	www.nlc.state.ne.us/libdev/revguid.html
NH	www.state.nh.us/nhsl/libstandards/index.html
NJ	www.njla.org/statements/ServiceStandards4.pdf
NM	www.nmcpr.state.nm.us/nmac/parts/title04/04.005.0002.htm
NV	http://dmla.clan.lib.nv.us/docs/nsla/lpd/state/
NY	http://nysgis.nysed.gov/libdev/ministan.htmwww.nysl.nysed.gov/libdev/edl/thirdpln.htm
OH	http://winslo.state.oh.us/services/LPD/standards.html
OK	Published in 1998, not available online, being revised in 2003.
OR	http://olaweb.org/pld/standards.html
PA	Act 164 not available online.
RI	www.lori.state.ri.us/libprograms/pl_standards/Minstand.htm

State	URL
SC	www.state.sc.us/scsl/pubs/PLstandards/
SD	www.usd.edu/sdla/PublicLibs/CA.htm
TN	Not available online. In process.
TX	www.txla.org/groups/plstand/plstand.html
UT	http://library.utah.gov/plstandards.html
VA	www.lva.lib.va.us/whatwedo/ldnd/govadmin/pfle/index.htm
VT	http://dol.state.vt.us/GOPHER_ROOT5/LIBRARIES/forms/standards_forms.htm
WA	None?
WI	www.dpi.state.wi.us/dlcl/pld/standard.html
WV	West Virginia Public Library Working Standards Manual (not available online)
WY	None

Pursuing Percentile Comparisons

INTRODUCTION

This chapter provides a consistent method of comparing your library to libraries of comparable size in the country based on thirty-nine input and output measures. Input measures include the things that a community puts into a library such as funding and staffing levels; output measures include the things that a library does such as circulation or annual patron visits.

Besides the measures suggested here, the library may wish to calculate additional measures as suggested in *Output Measures for Public Libraries*[1], or as indicated by state standards. Only a few of the PLA's output measures have national or state comparison figures. In addition, consider the Federal State Cooperative Service Peer Comparison Tool available on the Web from the National Center for Educational Statistics (NCES) (http://nces.ed.gov/surveys/libraries/publicpeer). According to NCES, the tool "allows the user to get information on a particular library, or to customize a peer group by selecting the key variables that are used to define it. The user can then view customized reports of the comparison between the library of interest and its peers, on a variety of variables as selected by the user."

The site also notes that the data available "have been reviewed and edited at the state and national levels, and verified as correct by each state's data coordinator. These data have not been imputed for nonresponse, so some data for some libraries may be missing. This may mean that some libraries will not be selected as peers."

The advantage of the Peer Comparison Tool is that it allows planners a greater degree of control over the broad range of parameters used to compare its library to others. The use of these parameters may make planners more comfortable, since they know they are comparing their data to that of "true peers." I believe that the Metrics Worksheet sample presented in the chapter provides a better and more consistent method of comparision than the Peer Comparision Tool, but some planners may wish to consider this as an alternative.

BRITISH PERFORMANCE INDICATORS COMPARED TO U.S. DATA

You may want to look at how libraries and other government services are measured and assessed in England and Wales. The national governments there have implemented a consistent set of comparison tools and evaluators that is in many ways very similar to the methods and tools presented in this chapter (See Figure 5–2).

Figure 5–2 England and Wales (Combined) Summary Library Statistics 1998/1989

Measure	75th percentile	Median	25th percentile	Average	U.S. average
Circulation per capita	9.5	8.0	6.9	8.2	7.6
Visits per capita	6.6	5.4	4.6	5.7	5.0
Materials expend. per capita ($US)	4.06	3.33	2.72	3.43	4.26
Total expend per capita ($US)	23.45	19.71	17.36	21.41	24.64

Since 1994 the Audit Commission has collected and published performance information on council, police, library and fire services in England and Wales, allowing researchers to see how performance has changed over time, as well as compare performance. The latest performance data, as well as data from as far back as 1993, can be downloaded as an Excel spreadsheet (www.bestvalueinspections.gov.uk and www.audit-commission.gov.uk/pis). There is also a program that allows you to compare a performance indicator across authorities and years. For example, you can look at the comparative circulation per capita across all the libraries you select and the years available in the database.

The table in Figure 5–2 provides the average, 75th percentile, median, and 25th percentile for Audit Commission performance indicators for libraries. A 75th percentile measurement for the circulation per capita in that table means that 75 percent of libraries do less than the 9.5 circulations per capita indicated in the table. For reference I have added the relevant data for the U.S.

The data for U.S. and U.K. library use is very similar. Circulation per capita is somewhat higher in the U.K. After adjusting for exchange rates, U.K. materials spending and total spending per capita are just a bit lower than found in the U.S. The input measures (materials and total spending per capita) and output measures (circulation and visits per capita) are quite comparable in both countries.

This comparison is important because Great Britain recently adopted national standards and the Audit Commission began publishing both a summary annual reports of library conditions and individualized ratings of libraries in 2000. This proves that national standards can be developed based on specific data very similar to that which is available in the U.S.

The Audit Commission, an independent body, bases the reports on statistical data, long-range plans, local government commitment to the library, and a site visit and assigns every library a score. The scoring chart displays performance in two dimensions. A horizontal axis shows how good the service is at present on a scale ranging from poor (no stars) to excellent (three stars). A vertical axis shows the improvement prospects over time of the service, also on a four-point scale. The narrative reports, which are about forty pages long, are very specific and quite blunt in their assessments and recommendations for improvement.

There is no agency to do this English standards type of assessment for U.S. libraries, although in earlier generations many state library agencies performed this type of assessment for individual libraries. However, using the Metrics Worksheet in Figure 5–4, as well as the other performance checklists provided in this book will allow a self-assessment based on consistent principles that will result in a plan rooted in objective data.

Metrics Worksheet

It is important to remember that the population numbers used here and in the tables in the appendix are the "Legal Service Area" figures recorded by each state library agency with the Federal State Cooperative System for libraries. This number nearly always differs from the current census population of the community supporting the library. Check with your state library agency on this number; otherwise, the per capita calculations you will derive in columns G and J in the Metrics Worksheet (see Figure 5–4) will not be comparable to those in the percentile tables presented. The population data is also available on the author's Web site (www.haplr-index.com) in the section on state comparisons.

The Metrics Worksheet, available as an Excel spreadsheet on the CD, includes thirty-nine benchmark measures a library can use to compare itself to other libraries in its population category. After library planners have done the calculations on the Metrics Worksheet, they can compare their library to other libraries in the Percentile Details sheets found in Appendix 2.

For instance, suppose that your library is in the over-500,000 population category. After you have worked out the numbers in the Metrics Worksheet, you will compare your library's numbers to those found in Figure 5–2, "Percentile Details for 500,000+ Population Libraries."

Turn to Figure 5–3, the Metrics Worksheet, now. library planners will need to collect the data indicated on the worksheet first.

The current population served by the library will be repeated numerous times in most rows of column F. The projected future population will be repeated in column I. Be sure that you use the service data as used by FSCS and your state library agency, not the census data population. The spreadsheet on the CD is set up to run the calculations automatically, but take care if you use the spreadsheet printed here to do the calculation on the basis indicated in column C.

Column D, HAPLR weight, is provided for reference only. It indicates the relative weight in the HAPLR ratings assigned to these measures. The other measures, while useful for comparison, are not included in the HAPLR ratings calculations. For further discussion on the HAPLR ratings, see Chapter 4 and Appendix 1.

Fill in the Current Amounts and the Future Amounts in Columns E and H. Future amounts are harder to calculate, since projecting three to five years into the future on such things as funding or staffing or library visits is nearly impossible.

The Metrics Worksheet divides the thiry-eight comparison items into six larger categories:

- Revenue, including Federal, Local, State, other

  1. Federal government—Funds from the Federal Government, usually Library Services and Technology Act (LSTA) grants

  2. Local government—Funds from the municipality or municipalities that fund the library (city, town, county, district, etc.)

  3. Other income—Income from other sources (fines, fees, donations, etc.)

  4. State government—Revenue from the state government

  5. Total income—1 through 4 above combined

- Expenditure, including capital, materials, and so forth

- Staffing, including staff with masters degrees

- Collection elements such as books, magazines, video, and audio

- Hours open

- Output measures such as circulation, visits, and program attendance

Figure 5–3 Worksheet for Input and Output Measures

A	B	C	D	E	F	G	H	I	J
				Current amount for this library			Future amount for this library		
Category	*Title*	*Measure*	*HAPLR weight*	*Current amount*	*Current pop. (or other measure)*	*Per capita*	*Future amount*	*Future pop. (or other measure)*	*Per capita*
a) Revenue	Federal govt	Per capita							
	Local government	Per capita							
	Other income	Per capita							
	State government	Per capita							
	Total income	Per capita							
b) Expend.	Capital expenditure	Per capita							
	Electronic access	Per capita							
	Electronic materials	Per capita	2						
	Materials collection	Per capita							
	Other operating	Per capita	2						
	Percent budget to materials	Ratio							
	Personnel-benefits	Per capita							
	Personnel-salaries	Per capita							
	Personnel-salary and benefits	Per capita							

A	B	C	D	Current amount for this library			Future amount for this library		
Category	Title	Measure	HAPLR weight	Current amount	Current pop. (or other measure)	Per capita	Future amount	Future pop. (or other measure)	Per capita
	Total expend. per circulation	Per circ.	3						
	Total expenditure	Per capita	3						
c) Staff	Master-degreed librarian	Per 1000 pop.							
	Nondegreed professional	Per 1000 pop.							
	Other staff	Per 1000 pop.							
	Total staff	Per 1000 pop.	2						
d) Collection	Audio	Per 1000 pop.							
	Book volumes	Per capita	1						
	Subscriptions	Per 1000 pop.	1						
	Video								
e) Hours	Hours open	Per bldg., per wk.							
	Total hours	All							

Figure 5–4 Sample Use of Worksheet and Percentile Charts

A	B	C	D	E	F	G
Category	*Title*	*Measure*	*This library*	*75th*	*50th*	*25th*
a) Revenue	Federal govt.	Per capita	$0.17	$0.22	$0.12	$0.02
	Local govt.	Per capita	$25.00	$32.61	$23.61	$16.73
	Other income	Per capita	$2.50	$3.20	$1.92	$0.99
	State govt.	Per capita	$2.50	$3.03	$1.71	$0.56
	Total income	Per capita	$29.17	$39.80	$28.50	$19.65
b) Expend.	Capital expenditure	Per capita	$3.33	$3.98	$0.73	$0.08
	Electronic access	Per capita	$0.83	$1.00	$0.58	$0.33
	Electronic materials	Per capita	$0.17	$0.35	$0.24	$0.07
	Materials collection	Per capita	$3.33	$5.63	$3.96	$2.79
	Other operating	Per capita	$4.17	$7.10	$5.11	$3.38
	Percent budget to materials		11.4%	18.0%	15.4%	12.9%
	Personnel: benefits	Per capita	$3.33	$5.21	$38.50	$2.32
	Personnel: salaries	Per capita	$12.50	$19.44	$13.15	$9.51
	Personnel: salary & benefits	Per capita	$15.83	$24.59	$16.26	$11.72
	Total expend per circulation	Per circ.	$2.92	$5.89	$4.29	$3.38
	Total expenditure	Per capita	$29.17	$38.50	$25.87	$19.33
c) Staff	Master degreed librarian	Per 1000 pop.	0.17	0.17	0.11	0.08
	Nondegreed professional	Per 1000 pop.	0.12	0.19	0.12	0.09
		Per 1000 pop.	0.40	0.43	0.30	0.20
		Per 1000 pop.	0.69	0.69	0.43	0.31
d) Collection	Audio	Per 1000 pop.	100.0	151.2	85.1	51.7
	Book volumes	Per capita	2.5	2.8	2.2	1.6
	Subscriptions	Per 1000 pop.	5.0	7.9	4.6	3.3
	Video	Per 1000 pop.	50.00	83.7	54.1	33.6
e) Hours	Hours open	Per bldg., per week	57.7	57.4	49.8	42.0
	Buildings	Number	20			
	Total hours	All		77,922	59,688	50,331

A	B	C	D	E	F	G
Category	Title	Measure	This library	75th	50th	25th
f) Output	Children circulation	Per capita	1.7	2.9	1.9	1.3
	Children prog. attend.	Per 1,000 pop.	166.7	201.4	122.6	90.8
	Circulation (frequency)	Per hour	100.0	105.4	77.8	59.6
	Circulation (staff)	Per staff hour	7.0	8.9	6.6	4.7
	Circulation (volume)	Per visit	10.0	1.9	1.4	1.1
	Collection Turnover		4.0	3.9	2.4	1.7
	Interlibrary loan IN	Per 1,000 pop.	20.0	20.7	8.0	2.7
	Interlibrary loan OUT	Per 1,000 pop.	23.3	12.5	4.5	1.6
	Reference	Per capita	1.7	2.0	1.4	0.8
	Total circulation	Per capita	10.0	8.9	5.0	3.9
	Visit (frequency)	Per hour	45.0	68.5	56.2	40.7
	Visits	Per capita	4.5	5.1	3.8	3.0

Using the Metrics Worksheet, library planners can generate Table 5–4. This library is in the 500,000 plus population category and it is being compared to libraries in the 75th, 50th, and 25th percentile in columns E through G. Its 17 cents per capita in Federal revenue places it between the 75th and 50th percentile for libraries of a comparable size.

After calculating where the library is now on each of the thirty-eight measures, it is time for library planners to target where they want to be by the end of the next planning cycle. For instance, the library illustrated here has the following under d) Collection: 100 audio titles for every 1,000 residents, 2.5 books per capita, 5 subscriptions per 1,000 residents, and 50 videos for every 1,000 residents. Subscriptions are at a lower percentile rate than the other three items. Subscriptions could therefore be targeted for improvement.

Using These Percentiles or Standards to Set Goals and Objectives

The goals and objectives in a long range plan need to be specific, measurable and time-related. Figure 2–8 is an example of how state-defined standards can be used to set the objective of meeting collection standards.

A number of states have defined tiers of standards for various input measures. The tiers usually range from basic to moderate, enhanced, and excellent—or some variation on that theme. This allows library planners to determine their aims for each category.

Here is an example of how to use state standards to develop objectives. When examining the data, the planners discover that the library has fewer books per capita, operating hours, total staff, and videos than the basic level recommended for libraries in their state. As a strategic direction, the library determines that it wants to get to the basic level within three years and then continue on to the moderate level within six years. Not every library can aim for the "excellent" level in such tiered standards—circumstances and financial constraints may mean that a library can realistically aim at only basic levels. The standards allow the library to note that it is, for instance, 6,000 volumes short of the mark for the moderate standard for book volumes. It can then set a six year target of net volume additions to reach its goal (adjusting for reasonable annual collection weeding, of course). If that means that the library needs to add 1,000 books per year, but its current book budget will only support 500 volumes, then the objective cannot be fulfilled without added funding. Figure 2–11 helps planners set budgets for these and similar situations.

Of course, lacking state standards, planners can use the Metrics Worksheet to measure potential efforts and develop objectives. Suppose, for instance, that the library discovers by using the Metrics Worksheet that it has far fewer library staff per 1,000 of population and is open fewer hours than 75 percent of comparably sized libraries. Effective planners could use Figure 2–8 to develop objectives appropriate to the deficiencies discovered and use Figure 2–11 to attempt to close the gap over a period of years.

Remember that setting goals and objectives that require additional funding means the library's funding body must be clearly informed of the deficiencies and must agree to use added funding to address them. Planners must address shortcomings, even if it makes some group members uncomfortable about those deficiencies and the potential costs of rectifying them.

136

Conclusion

This chapter has provided:

- an overview of the history and current status of public library standards in the U.S. Most states have library standards, but if your state does not, it is advisable to look at those the do. Planners should also look to the percentile measures in this chapter and Appendix 2 for guidance;

- a consideration of the distinction between numerical and prescriptive standards. Numerical standards ask library planners to aim at a set amount of books or staff per capita. Prescriptive standards ask library planner to assure that certain conditions apply to the library: that the library has a collection development policy, is legally organized, and so forth;

- a checklist and database of standards and their location on the Web;

- an outlined method libraries can use to set specific numerical targets for key input and output measures;

- a consistent set of metrics for examining measures on thirty-eight factors for all libraries of similar size in the country. Libraries should consult Appendix 2 for the comparative data for their specific population size;

- the advantages of the measures included in the Metrics Worksheet (Figure 5–3) in this chapter so that the library can compare itself to all other libraries in its population category on each of the thirty-eight measures listed. The worksheet is available as an Excel spreadsheet on the CD.

Updated information, when available, will be posted to the author's Web site (http://haplr-index.com).

Note

1. Van House, Nancy A., et al. 1987. *Output Measures for Public Libraries: A Manual of Standardized Procedures*, 2nd ed. Chicago: American Library Association.

Chapter 6
Integrating Financial and Governance Issues into the Plan

Overview

"Sunlight is the best disinfectant," said U.S. Supreme Court Justice Louis Brandeis. Library officials should keep that dictum in mind at all points when planning library finances. This chapter covers financial and governance issues in the context of long-range planning and policy development rather than other day-to-day issues. It deals with strategic budget issues, not accounting or fiscal details. Major changes in how a library is governed or in its financial basis are rare, but it is important for planners to look closely at all the related issues. Budget and financial planning is just as important as planning for new programs or services, but in the library literature on planning, it is often overlooked.

Most of the information in this chapter is for the administration, library board, and possibly the governing body. The author of the plan will want to read this information to shed light on the issues involved, but many of the planning committee members can either skim or entirely skip some of the issues presented in this chapter. Because state laws differ widely in the types of library structures they allow and the types of library governance permitted, this chapter covers some of the related issues that library planners must consider about library governance and administration.

There are many books solely on the topic of budgeting in public libraries, and the bibliography lists recommended titles.

INTRODUCTION

Only a few libraries in the U.S. have direct taxing authority; a few others have a sufficient endowment and can avoid asking for funds from tax authorities; and some, such as some of the district libraries in New York State, must seek annual referendum authority directly from the voters. Most public libraries, however, must submit both their annual operating and capital budget requests to a funding authority or authorities. Often a referendum is required for major building programs as well.

The single most important policy document for any agency is its budget. No matter how much planning and projecting we do, if something is not translated into a budgeted item, it is not ordinarily done. During the course of the planning effort, the planners must make an effort to identify realistic costs for the goals they are setting. A long-range plan without a budget is almost as bad as no plan at all—and it is likely that municipal officials and boards will treat it as such.

RELATIONS WITH FUNDING AGENCY AND THE CONTROL AND CUSTODY OF FUNDS

The guidelines and issues discussed here will not be true for every library in the U.S. Be sure to check on the specific legal and budgetary relationships between your library and the funding authorities before following the advice here. State library agencies and regional library systems will be the best authorities to consult.

In most cases, there are state statutes that give the library board *exclusive control* over the expenditure of the library budget after the city council or other funding authority approves it. Library boards have historically been given broader independence and latitude than other municipal agencies because of concerns for first amendment rights or intellectual freedom issues, among other things. For most libraries this means that alderpersons, city managers, mayors or other officials cannot and should not attempt to define how individual line items in the operating budget are spent. The funding authority entrusts specific line item spending decisions to the library board. At times, there are exceptions for parts of the budget such as salaries, especially if collective bargaining is part of the equation. This exception may be either statutory or simply the decision of the library board and administration to follow the general personnel policies of the city or county of which they are a part.

Exclusive control is not the same as *exclusive custody*. State laws frequently require the deposit of all public funds in a municipal or county account administered by a properly certified and bonded individual. Most often private funds such as donations and bequests can be retained and administered by library boards or sometimes by a separately established Friends group or a Foundation. It is important for the administration and board to ensure that all funds are handled legally and appropriately, whether by the board, the governing body, or by Friends or Foundations. For more information on Friends and Foundations, see the section on those issues in this chapter.

Even in those cases where a library law allows the library board to have custody of the public funds under its control, it is simply good fiscal practice to have those funds administered by a properly certified and bonded individual. When a board handles funds separately, it is imperative that a separate audit firm audits them annually according to the Generally Accepted Accounting Principles. There is more information on audit requirements in the audit section of this chapter.

TYPES OF TAXATION

A library tax, or any local tax, can take a wide variety of forms. The mill rate or millage tax on property is the most common in most areas of the country but is by no means the only form of library support. Here are the major types of tax revenue available to libraries (fees and fines for use, gifts, bequests, and grants are excluded):

- State and federal revenue sharing to municipalities

- Direct state aid to libraries

- Property tax or millage

- Sales tax

- Income tax

- Fines, forfeitures, intangibles

- Lottery proceeds

STATE AND FEDERAL SHARED REVENUES

With the exception of the property tax, local communities must usually rely on their state to collect the other taxes listed here. In many states, sending back the proceeds generated locally on sales or income taxes would mean wide disparities, with richer or more commercial centers getting most of the money. As a result, many states have shared revenue programs that redistribute state revenues back to localities on a formula basis. The formulas vary widely, but the attempt is usually to even out some of the disparities that would otherwise occur and to distribute more to need communities.

MILL OR MILLAGE RATES (PROPERTY TAX)

Most library taxes are property taxes. Real estate is assessed with a hypothetical market value that is supposed to represent the sales value of the property. Theoretically, a home that sells for $100,000 should be assessed for property tax purposes at $100,000; however, since there is no way to absolutely assess the value of a property except by selling it, property values can vary more or less from the "real" value. Much depends on the assessor, the assessment policy of the jurisdiction, and the state.

Keeping your own property's rate low while new homes are being built nearby keeps your tax low and transfers the cost to other newer homes and properties. Some states (Wisconsin, for example) force local assessors to reevaluate properties periodically if a sample of sales of existing homes differs by a fixed percent from the assessed value.

The term "mill rate" or "millage rate" comes from the Latin for "thousand." It means a tax rate per $1,000 of assessed value of the property. A tax assessor sets the value of your home at $100,000 and the tax rate is expressed per $1,000 of value (mill rate). A mill rate of $1.00 per $1,000 will generate a tax of $100 on a $100,000 home, $200 on a $200,000 home, $300 on a $300,000 home and so forth.

If a taxing district has an aggregate value of $100,000,000 and there is a need for $200,000, that is referred to as a need for a $200,000 tax or tax levy. The tax rate in the district is expressed as a mill rate or millage rate on all taxable property—a $2.00 mill rate ($200,000 divided by the aggregate value of the district of $100,000,000 equals $2.00 per thousand of property value).

Politicians like mill rate comparisons because the value of real estate is almost constantly rising because of inflation and new construction. The rate per $1,000 can remain stable or even decline, leading to headlines about declining tax rates. This is true even though the total tax levy amount is increasing. If the total tax base of new and existing properties grows 10 percent, the same mill rate generates 10 percent more money. If the base grows 20 percent and the tax levy goes up only 10 percent (still higher than the rate of current inflation, of course) the mill rate will decline, leading to positive headlines.

Property tax levies are probably the most stable and least volatile form of taxation, a reason for libraries to favor them.

SALES TAXES

Next, look to the sales tax. The sales tax is more volatile, rising and falling with economic conditions far more so than the property tax. Some jurisdictions will get more benefit from a sales tax than others; retail centers and resort areas raise more in sales taxes than rural towns or suburbs. Nevertheless, property taxes are widely unpopular and many are looking for alternatives.

LOCAL INCOME TAXES

Another possible library tax is the income tax. A local purpose income tax is less common than either sales or property taxes. The tax itself is usually collected by the state with the annual income tax and distributed back to the local municipality. Most policy observers consider the income tax to be the least regressive because it taxes most those with the greatest ability to pay. When used locally, however, it has the unfortunate effect of providing an incentive for moving to a community without a local purpose income tax.

FINES, FORFEITURES, INTANGIBLES

A very few libraries also receive money from fines, fees, and civil forfeitures. Until thirty-five years ago, Ohio libraries were supported by an "intangibles tax" on bonds, stocks, and jewelry. All school libraries in Wisconsin get their book funds from this type of revenue, but it is far less common for public libraries. The advantage for the library is not being included in the more widely unpopular property, sales, or income tax. Those getting fines in civil and criminal court get a lot less sympathy in the court of public opinion if they object to part of their fines going to pay for a library.

AUDITS AND GASB 34

The annual audit, or Comprehensive Annual Financial Review (CAFR), is usually something dreaded by library staff, and the resulting report usually gets little attention by library boards or even city councils.

GASB 34 is a new set of accounting rules considered by accountants to be the most monumental change in government financial reporting in U.S. history.[1] By June of 1999 the rules began to apply to the largest jurisdictions, and even the smallest jurisdictions were required to use the new standards by June of 2003.

GASB 34 forces public sector agencies to use accrual accounting. Traditionally, state and local governmental agencies have used cash or modified accrual accounting methods to report infrastructure assets like roads, bridges, water and sewer facilities and, of course, libraries. Under the old rules, the capital cost of an infrastructure investment appeared in an agency's annual financial report during the year in which the cost of construction was incurred.

Using cash or modified accrual accounting methods, the value of all physical assets is effectively off the books. In reality, physical assets such as roads, bridges, and library buildings continue to have value long after agencies have incurred the cost of construction. Just as cars depreciate, the value or usefulness of roads, bridges, and libraries declines over the course of many years. GASB 34 requires libraries to use the type of accounting required of most businesses, one that keeps infrastructure assets on the books.

The library manager who understands the effect of capital costs on the jurisdiction's bond rating and who plays the cards right could have an advantage in the ever present struggle for municipal resources.

A new section under GASB 34, "Management Discussion and Analysis," will be required in all audits. It is supposed to provide for elected officials, bondholders, and the public an "easy to read" assessment of the financial results for the entity for the previous year. Consider the following situations and whether they would help or hinder the ongoing development of *your* library program.

146

The library passed a special bond issue in 1999 that included money for materials. Recent flooding damage to the entire headquarters collection was not covered by insurance. Prospective bond buyers should consider this fact when considering purchase of the newly proposed special district bonds for additional branches and collections.

How do you suppose the library district's bond rating will fare?

The public works commission and the library board both report that their facilities are in need of urgent repair. Public works supplied the city council with comprehensive alternative strategies for current and future values of investment in the next ten years. The library board, although it has complete architectural plans, is still reevaluating alternative investment strategies under the new accounting rules.

Which city department gets the capital improvement go-ahead from the city council?

If the library is in disrepair, the collection inadequate, and the service sporadic, this should be noted in the Management Discussion and Analysis section of the library or municipality's audit. Will it be? Only if library staff are aware of the requirements and use them to their advantage.

POLITICAL CONTEXT OF THE BUDGET

It is important to consider theory, practice, and political reality when considering budget issues. Sometimes city councils, county commissions, city managers, or even municipal budget officers overstep their bounds and attempt to dictate how funds are spent, leading to potential conflict between the municipality on one hand and the library board and administration on the other.

Those on the library side must consider the costs and benefits implicit in any potential conflict over budget authority. If the municipal authority's attempt to dictate the budget will set a precedent that makes it nearly impossible to run a good library, then there is one "answer"—fight to retain the library's autonomy.

However, if the issue is minor or the political fallout has the potential to be a long-term disaster to future budgets, there is another answer—reassert the library's autonomy, but accede to the specific action demanded.

Exposing either side in a conflict to public humiliation is bad negotiating strategy and worse politics. If the city council or mayor is to back down, care must be taken to provide political cover. The same holds true for the library administration or board. Often it is enough to simply assert the exclusive control of the library board on the issue but then proceed to do what is being asked.

When driving, one always avoids a head-on crash. In library work, the head-on confrontation about a budget is only advisable if the principle is critical to the library's ability to achieve its purpose. Politics is the art of compromise, and budgeting is the most political piece of that art.

Openness in Budgeting

A library budget should never be a shell-and-pea game. Sometimes library officials are tempted to conceal the extent of their revenues from other sources in order to maximize the revenue they can get from the city or county board. City councils, in turn, attempt to minimize the tax burden by using what are deemed windfall revenues at libraries. Library officials should always avoid the temptation to hide funds or anticipated revenues from municipal officials in order to maximize the budget. Doing the wrong thing for a good reason is still the wrong thing.

There are many possible reasons for a sudden increase in funding to a library. For example, fines or state funding could increase unexpectedly, or the library may receive an unexpected gift or bequest that specifies that tax effort cannot be diminished. Whatever the reason for the new source of revenue, there may be a temptation to move funds around in the trust funds, gift funds, or elsewhere to conceal the windfall and assure a continued flow of funding from the city or county. There are legitimate and necessary purposes for library special funds, but they are not there to make it possible to conceal revenues. Full disclosure of all anticipated sources of revenue for the library is the only proper course of action.

There are often a number of funds set up for a library that serve valid accounting and budget purposes. They are set up to illuminate, not obfuscate. Library planners should remember Judge Brandeis' maxim: "Sunlight is the best disinfectant," and plan accordingly.

FUND TYPES

Library boards, administrators, and municipal authorities have a tendency towards favoring the status quo in budgetary and financial matters. Remember that just because a specific trust or building fund is set up in a particular way, that does not make it right. It may have been proper at one time, under different state laws, municipal ordinances, or accounting principles, but if it is not proper now, it must be changed. Library planners will find G. Stevenson's *Accounting for Libraries*[2] an excellent source for accounting information.

Don't let this happen to your library:

Not long ago an honest individual found an uncashed bond from the 1950s. By 2000, it would have been worth enough to build a new library in a small town had it been reinvested when necessary; but it was not reinvested and it had only its 1955 redemption value. What happened? Why had the funds not been reinvested?

The board entrusted a long-standing member with the gift funds. As time passed, others, including the administration, lost track of the funds, and when the member died, the bond remained tucked away in some papers that were part of an estate. It was lost until a rummage sale years later. The bond had some current value, but the amount of lost interest over fifty years was staggering.

While this particular story is apocryphal, there are all too many like it that are true. The moral is that trust funds and foundations must be properly established according to state laws. There should always be more than one individual involved, the officers of the trust should be bonded as required by law, and the financial position of the trust must be regularly reported in a comprehensible and audited report that goes to the library board, local officials, state officials, and the public at large through legal notices.

Always obtain legal assistance when setting up special funds for a library. State laws covering how a fund is to be established, governed, and maintained can vary considerably. Community foundations are usually set up to provide funding vehicles for a variety of public service and arts organizations in a community.

Auditors, state law, or common practice within the city or county may require many libraries to establish various funds in specific forms. A critical part of any long-range plan review is to periodically review the types of funds and how they are handled. This is especially important if the library or community fund practices have not been reviewed since the changes required under the GASB 34.

The types of funds for a library will vary depending on the type of library organization involved. Special districts often have a more extensive fund structure than a library within a municipality, for instance. The review should proceed with that context in mind.

The most common types of funds found in libraries are:

- General revenue (or operating) fund
- Special revenue funds
- Proprietary funds
- Enterprise funds
- Building and capita funds
- Trust Funds

GENERAL REVENUE (OR OPERATING) FUND

In many cases the general revenue or operating fund will be the only fund used by a library. The most critical question to ask is this: what happens to lapsed funds? The converse of the question, or course, is: what happens if the library spends more than the budget allowed?

Some states and localities allow libraries to carry over their fund balance from one operating year to the next; others do not. In the former case the fund balance or reserve account can grow without proper planning, or it can quickly be depleted without sufficient care.

There are a great number of horror stories surrounding fund balance issues. One library hired a new director who did not fully understand that fund balances should be spent down, if at all, for one-time projects. The rest of the staff and board were amazed to see the levels of new staffing and materials spending this new director initiated, thinking perhaps that the previous director had just been too miserly. It was too late when they noticed that the library's entire reserve fund, including the gift fund, was gone. Making up for the hole in that budget was painful.

Another library's board and director believed that all unspent money for a given year went into their building fund. They kept track of the totals and the expected interest earnings, looking forward to the happy day when they could begin the building. The only trouble was that their view of the world was not the same as that of the city. From the standpoint of the city finance director and the city's annual audit, unspent library funds lapsed into the general municipal fund, not into a separate library-building fund. It was a rude awakening for the board and the director. They still have no building.

Understand how funds are handled in your community and plan accordingly.

SPECIAL REVENUE FUNDS

Not all libraries have special revenue funds, but for those that do, this section touches briefly on three types:

- Trust, Gift, Endowment Funds

- Building and capital funds

- Enterprise funds

Accountants distinguish special revenue funds from the general revenue fund for the library. Sometimes the audit or CAFR for the municipality has these funds contained in the special funds for other municipal departments rather than separately.

Many libraries have trust funds, gift funds and, more rarely, endowment funds. These funds usually allow members of the public to donate funds for library materials, equipment, programs, and even buildings. The library board is sometimes the fiscal agent for these funds, and at other times it is the municipality or a separate foundation. Sometimes the intent is to use only the interest earned on funds rather than the principal; at other times, the funds are intended to be self-liquidating on an annual basis. The source of the revenues mentioned here is private rather than governmental.

Building and capital funds are established to plan for or pay off long-term debt for a library building. Such funds can frequently contain a mix of tax revenues, earned interest, and private donations towards a building. In a municipal audit or in a district library audit, bonding authorities will pay special attention to these funds. There have been major changes in requirements for the CAFR by the GASB.

Enterprise funds are the least common type of fund to find in most libraries. Sometimes an enterprise fund is established to allow the replacement of supplies and equipment by using the revenue generated by a specific library program or service such as proceeds from the photocopier or rental programs for audiovisual equipment. Often the revenue from such programs reverts to the municipality's general revenue fund, but not all municipalities handle funds in this way. Find out how things are handled locally and make future plans appropriate to your library for the future.

TYPES OF FUND-HANDLING ORGANIZATIONS

There are three types of fund-handling organizations to consider:

- Friends Groups
- Library Foundations
- Community Foundations

Friends Groups

Friends Groups are usually set up to as a dues-supported group that provides both funding and volunteer support for library promotion activities and building campaigns. While Friends groups can be critical to referendum campaigns and often provide substantial fund campaigns, they are not usually able to handle the level of fund raising needed for an entire building. Library planners who are considering Friends groups must consider the following:

- Working with friends' activities can be very time consuming for staff.

- Conflicts and rivalries often develop between friends, library boards, library foundations, and municipal boards.

- Separate audit and bookkeeping requirements can add to library staff burdens.

    For help in establishing a friends group, visit www.folusa.org.

Library Foundations

Library foundations are set up under state laws as a separate legal entity to receive gifts, donations, and bequests either as a limited capital campaign or an ongoing endowment to support library activities. With a library foundation, as opposed to a community foundation, there is more control over investment strategy and timing of distributions. Library planners who are considering foundations must consider the following:

- Foundation activities can be very time consuming for staff.

- Conflicts can develop between foundation boards, library boards, friends groups and municipal boards.

- Separate audits are usually required.

- Separate bookkeeping requirements can add to library staff burdens.

Community Foundations

Community foundations are set up for a variety of civic, charitable, and arts activities in a community. The separate auditing and bookkeeping functions of a library foundation are not needed because the organization does this (at a fee, of course) for all the participating organizations. Library planners who are considering community foundations must consider the following:

- Donors may be more reluctant to give money to a general organization than a library-specific one.

- The library board may not have the degree of control it needs over investment strategies, withdrawal terms, and use of funds in an emergency.

- Fees for handling of funds and administration can be quite substantial.

- Community foundations are less common in rural areas.

Budget Types

Be certain that the type of budget currently in use by the library is the type prefered by the funding authority. If the city or county prefers program budgets and the library is still using line items, the total budget is not going to get as positive a response as expected.

Financial administration and budgeting go through periodic changes. Some of the changes are fads. There are three basic types of budgets currently in use by most libraries. They are, in decreasing levels of use:

- Line item budget
- Program budget
- Zero-based budget

Line item budgets are usually the easiest to set up and administer and they have been in use for the longest amount of time. Line item budgets indicate broad categories of revenue (local, state, fines and fees, etc.) and expenditures (staff, books, utilities, etc.).

Program budgets are intended to help authorities respond to programs rather than line items—reference or children's services rather than electric bills or book budgets. Program budgets are harder to set up and monitor, and library staff frequently resist the attempts. They do offer library staff the opportunity to make reasoned and compelling cases for expanding or contracting programs.

Zero-based budgeting is much less in vogue today, but some communities still use it. The theory behind the form is that agencies should build their programs up from zero every year, defining the benefits of each new "decision package" as it is introduced. In practice, most communities do not ask departments to go all the way back to zero, but they do often expect new decision packages above a certain baseline or "cost to continue business as usual."

The important issue for planners is that budget planning must take into consideration the needs and preferences of the funding authority. Resistance on form will usually be met with resistance on funding. Go with the flow when possible.

OPERATING AND CAPITAL BUDGETS

In nearly all communities, the budget planning is divided into two main categories: operating budgets and capital budgets. Even library boards with their own taxing authority, like those in library districts, usually make the distinction.

Funding authorities usually have a Capital Improvement Plan and process. This means that if the library needs a new building, shelving, or circulation system, it must get its project in line with those of other municipal departments. Such plans typically extend out three to ten years. Getting on the list for a given year is no guarantee of future funding, since unforeseen contingencies may change municipal priorities. Nevertheless, usually library planners are pleased when a building or other capital asset project is put on the list for future funding.

Notice that municipalities usually have multi-year plans for capital funding but only a single (or, at best, three-year) plan for operating budgets. This very often sets up a dilemma for library planners—the library can present to the municipality its budget plans for a new building or branch but not for the staff needed to run it or the materials needed to stock it.

Many libraries have fallen victim to this capital/operating budget problem. In their desire to get the building on the schedule and built, administrators and boards neglect to mention the inevitable future need for added staff, utilities, and books. The board and administration are often fearful that if they mention the new costs they will kill the chances for the building. Some members believe that economic circumstances will be better in the future or that all the added use and community enthusiasm will make the future requests for operating money for the building less troublesome.

Then, after the ribbon cutting and the celebrating, there will be another operating budget submitted with calls for expanded staff and other costs. The city council (often with many new members since the original capital budget was approved years before) is shocked to discover that, having spent enormous sums for the building, they are now asked to spend even more to heat and staff it. To avoid this outcome, produce a long-range plan that cites the ongoing costs, as well as the capital costs.

What About Budgets in the Red?

Planning can include dealing with state and national issues through lobbying, as well as coming up with new and creative solutions for funding. In the event of a budget crisis, the administration and board will want to convince themselves and the public that everything possible has been done to spend wisely. This section, parts of which were originally published as the author's cover story for the March 2003 issue of *American Libraries,* provides some starting points for responding to budget crises.

Something that has kept many of us going as most of the dot-coms went bust is this: we have a business plan that has stood the test of time. Generations of librarians have believed passionately in our plan; it has inspired countless library users and city councils because of its simple elegance. Libraries have a bargain with history to share knowledge for those seeking wisdom, and we keep that promise—whether it is with print or with nonprint (now called electronic) sources—at bargain prices. For this, society has rewarded us for over a hundred years. The rewards have not been much, it's true, but we have a staying power that others with less clear business plans, like those at docoms, never achieved.

Many states faced major budget crises because of the economic downturn, a downturn that many blame in large part on the 9/11 terrorist attacks. As states and local government deal with their budget problems, librarians and the public must remind political leaders that public library services are also important, even when stacked against critical emergency services and responses to terrorism.

During World War II, emergency services such as air raid systems took priority over local libraries, but they did not eclipse them. Library supporters successfully made the case for the important place of the library in wartime budgets, just as they had for Depression relief. In a true democracy, then as now, elected leaders must provide for all types of homeland security, including a secure place in their budgets for our public libraries.

The idea of free public library service still resonates widely with the American public. The ALA Survey on Library Use in Chapter 3 found that 91 percent of people believe that libraries will continue to be a necessary service even in the face of the growing availability of computers. At least 40 percent considered the library the most important tax-supported service provided by local government.[3] That report and those figures need much wider distribution to help forestall the state and local budget cutters. We can—we must—focus on developing new strategies and tactics to sustain that business plan, that bargain with history, for our time. Only then can we deliver on the library's true potential. Only then can we answer to budgets in the red.

PLANNED GIVING AND FOUNDATIONS

Library foundation programs can assist libraries through budget problems, but there are a number of caveats. Too often the local city or county expects the library to substitute donated funds for tax funds, leaving the library no better or worse off than before the gift was given. Donors won't donate without an assurance that their money will go towards library improvement rather than tax abatement and library staff have little incentive to do foundation development work if the end result is to be at roughly the same level of funding as before.

Clear statements passed by the library board are essential to assure the continued flow of donations. Community foundations that manage funds for a number of charitable groups are one way to minimize the extra work of record-keeping involved in a dedicated, stand-alone library foundation. State and regional library staff should organize information and training for library boards and administrations on the pros and cons of community foundations, planned giving, and other types of gift assistance.

E-COMMERCE INITIATIVES

Very few libraries have taken advantage of the Internet-based options for increasing the flow of small-scale contributions. Library associations at the state and national levels feature examples of such programs. One way other Web sites allow contributions is to use a tool like the Amazon Honor System, which allows individuals to use Amazon.com payment technology to make payments to Web sites as small as $1.00. If Amazon can do it, why can't the ALA? A tool allowing library fans, of which there are many, to donate small sums to their favorite library could be a boon to both the association and local libraries. Imagine the ALA @your library campaign with a dollar sign added in for good measure! However, libraries should consider the benefits, pitfalls, and legal constraints of such programs. For more information, see "Library Fundraising On the Web: A Practical Guide for Libraries" (www.lights.com/how-to/libraries.html).

REENGINEERING THE BUDGET

Does your library budget presentation look much the same as it did five years ago with much the same results? Maybe it is time for a budgetary facelift. The funding authorities, whether they are city councils or the voters at large for a referendum, may be demanding a different take on the budget presentation. In the wider context of budgets at the municipal level, budget officers are now demanding accountability factors and outcome measures in municipal budgets.

Even though the budget is the most important policy document for the library, lethargy, inertia, or an appeal to a library board's autonomy and prerogatives have led libraries to resist the forces for changing the look and feel of the library budget. Remember—it is as important to make the plan, but perhaps even more important to include it in your budget.

GRANTS

In most states, the most likely source of grant money is the Federal Library Services and Technology Act (LSTA), administered by each state's library agency.

Grant making agencies are usually seeking to augment local spending and use targeted funds for experimental purposes to enhance their own objectives. This is true of nearly all grant making agencies, including the state-administered LSTA—they rarely make funding available to substitute for a shortfall of state or local funding. It follows that grants are not, for the most part, much help for libraries in the red because of a loss of state or local funding. Nonetheless, grant revenue, if carefully worked into a library's overall profile, can help alleviate funding problems, if only for a time.

Contact your state library agency for the rules on funding under the Federal LSTA grant program. The IMLS (www.imls.gov/grants/index.htm) provides for some limited direct funding to public libraries through national leadership grants and grants for cooperation between libraries and museums.

FUND RAISING CONSULTANTS

Libraries decide to hire a fund raising consultant for a variety of reasons. Most often the motivation is the need for a new building and the inability to get the local funding authority to authorize bonding authority. At other times the motivation comes when a board, administrator, or Friends group identifies a need to enhance services beyond what is possible under current tax structures.

Whatever the motivation or need, seeking a fund raising consultant can present a number of problems.

Libraries have sometimes found that the cost of the fund raising consultant's time can be as much or more than the funding raised. Retaining a fund raiser often lets friends, trustees and foundation members "off the hook" and they feel less inclined to do aggressive fundraising on their own. Often there are self-styled local residents who can convince library trustees or local city councilors that they are "fund raisers" when in fact they have little experience or skill in the area—turning them down and getting a professional can cause local political problems. Contact your regional or state library agency on securing a qualified fund raiser.

USER FEES

As a library planner, you may see library trustees, city council members, and even library staff members move towards library fees whenever the economy is in recession. In their statement "Economic Barriers to Information Access" (www.ala.org/alaorg/oif/econ_bar.html), the ALA opposes the charging of user fees for the provision of information by all libraries and information services that receive their major support from public funds. Many states also expressly prohibit most types of user fees for public library services in their statutes, so in most cases, a move towards wider user fees will first require a change in state law.

Most library statutes allow for limited library charges:

- fines for overdue materials
- fees for replacement of lost items
- fees for photocopies and faxes
- fees for some value-added databases

VALUE PURCHASING

Buying in bulk, based on a contract with a vendor, will always save money. Libraries need to seek the best venues for value purchasing in order to get the best deals. In some cases this will be part of a state purchasing contract; in other cases it will mean buying into a regional, county, or local purchasing consortium. If no such consortium exists for the library, it may be time for the library to initiate one.

Are Impact Fees the Right Thing?

In larger units of service and growing areas, the use of an impact fee—a property tax assessment placed on a home while it is being built—will be a very effective tool in library funding and development. This section of the chapter provides a discussion on this planning and funding tool.

The theory behind impact fees is that new residents impose an impact on the library that should be borne by the new resident rather than current residents. The cost is usually rolled into the purchase price of the home. State law must authorize the impact fees for library purposes and the community must endorse the proposed fees based on a plan ordinarily drawn up by the library or its agents. Impact fees are far more workable in growing areas. Note that real estate agents and developers often oppose impact fees and that governing bodies have mixed responses. They have much deeper lobbying pockets than libraries do, so the political aspects of an impact fee strategy must be considered on a state-by-state basis.

It is important to look at model state laws, model local ordinances, and specific examples of successful impact fee development. The CD includes an Impact Fee Calculator.

Draft of a Transfer of Funds Ordinance

State law will normally require a specific local ordinance to institute an impact fee. This example references statutes that may or may not exist in your state. Check on that fundamental point before using the document.

WHEREAS the City Board of the City of Anywhereville imposes impact fees in accordance with State Stat./_____ pursuant to Anywhereville Municipal Code/____; and

WHEREAS a separate impact fund for public library improvements exists pursuant to Anywhereville Municipal Code/____(6) which consists of impact fees collected by the City for the purpose of paying the capital costs of public library improvements; and

WHEREAS Anywhereville Municipal Code/____ authorizes the use of monies collected per its terms for capital costs for new, expanded or improved public facilities which are related to the effects of general population growth in the City of Anywhereville; and

WHEREAS the City of Anywhereville has experienced such population growth and has made necessary improvements to the City's public library system pursuant to Exhibit A, attached hereto and made a part hereof by reference, in conformance with the Public Facilities Needs Assessment; and

WHEREAS the capital costs for the expenditures shown on said exhibit were paid by the City of Anywhereville Public Library System from various accounts as listed in said Exhibit A, and properly consist of public library system improvements capital costs:

NOW, THEREFORE, BE IT RESOLVED by the City Board of the City of Anywhereville, that, pursuant to the above, $ _____ shall be transferred from the City of Anywhereville Public Library Improvements Impact Fee Fund to the City of Anywhereville Public Library System Operating Account and $_____shall be transferred from the City of Anywhereville Public Library Improvements Impact Fee Fund to the City of Anywhereville Public Library System Fundraising Account to reimburse the library system for the capital costs for public library improvements expended through_____, having made the findings as follows:

These expenditures for these items bear a rational relationship to the need for new, expanded or improved public library facilities created by land development within the City of Anywhereville and the attendant population growth; and

The costs of these capital improvements do not exceed the proportionate share of the capital costs to serve land development compared to existing uses of land within the City; and these costs are actual and not estimated capital cost items; and

There are no special charges or offsets against these expenditures, and there are no federal or state contributions of any nature toward the acquisition of these capital assets; and

These capital costs were not incurred for the purpose of addressing existing deficiencies; and the City finds that it is in the best interest of the public library system of the City of Anywhereville to reimburse the public library system accounts for these capital costs. See Appendix 3 for a sample plan.

Considering Governance Issues

Be clear about the type of library for which you are planning; the group should always ask whether the current type of organization is the most appropriate for this library and the current population served. Most of the time the group will agree that no organizational change is needed or wanted.

A library cannot go from a village or township library to a city library unless its parent municipality changes from a village or township to a city. Some types of library organizations—the special district, for instance—are not even possible in some states. Those considering other forms of library organization should refer to Chapter 8 on District or Multi-jurisdictional libraries.

Types of Public Libraries

The Federal State Cooperative Service identifies the following types of libraries.

Figure 6–1 Types of Public Libraries in the U.S.

Type	Characteristics
Municipal	Almost every state has this, the most common type of library organization-1/2 of all libraries and 1/3 of the U.S. population. It is usually governed by a board appointed by the municipality. Forms vary. In a few cases, state law allows for election of boards or direct taxing authority; in other cases, the library is a direct department of the city, usually run by a city or city manager.
County or parish	All but 12 states have county, city county, or parish libraries. The second most common form of library organization. Taxing and governance forms vary. In a few cases, state law allows for election of boards or direct taxing authority. In other cases, the library is a direct department of the county, usually run by a county manager.
City and county	This hybrid type of one and two above is found in only 87 instances in 9 states. Ownership of the building, equipment and materials in such arrangements often presents challenges. Governance and taxing authority issues are also usually challenging, unless the library board is elected and/or has taxing authority, a rare occurrence.
Multi-jurisdictional	Many multi-jurisdictional libraries are multicounty organizations; in other cases, such arrangements encompass one or more municipalities. Multi-jurisdictional libraries do not usually have either elected boards or taxing authority.
Nonprofit or agency	The New England and Mid-Atlantic states have most of this type of library organization. Many have longstanding endowments to cover a substantial part of the operating costs. Board appointment is usually by the board itself rather than by the municipality. Some of these types of libraries are now substantially tax supported but still retain the non-profit status.
Tribal	Native American tribes run 23 tribal libraries, usually on reservations. They are located in Alaska, Arizona, New Mexico, New York, and Wisconsin. The governance, funding, board organization and relationship to regional or state library agencies vary widely, depending on the tribe. Changing from or to this type of organization is, of course, not an option.
School district	School Districts run 306 libraries in 7 states. They are usually well funded by comparison to other types of libraries. Sometimes this type of library is what is called a "joint use" library, meaning that the facility is used for both school library and public library purposes. At other times the school district runs a public library in s geographical area of a school district.
Special district	Only 19 states allow for the formation of special districts and there are 741 such libraries. The board usually has taxing authority and is often elected rather than appointed. Per capita funding and sage data are much higher than for most municipal libraries.
Other	For some reason the state library agency for Pennsylvania defines every library in that state under "other."

Figure 6–2 Distribution of Library Types in the U.S.

State	City/County	Municipal	County/Parish	Mult-juris-dictional	Native Amer Tribal	Nonprofit or agency	Other	School District	Special District	Grand Total
AK		32	11	3	4	15				65
AL		142	16	39					2	199
AR		8	10	19			1			38
AZ		27	1	2					10	40
CA		110	47	6					12	175
CO		39	18	1		1	9		42	110
CT		98				95				193
DC		1								1
DE		2	12						16	30
FL	2	29	33	11					1	76
GA			20	37						57
HI							1			1
IA		474	3				1			478
ID		67				1		4	25	97
IL		272					50		296	618
IN		27	46	161			2			236
KS		269	14	2			2		7	294
KY		2	8	3					103	116
LA	1	2	59	2					1	65
MA		330				24				354
MD			24							24
ME		92				137				229
MI		211	22					20	125	378
MN	50	64	4	3		1	8			130
MO	5	85	39	14		6	3			152
MS	8	2	21	17						48
MT		29	27	21					2	79
NC		10	43	17		5				75
ND	6	43	9	11						69
NE		198	7				2			207
NH		204		1		5				710
NJ		232	14	6		55				307

State	City/County	Municipal	County/Parish	Mult-juris-dictional	Native Amer. Tribal	Nonprofit or agency	Other	School District	Special District	Grand Total
NM		48	2	1	9	3	1			64
NV		2	11	1					8	22
NY		211	8		3	362	1	128	27	740
OH		24	58			18		150		250
OK		102	5	6						113
OR		87	17			2		1	14	121
PA							457			457
RI		24				24				48
SC		1	35	4						40
SD		46	12	19						77
TN		12	118				12			142
TX	12	277	148	8		72	1		2	520
UT	1	41	27							69
VA		23	40	26			1			90
VT		90		10		51			1	152
WA		40							19	59
WI	2	331	14	24	5			1		377
WV		48	30	17				2		97
WY			23							23
Totals	87	4,508	1,056	490	23	877	552	306	713	8.612

TYPES OF BOARDS AND DUTIES

State law, past practices, and the specific conditions of the library all make a difference in the best type of governance for a particular library. The library board takes many forms. For the majority of libraries, it is a policy-making body that will adopt the long-range plan and monitor its implementation. The city and/or county elected bodies appoint most of those boards, but some states allow for the election of library boards in a library district with taxing authority. If the library has received substantial endowments over the years the board may be a self-replicating agency that handles a private trust account. Some counties and cities have a strong tradition of city or county managers; in those cases, the library director reports for legal, financial, and administrative purpose to the city or county manager, and the library board is advisory only.

Investigate the type of library board involved, assure that it is the best for the library, and then assure that by-laws and policies are in order for your ideal board type. The planning committee should make sure that all the players in the library drama understand their roles and responsibilities. For example, if the city council believes that the library board is advisory only, but the board actually has policy making authority, there is bound to be conflict. A board that thinks it is just giving advice when it should be governing will leave itself open for problems.

FORM OF LIBRARY BOARD

Determine the current form, and the ideal form for your library:

- Advisory board

- Policy making board

- Managerial board

- Autonomous board for an association library with and endowment

- Autonomous board without taxing authority (elected or appointed)

- Autonomous board with taxing authority (elected or appointed)

    Library trustee duties vary from state to state and board to board, but most boards have the power to:

- Adopt bylaws and rules for the board's governance

- Exercise exclusive control over the building and grounds of the library

- Control the expenditure of all funds credited to the library fund

- Appoint a library director (and delegate the hiring of other staff to the director)

- Remove the library director

- Develop and approve the personnel policy, including the salary and benefit policy of the library

- Adopt an annual library budget

- Adopt rules and regulations regarding the use of the library

- Exclude from the use of the library anyone who willfully violates the board's rules and regulations

- Determine the policy for selection of library materials for inclusion in the library's collection

- Assess community needs and plan for the future

- Advocate for the library to municipal boards, civic groups, and the public at large

Figure 6–3 Board Bylaws Checklist

Area	Yes	No	Comments
The bylaws specify the board officers, their terms, powers, and responsibilities.			
The bylaws define the expected meeting frequency for the full board as well as any subcommittees. Procedures for emergency or special meetings are outlined.			
The bylaws specify the rules of order that will govern the board. (Usually the rules are Robert's Rules of Order.)			
The bylaws define standing committees, their appointment and responsibilities, as well as the same for ad hoc committees.			
A clear statement on conflict of interest is included and it is consistent with state and local legal requirements.			
The determination of a quorum is defined clearly.			
The bylaws outline the relationship between the board and the library director regarding hiring, firing and supervisory practices. They also address these issues as they relate to the staff.			
The bylaws clearly detail the relationship with the appointing authority (or authorities).			
There is a clear method for filling vacancies.			
Term limitations, if any, are stated.			
The reasons and methods for removal of members or officers are stated.			

Area	Yes	No	Comments
The bylaws specify meeting attendance requirements, and the method for removing trustees for nonattendance is included.			
The bylaws specify that the board will adhere to state and local laws regarding open meetings, privacy of records, insurance and bonding of officers, and so forth.			
The method and timeframe for amending the bylaws is stated.			

Conclusion

This chapter has provided:

- coverage of some of the issues that library planners must consider about library governance, administration and finances. The planning group should be clear about the type of library for which they are planning. The group should always ask whether the current type of organization is the most appropriate for this library and its library population served at this time. It is rare for a library to change something as fundamental as the type of governance involved and a change requires major legal hurdles that go beyond the scope of a planning committee's jurisdiction;

- an overview of strategic budgeting and financial issues in the context of long-range planning and policy development;

- information to help planners put the entire plan on sound financial footing;

- a consideration of various of fund handling organizations, budget presentation types, taxation types, and suggested budget augmentation.

Notes

1.   For further information see Thomas J. Hennen Jr.'s article, "Do You Know the Real Value of Your Library?" *Library Journal* 126:11 (15 June 2001):48–51.

2.   Smith, G. Stevenson. 1999. *Accounting for Libraries and Other Not-for-Profit Organizations*, 2nd ed. Chicago: American Library Association.

3.   The survey questions indicated here are from a national survey commissioned by the American Library Association. KRC Research and Consulting conducted the "@ your library: Attitudes Toward Public Libraries" study. The random study of attitudes and beliefs about their libraries found that most that most Americans are highly satisfied with their current library services, would be happy to pay more than they currently pay for library service, and few believe that the Internet will substitute for library services any time soon. It polled about 1,000 adult Americans in a national random-sample telephone survey conducted March 8–11, 2002. The estimated margin of error was 3 percent.

Chapter 7

Defining Major Planning Sections

Space Needs Assessment
Public Library Space Needs
Public Library Space Needs: Worksheet
Reader Seating Calculation
Public Access Workstation Calculations
Staff Workstation Calculations for a Library
Estimating Capital Costs for Building and Equipment
Specific Library Cost Estimates
Capital Cost Calculator on the CD
Instructions for the "Capital Cost Calculator"
Staffing and Personnel Issues
The Balancing Act
Personnel Comparisons
Training Issues
Other Service Issues
Special Needs
Reference
Children's Services
Branch Service
Disaster Preparations
Conclusion

List of Figures

Overview

There are at least two possible ways to organize the written plan. The ALA Planning series recommends grouping goals and objectives beneath the service responses that a library has chosen. I recommend grouping them by activity sections as follows:

- Electronic Services

- Collection Development

- Technology

- Access and Facilities

- Staffing and Personnel

- Other Service Issues

Both the role method and the activity method have shortcomings. Grouping goals and objectives by roles has a certain logical consistency and appeal but in practice can result in any number of goals and objectives that are left hanging in a "miscellaneous" or "other" category. Goals and objectives are then forced into role sections to which they are only marginally related. Grouping goals by activity rather than roles allows like activities to be discussed and considered together but such groupings can beg the question about what role is being served by each activity.

This chapter discusses each of the activity sections and suggests how to plan effectively in each case. The charts and spreadsheets indicated are available on the accompanying CD. The appendix section includes sample plans organized in each of the suggested methods; The Brookfield Public Library plan is organized by topic and the St. Joseph Public Library is organized by role.

Electronic Services

In this new millennium, no other topic is quite as uncertain as electronic services planning. There are few accepted evaluation measures, so this section presents some of the measures that library leaders are advancing and suggests strategies for library planners.

Balancing the Books and Bytes

There are several major issues planners will need to consider regarding electronic resources. Vicki L. Gregory's *Selecting and Managing Electronic Resources* provides further information on developing electronic resources. Bertot, McClure and Ryan provide much useful information on measures for electronic resources in the manual *Statistics and Performance Measures for Public Library Networked Services.*

All planning literature insists that objectives should be specific and *measurable*. Electronic resources are harder to compare and measure than most library resources and services, and there is little reliable comparative data on electronic resources that planners can use to gauge their own operations. In addition, the costs for such things as full-text databases vary quite widely, since vendors are still trying to learn what the library market will pay for these new tools.

Even though the balance of print and electronic resources will be difficult to assess, develop a strategic statement that includes a pledge to balance the "books and bytes." Library stakeholders will be concerned with how the library plans to balance the costs of the two formats.

There are three large categories for modern library collections: print materials (including archival material), audiovisual materials, and electronic resources. Librarians have had a lot more time to develop benchmarks and guidelines for print material than for audiovisual or electronic materials. When it comes to audiovisual material, we have seen many formats come and go, from filmstrips to vinyl records and, soon it seems, audiotapes. At least these formats are tangible—planners can, with relative ease, compare the number of videos their library has to those in the state, the nation, or their self-defined peer group.

Electronic resources, for example full-text databases that a library subscribes to or owns, depend, for the most part, on the use of a personal computer or workstation. Many electronic resources vendors and suppliers now distribute Internet-based products (i.e.

Ebsco Host Web) but some still sell products on CD-ROM. Electronic resources can be used by patrons within the library and at remote locations. Not included under electronic resources for the purposes of this chapter are the automated circulation system, its local or wide area network, or its general technology infrastructure; these topics are covered in the technology section in this chapter.

Library planners must consider several points regarding electronic resources.

- First, should planners consider electronic resources separate from the rest of the collection for purposes of budget allocation and collection development policy?

- Second, given the library's role, can access to resources be an effective substitute for the item itself? Can the library eliminate the print copies of the magazine or periodical when subscribing to its electronic equivalent?

- Third, how do we measure success in electronic resources without any standard and agreed-upon measures?

In answer to the first question, most libraries will want to consider electronic resources separately from the rest of the collection for budget and collection development purposes. The very structure of the marketplace dictates the answer in most cases. Libraries usually end up buying electronic resources from vendors other than those that provide traditionally print resources, so they usually need to budget separately.

Whether or not the electronic resource can substitute for the print item will depend on the needs and desires of the user. Switching to electronic-only is useful currently for only some resources. Recreational fiction and most lengthy nonfiction are not suitable in electronic form to most users. On the other hand many, though not all, reference resources are suitable in electronic form. Effective planners will plan accordingly.

The following pages will deal with the major challenges posed by the third question—how library planners can measure and evaluate the use of electronic resources. Over the course of many years we have developed measures of library circulation, visits, and other traditional items, but tracking electronic use is considerably tougher. Effective library planners will pay particular attention to this aspect of library planning and development.

Check Those Costs

Selecting and subscribing to full-text databases can be a tricky business. Planners need to be aware that the vendors usually have considerable latitude in pricing their products. Negotiate—the first price quoted is seldom the best price. Working with a group of libraries in the region or state will ordinarily improve the cost of the database, but collaboration also reduces the individual library's selection choices.

Vendors can sell a variety of full-text database packages, from a license for a single concurrent user, to any number of multiple concurrent users, to unlimited users. Charges depend on the license you choose and perhaps on the population you serve. Check your agreement carefully for these and other restrictions. It is also possible to negotiate remote access to such value-added databases for patrons, provided the library's automated system allows for it and the vendor is able to set up such a system.

What to Count for E-Metrics

Most of us have a fairly good idea about how to fill out the annual state library survey regarding our library's statistics—except when it comes to reporting anything to do with electronic resources or e-metrics. When it comes to e-metrics, many libraries can be expected to have difficulties defining the data they will collect. Is it any wonder? We have had generations to define the meaning of "reference transactions," "circulations" or "visits," but we have had barely a decade to define the meaning of "database sessions" or "public access workstations." Despite the difficulties, counting carefully is important for effective planning.

Library professionals have been debating how electronic resources should be counted and measured for a number of years. While the debate is by no means over, the 2001 publication of *Statistics and Performance Measures for Public Library Networked Services* by Charles McClure and Carlo Bertot almost certainly stands as milepost in the search for such measures. Figures 7–1 and 7–2 include the measures and the statistics McClure and Bertot recommend.It will probably be some time before these measures are collected consistently on a national scale but some states have begun collecting some of them. There is bound to be a period of adjustment on such measures; some libraries will read the guidelines differently than others and the counts will be radically different. Over time librarians will compare the numbers, ask the questions, and bring consistency to the collection and reporting of data.

Some of the measures will be discarded because they are too much trouble to keep; others will be modified; still others will be added as libraries continue on this course. Consider the experience of libraries with the measure of "in-house use of materials" recommended in 1981 for the ALA Output Measures. Many libraries tried to collect this information and some states began requiring that libraries put it in their annual reports, but it proved too time consuming. Even though it is a useful measure, it was eventually dropped from the required list of data elements in most states. A similar outcome is likely here. Measures that can be compared across many libraries and are easily collected and standardized are likely to remain.

Figure 7–1 Proposed Performance and Composite Measures

Proposed performance and composite measures	Proposed definition
Public access workstation per some amount of the legal service population	The ratio of the legal service area population to # Public access workstations (e.g., XYZ library provides 1 public access workstation per 3,000 legal service population).
Average use per workstation	The ratio of the number of public access workstation users to the number of public access workstations.
Total reference use	Combine traditional measures of reference service with electronic measures.
% Virtual reference to total reference questions	Percentage of virtual reference transactions to total reference questions (both electronic and face-to-face).
Level of public service effort in servicing information technology	The percent of a public library's total public service staff time spent serving the public that is spent servicing IT during a sample period.
Total library visits	Physical visits to the library (i.e., turnstile count) and virtual visits combined into one total.
% Remote library visits	The percent of virtual visits to total library visits (virtual plus physical library visits).
% Registered borrowers receiving information technology training	The percentage of registered borrowers receiving IT training annually from the public library.
User information technology training as % of total reference use	The number of users trained in IT as a percent of total reference use.
Hours of formal information technology training per staff member	The average number of hours of formal IT training a public library staff member receives per year. Staff counted includes professional, paraprofessional, and volunteer staff as well as board members.
Total library material use	This composite measure combines the circulation and use figures for all of the paper, multimedia and electronic collections that the public library owns or provides access.
# Electronic database views as a % of total library material use	This performance measure compares use of licensed databases to the total library material use.
Total amount network services provided	This composite figure combines several new data elements including: # Virtual visits to networked library resources, # Electronic database views, # Users trained in IT, and # Virtual reference transactions.

Figure 7–2 Proposed Electronic Data Elements/Statistics

Public Access Workstations	
Data element/statistic	**Definition**
# Public access workstations	Count of the number of public access graphical workstations that connect to the Internet. Workstations may include personal computers, "thin clients," graphical terminals, or networked computers if they are connected to the Internet and publicly accessible. **NISO Definition:** Library owned public access graphical workstations that connect to the Internet for a dedicated purpose (to access an OPAC or specific database) or multiple purposes. NISO Link: http://www.niso.org/emetrics/current/category7.7.html
# of Public access workstation users	Count of the number of users of all of the library's graphical public access workstations connected to the Internet. NISO Definition: Annual count of the number of users of all of the library's graphical public access workstations connected to the Internet computed from a one-week sample. (Branch Level Statistic) NISO Link: www.niso.org/emetrics/current/category7.7.html
Maximum speed of public access Internet workstations	Indication of the maximum speed of public Internet access, e.g., 56kbps, ISDN, T1. NISO Definition: None NISO Link: None

180

Databases	
# Unique electronic titles	Total count of the number of unique online database titles available at the library. **NISO Definition:** Content in the electronic collection that is delivered to a user. The subcategories that follow provide for a detailed breakdown by type of content delivered (full-content unit, or descriptive record) and system delivering the content (Library Collection, Commercial Service or OPAC). **NISO Link:** www.niso.org/emetrics/current/subcategory7.8.1.html
# Database sessions (definition adapted from proposed ICOLC standard)	Total count of the number of sessions (logins) initiated to the online databases. **NISO Definition:** A session is defined as a successful request of an online service or library s online catalog. It is one cycle of user activities that typically starts when a user connects to the service or database and ends by terminating activity that is either explicit (by leaving the service through exit or log-out) or implicit (timeout due to user inactivity). The NISO standard distinguishes between various types of sessions. **NISO Link:** www.niso.org/emetrics/current/subcategory7.8.1.html
# Database queries/searches (definition adapted from proposed ICOLC standard)	Total count of the number of searches conducted in the library's online databases. Subsequent activities by users (e.g., browsing, printing) are not considered part of the search process. **International Coalition of Library Consortia (ICOLC) Standard:** www.library.yale.edu/consortia/webstats.html
# Items examined	Total count of the number of online database content views (e.g., abstracts, full-text articles). See ICOLC Standard above.

Electronic services	
# Virtual reference transactions	Count of the number of reference questions received electronically (e.g., via e-mail, WWW form, etc.) excluding phone and fax. **NISO Definition:** Virtual reference transactions conducted via e-mail, Web site, or other network-based medium designed to support virtual reference. (ARL E-metrics; Bertot, McClure, Ryan). Note: Includes questions either received or responded to. **NISO Link:** www.niso.org/emetrics/current/subcategory7.3.1.html
Public service time spent servicing information technology)	Count of the public service staff time spent in installation, repair, maintenance, servicing, and recovering from information technology resource and service activity. For example, fixing printer jams, adding paper to printers and copying machines, re-booting frozen software, installation of new or upgraded software or hardware, etc. **NISO Definition**: None **NISO Link:** None
Virtual visits	
# Virtual visits to networked library resources	A visit occurs when an external user connects to a networked library resource for any length of time or purpose (regardless of the number of pages or elements viewed). Examples of a networked library resource include a library OPAC or a library web page. In the case of a user visit to a library web site a user who looks at 16 pages and 54 graphic images registers one visit on the Web server. NISO Committee AY, Library Statistics Standard Z39 .7-2002draft:http://216.239.39.104/search?q=cache:dDc0 QZcW92wJ:www.niso.org/emetrics/appendixC.pdf+site :www.niso.org+virtual+visits&hl=en&ie=UTF-8
# Virtual visits excluding in-library use	This takes the # virtual visits to networked library resources statistic and subtracts the in-library use of these network resources. Excluded, for example, would be the visits made by library users within the library using the public access workstations provided. **NISO Definition:** None **NISO Link:** None

Training	
# Users trained in information technology	Count of the number of users trained in the use of information technology or resources obtainable using information technology in structured, informal, and electronically delivered training sessions conducted or sponsored by the library. Structured means a course with a designed curriculum intended to demonstrate the use of a technology such as the Web, Internet searching, library workstation, personal computing, etc. Informal includes contacts with users by library staff intended to demonstrate the use of library workstations, aspects of the applications available on those workstations, etc. An electronically delivered user training session might involve a Internet based course or distance learning, computerized learning module, or instructional video related to use of information technology or resources obtainable using information technology. Sponsored means that the library plays some role (not limited to training) in the training session. **NISO Definition:** A count of the number of users instructed and the hours of instruction offered in the use of information technology or resources obtainable using information technology in structured sessions—either delivered in the library using a computer lab or other instructional setting or delivered electronically through online-based instruction. (Bertot, McClure, Davis). **NISO Link:** www.niso.org/emetrics/current/subcategory7.9.2.html
# Hours of information technology user training	Count of the number of hours spent training users in the use of information technology or resources obtainable using information technology in structured, informal, and electronically delivered training sessions conducted or sponsored by the library. **NISO Definition:** None **NISO Link:** None
# Staff trained in information technology	Count of the total number of staff receiving formal training in the management or use of information technology or resources obtainable using information technology. Formal means a session, conference, workshop, instructional learning module, distance learning program, or course with a designed structure or curriculum intended to demonstrate the use of information technology or resources obtainable using information technology. **NISO Definition:** None **NISO Link:** None
# Hours of formal information technology staff training	Count of the total number of hours library staff engaged in formal training in the management or use of information technology or resources obtainable using information technology. **NISO Definition:** None **NISO Link:** None

NATIONAL ELECTRONIC RESOURCE DATA

The FSCS has begun collecting some data elements on a national level (http://nces.ed.gov/pubs2003/2003398.pdf). By 2002, at least 80 percent of U.S. libraries were able to report on a few measures for 2001 activities. The tables below indicate averages and per capita comparisons for those libraries measuring electronic use—but the averages do not tell the whole story, of course. The data are reported as electronic uses per typical week, but the plan is to annualize the numbers in the next edition to parallel all other data reporting.

The FSCS provides directions for collecting data on the number of users of electronic resources per typical week:

> Count the number of users using electronic resources in the library in a typical week. Electronic resources include, but are not limited to, Internet (WWW, email, telnet, other), online indexes, CD-ROM reference sources, software, and the online catalog. Do not include staff use of these resources. Note: The number of users may be counted manually, using registration logs. Count each user that uses electronic resources, regardless of the amount of time spent on the computer. A user who uses the library's electronic resources three times a week would count as three customers. Software such as "Historian" can also be used to track the number of users at each public terminal.

Examination of the data indicates huge library by library variations that are probably the result of differing interpretations of the definitions on electronic use from FSCS. For example, while the average in all population categories hovers at about 1.0 use per capita annually, the difference between the 5th and 95th percentile can vary by a factor of fifty or sixty to one! Surely there are differences between the availability of these resources, but the differences in that range seems to indicate the need for further clarification of the definitions and reporting requirements.

The available data is not yet complete enough for thorough analysis, but let's see what the statistics are beginning to indicate. In 2002:

- Just 80 percent, or 7,291 libraries, reported electronic resources use.

  o By population category the reporting ratio ranged between 60 percent and 83 percent.

- By the reported data, nationwide library collection expenditure per electronic use averaged 94 cents as compared to 50 cents for collection expenditure per circulation.

  o At least for now, spending on electronic resources appears less cost effective than spending on traditional collections.

- The average annual electronic use was about 1.0 per capita, although it varies widely by population category. The electronic resources rate in 2001 is:

  o about the same rate as that for reference queries,

  o about one electronic use for every four library visits, and

  o about one electronic use for every six circulations.

Figure 7–3 Libraries Reporting Electronic Use in 2001

Population category	Number of libraries	Percent of libraries in this population category reporting electronic use
a) 500 K (Over 500,000)	47	62%
b) 250 k (250,000 to 499,999)	57	60%
c) 100 k (100,000 to 249,999)	234	72%
d) 50 k (50,000 to 99,999)	418	77%
e) 25 k (25,000 to 49,999)	738	81%
f) 10 k (10,000 to 24,999)	1,449	82%
g) 5 k (5,000 to 9,999)	1,195	83%
h) 2.5 k (2,500 to 4,999)	1,075	82%
i) 1 k (1,000 to 2,499)	1,285	79%
j) 0 k (Under 1,000)	793	76%
Combined	7,291	80%

The year 2001 was the first year that FSCS reported electronic resource use. This chart demonstrates electronic use reporting by

185

libraries in 2001. About 80 percent of libraries nationwide report electronic use according to the definitions agreed to by the state data coordinators and the FSCS. Many more libraries provide access to electronic resources but were not able to report that use in the form required by FSCS.

Figure 7–4 Average Expenditures per Circulation and Electronic Use (2001)

Population category	Total annual electronic resource uses	Total annual circulation	Collection expenditure per electronic use	Collection expenditure per circulation
a) 500 K	57,425,888	286,777,918	$0.81	$0.66
b) 250 k	21,822,008	118,157,546	$0.94	$0.51
c) 100 k	29,117,296	200,814,357	$1.10	$0.45
d) 50 k	29,346,668	175,284,157	$0.93	$0.43
e) 25 k	23,695,464	163,970,570	$1.02	$0.46
f) 10 k	23,178,376	163,556,526	$0.99	$0.42
g) 5 k	7,864,896	62,680,936	$1.00	$0.43
h) 2.5 k	3,801,408	28,384,346	$0.80	$0.43
i) 1 k	2,387,632	17,300,621	$0.95	$0.43
j) 0 k	757,276	4,473,932	$0.85	$0.46
Averages	199,396,912	1,221,400,909	$0.94	$0.50

This table compares direct collection expenditures and electronic use expenditures at the 7,291 libraries that report electronic use information. Electronic resources include, but are not limited to, the Internet (WWW, email, telnet, other), online indexes, CD-ROM reference sources, software, and the online catalog.

Figure 7–5 Per Capita Comparisons for Electronic Use, Reference, Visits, and Circulation (2001)

Population category	Electronic resource use	Reference	Visits	Circulation
a) 500 K	1.2	1.6	4.1	6.1
b) 250 k	1.1	1.1	3.9	6.3
c) 100 k	0.8	0.9	3.9	6.0
d) 50 k	1.0	0.8	4.2	6.4
e) 25 k	0.9	0.8	4.7	6.7
f) 10 k	1.0	0.8	5.1	7.2
g) 5 k	0.9	0.8	4.9	7.2
h) 2.5 k	1.0	0.8	4.7	7.3
i) 1 k	1.1	0.9	5.0	8.0
j) 0 k	1.6	1.0	6.1	9.3
Combined	1.0	1.1	4.3	6.4

This table compares the per capita electronic use rates to the more traditional measures of reference, visits, and circulation in the 7,291 libraries reporting electronic use.

USING COMPARATIVE ELECTRONIC SERVICES DATA

The data in Figures 7–1 and 7–2 should help effective planners to set appropriate measures and benchmarks for their libraries. Most libraries are submitting their data for funding, electronic use, and circulation, which allows for easy comparison. If your library's collection expenditure per electronic use or your collection expenditure per circulation differs markedly from the national data for your population category, further investigation is in order. Is it because the library has a greater commitment to electronic services or because the library is reporting data in manner that is at odds with the FSCS definitions?

Use the Percentile Tables in Appendix 2 to check the comparative data for your library's population category for each of the following measures:

- Electronic materials— expenditures
- Electronic access— items
- Electronic materials
- Annual electronic access

If your library's data is above the 95th percentile or below the 5th percentile for any or all of the indicated measures, then it is time to assure the planning group that it is getting solid data rather than misunderstood results. If, for instance, your library's electronic materials expenditure per capita, the number of sessions by an individual on a given database or resource, and number of electronic materials accessed are at the 25th percentile but the annual electronic access is at the 95th percentile, it is likely that some inaccurate counting of the electronic access is taking place.

Make efforts to fix the data reporting structure. It is pointless to write objectives for electronic access if the data being used are faulty. Please bear in mind that using electronic measures is a very new activity for all libraries. Corrections on the methods for data reporting should not result in any recriminations or accusations. The data definitions are difficult to follow and any mistaken measurement has almost certainly resulted from misunderstanding rather than malice. Your goal should be to get the numbers right to help the library effectively gauge progress on electronic measures in the future.

EQUINOX ITEMS FOR ELECTRONIC MEASUREMENT

The issue of what to count for electronic measures has also been investigated in Europe. One example is the EQUINOX Library Performance Measurement and Quality Management System (http://equinox.dcu.ie/reports/d2_5.html#Conclusions).

The EQUINOX Web site notes that: "The potential market for the EQUINOX system comprises all libraries of all types worldwide—potentially many hundreds of thousands. However, only those libraries with IT systems in place are likely to be interested in adding an equally sophisticated management tool of this type."

The program conducted a peer review process to develop a standard set of indicators as follows:

- Percentage of the population reached by electronic library services

- Number of sessions on each electronic library service per member of the target population

- Number of remote sessions on electronic library services per member of the population to be served

- Number of documents and entries (records) viewed per session for each electronic library service

- Cost per session for each electronic library service

- Cost per document or entry (record) viewed for each electronic library service

- Percentage of information requests submitted electronically

- Rate of use for library computer workstations

- Number of library computer workstation hours available per member of the population to be served

- Percentage of rejected sessions versus total attempted sessions

- Percentage of total acquisitions expenditure spent on acquisition of electronic library services

- Number of attendances at formal electronic library service training lessons per member of the population to be served

- Percentage of library staff developing, managing, and providing ELS and user training versus percentage of total library staff

- Amount of user satisfaction with electronic library services

Collection Development

This section will help library planners develop the tools necessary for effective collection developmentby asking them to consider the following issues:

- Review and adoption of collection development policy

- Measurement and evaluation of the collection

- Allocation of materials budgets to collection types and categories

- Input of the public on collection development

- Issues of intellectual freedom

OVERVIEW

The checklist in Chapter 9 will help to determine if the library's current policies and plans are adequate. Write goals and objectives to address any gaps. Developing the needed strategies, goals, objectives and measures will challenge library planners to ask fundamental questions about the library and the community it serves. The debate about selecting materials for quality as opposed to user demand is an old one, but that does not make it any less important to library planners today. Planners have to agree on the right strategy for their own library, today and in the future.

COLLECTION DEVELOPMENT POLICY REVIEW AND ADOPTION

All too often libraries ignore either the initial creation of a collection development policy or the necessary revisions. There should be formal adoption of a clear set of policies regarding the type of collection for the libraryand the governing body of the library should review and revise the policies on a regular basis. No long range planning process is complete until the library board undertakes this review. If the planning committee neglects to discuss the collection development policy, it is incumbent on either the library director or the library board to insist on such a review.

One common debate among library planners is how to organize the collection development policies—by type of material, format, or by subject. Many collection development policies deal with guidelines for various types of fiction and categories of nonfiction for print separated by types and classes, with separate policies for other types of media like CD-ROMs, audiotapes, or even electronic resources.

Many planners would agree that, in the abstract, it would be preferable to be as holistic and inclusive as possible so that broad principles of selection, weeding, and budgets would apply across formats and types in the policy. The reality is usually that the policies have developed incrementally over time and that the inclusion of new formats requires a new section of the policy manual. Trying to force them all into an integrated holistic arrangement may be more trouble than it is worth. Furthermore, some collection development criteria really are specific to the fiction genre or the material format.

The most important thing to bear in mind about a collection development policy is that it is an important *communication* document. Through the document, the library makes clear to the board, the administration, the selection staff, the public at large, the governing body, and even the potential censors, what materials will be selected as well as how and when materials will be retained. The plannning committee is not usually responsible for reviewing the collection development policies or suggesting revisions, but they are responsible for assuring that the task is undertaken by the library staff and board.

Measurement and Evaluation of the Collection

Library collections and plans need continuous quantitative and qualitative evaluation. This section will consider the quantitative aspects first, then the qualitative.

Quantitative Measures

Plans can and should state quantitative objectives with reference to numerical state standards if they exist. If state standards are absent or insufficient, consider using the percentile comparisons in Chapter 5. When considering standards, library planners should state the objectives for collection development in terms of such things as numbers of volumes added or periodical subscriptions and plan the current and projected budget to meet any stated numerical objectives. Making such numerical comparisons can be painful for library planners—especially if a library is sadly deficient—but the comparisons must be made.

Planners will also want to consider collection use statistics as indirect measures of the collection. The percentile comparisons found in Chapter 5 will be useful. If standard measures for the library on circulation per capita or per visit vary substantially from those of similar libraries, perhaps this means that better marketing is needed to attract more people into the library. Or perhaps the building and collection are not drawing a reasonable number of visits. Unless a library is unusual for other reasons, a low turnover rate for a library of its size may be an indicator of the need for weeding, while a very high one may call for substantial additions to the collection.

Qualitative Measures

Checking standard lists and user surveys are the two main ways libraries measure qualitative aspects of the collection. Neither works perfectly, of course. Comparing the collection to standard lists is simpler than surveying users but has the disadvantage of being a one-size-fits-all approach. The community served by the library may differ radically from those served by standard lists. Surveys are difficult to develop and use appropriately. Library users ordinarily express satisfaction with the library collection and cannot define the types of materials that are missing that they would use.

Checklists

There are several examples of standard lists in the bibliography under "Collection and Resources." Probably the best known list with the longest history is the H.W. Wilson company's *Public Library Catalog*, which began with the 1908 version of the *Fiction Catalog*. In 1918 H.W. Wilson published the first of several installments for the *Standard Catalog*, which the company compiled in 1934 and later renamed the *Public Library Catalog*. Today the *Public Library Catalog* and its companion *Fiction Catalog* are available in both print and online form.

In addition, the professional library periodicals all feature checklists and recommended titles by topic and by format on a regular basis. Library planners will want to consider how to use these selection and checklist tools in their operations. The library's collection development policy should speak to which standard tools, if any, will be used and how. Effective long range planning will indicate the current methods in use and outline any projected changes.

Surveys

Library planners should approach the subject of developing new surveys with extreme care. In all but the largest public libraries, it is next to impossible to develop in-house any statistically significant and truly valid surveys on collection use or nearly any other type of library service. If the planning team, the board, and the administration are willing to accept from the start that these surveys are not valid for statistical purposes, then the surveys may be useful in other ways—but run that idea by the groups before proceeding, not after. When approaching a collection development survey, consider the "Data Relevancy Test" in Figure 4–1.

Staff surveys can be helpful, but they have their limits. Staff at the circulation desk will know what the public is seeking and interlibrary loan staff can help identify holes in the collection. Professionally developed telephone or mail surveys can provide excellent planning information, but are usually quite expensive. Libraries often compromise and use in-library surveys, especially when considering collection development. Another possibility is the use of Web-based surveys. As noted in Chapter 3, *Instant Web Forms and Surveys for Public Libraries* (see "Outcome Assessment" section in the bibliography) will be a good source for such surveys.

ALLOCATION OF MATERIALS BUDGETS TO COLLECTION TYPES AND CATEGORIES

There is probably only one truism of allocation of materials budgets—if everyone on the staff and in the public agrees that the library is fairly and adequately funding their favorite genre, area, or material format, then you are in the *Twilight Zone*, not a public library.

Some libraries allocate materials budgets by format: books, periodicals, videos, and so forth. Others do so by functional area: children, adults, young adult and so on. Libraries tend to base materials allocations on tradition, annual circulation rates, chosen priorities, or even on internal and external politics. The important thing for library planners to do is to acknowledge the potential variations, declare the library's chosen method, and outline the budget results in the long range-planning document.

Another issue that planners will want to consider is the proportion of the budget that goes to library materials. The percentile comparisons in Chapter 5 provide information on the percent of their total budgets that libraries of various population sizes allocate to materials. Many libraries try to aim for a fixed portion of the budget earmarked for materials—usually 15 to 20 percent of the operating budget total. However, the planners should bear a number of things in mind before they adopt a goal blindly. A library that finds itself with a substandard current collection will need to devote a larger percentage for a number of years to catch up. Take care what you count as materials expenditures. Although the state data coordinators usually take great care to have consistent reporting, sometimes expenditures get into the wrong category or end up "off" the ledger. For example some contract expenditures for electronic resources, especially if they are purchased through a regional or state consortium, are missed as collection expenditures. Sometimes Friends groups or foundations spend money toward materials that are not counted to the library's credit. Even materials spending from the library's own gift fund may be missed depending on the local accounting practices.

INTELLECTUAL FREEDOM ISSUES

A collection development policy that does not acknowledge intellectual freedom issues and laws is simply deficient. Library planners must consider the evolving local, state, and national changes regarding privacy and intellectual freedom. The various versions of the federal Child Internet Protection Act (CIPA) and the USA PATRIOT Act have presented new challenges to the library community since the turn of the millennium. Consider the related issues of filters, intellectual freedom, and privacy with great care and seek legal counsel before plans are made final.

Two recent books will help planners in this matter: Barbara Jones' *Libraries, Access, and Intellectual Freedom* and Mark

Smith's *Internet Policy Handbook for Libraries* (See "Internet and Automation Technology" in the bibliography for details). Jones takes the ALA's position on Intellectual Freedom, but Smith believes that at times libraries may end up restricting access and he allows for the development of intellectual freedom policies in a professional and careful manner.

Technology

Library planners should consider present and future technology issues as part of library planning, but should not let technology become the sole focus of planning. The emphasis here is on planning for the tools that deliver content to the user rather than on the electronic content—the Local Area Network (LAN) rather than a full-text database, for instance. Topics include:

- Obsolescence planning

- Technology planning and the e-rate

- Integrated automation systems

- Online catalogs

- Wireless or wired systems

- Virtual references

- Web pages, blogs, etc.

PLANNING FOR OBSOLESCENCE

On seeing his obituary mistakenly published in a newspaper, Mark Twain remarked: "The news of my death has been greatly exaggerated." Those of us who have been in libraries for some time know the feeling. The news of the death of libraries has been heralded because of paperbacks, movies, TV, photocopiers, personal computers, and now, of course, the Internet. We have also watched as countless technologies came and went, from 45 RPM records, to reel to reel tape, to 16 mm film, to filmstrips, to 5 1/4-inch floppy disks—to name but a few.

Our card catalogs are mostly gone, and the reference collection is far less tangible since the advent of online databases. Library planners have no choice but to plan for the inevitable obsolescence of the tools and technologies with which they work. It is best to "lean into it" and go with the flow rather than try to resist or to slow things down.

TECHNOLOGY PLANS

In the mid 1990s the Clinton administration set a widely publicized goal to get all schools and public libraries in the country hooked up to the Internet by 2000. The program largely achieved its goal thanks to federal funding from the Universal Service Fund "revenue enhancement" on phone bills generated millions of dollars in "E-rate Funds" for schools and libraries. By 2000, most of the 9,000 public libraries had high-speed access to the Internet. Another less publicized aspect of the program was the requirement that libraries adopt technology plans.

Figures 7–6 through 7–9 provide a restatement of the type of information that the E-rate program originally required for a library technology plan. Libraries serving over 100,000 in population or with multiple branches and bookmobiles will need a more extensive template for a technology plan, especially in regards to the LAN, but the basic elements will remain the same.

Figure 7–6. Technology Plan Narrative Description

Provide a brief description of the library, including population served, annual budget, annual technology budget, annual circulation, and other relevant information.
Name of library: Narrative description:

Figure 7–7. Technology Plan for Budget, Phones, and Workstations

Budget area	Vendor or notation	Year 1 budget	Year 2 budget	Year 3 budget
Automated circulation/catalog—vendor				
Other automation software—vendor				
Database/CD-ROM products				
On-line database subscriptions				
Annual telephone bill				
Budget for computer equipment				
Internet service provider costs				
Local area network costs				
Totals				
Telephone line access				
Number of phone lines				
Number of phones				
Computer workstations in Library				
Number of locally owned computer stations				
Number of locally owned stations on the local area network				
Number of locally owned workstations with graphical capacity for the Internet and full text databases				
Number of locally owned workstations with graphical capacity for the library catalog				

Figure 7–8 Technology Plan for General Issues

Question	Yes	No	Comments
Do you have a LAN? (Local Area Network)			
Describe internal connections, if any, a library already has or anticipates installing for a LAN or network. **The building is wired with twisted pair cable to handle Ethernet 10-100. The Novell network is Ethernet 10/Hub. The Windows NT network is Ethernet 0/Hub.**			
Describe your software for LAN and telecommunication connections currently available or budgeted. • **Novell and Windows NT Servers, which are bridges for certain information to pass from one network to the other** • **T-1 Access to the Internet for Integrated Automation System and for Internet Access; DSL is being considered for the future**			
Describe any existing or budgeted maintenance contracts to maintain computers or networks. • **Integrated Automation System vendor maintenance contract** • **ZYX Consulting provides WAN support by maintenance contract and workstation maintenance on an as needed basis**			
Do you know about the capacity of the library's electrical system to handle simultaneous uses? **Local electrical contractor, ABC Electrical, has examined current configuration and has assured library staff that the current electrical capacity is more than adequate to handle at least a 50% increase in workstation capacity.**			
Indicate the experience and training of staff in the use of the equipment and list needed training. **Staff have received training on Windows NT and various software Databases and CD-ROMs that the library has in-house. Additional training is needed on the Internet for full text databases and for virtual reference software.**			
Other wiring planning data • **Square feet in library: 12,412** • **Number of floors: 2** • **Estimated linear feet of cabling needed: 6,000** • **Construction type: brick frame, solid walls, cement floors, dropped ceilings** • **Current phone company: Ameritech/World Com/Not Your Father's Baby Bell** • **Type of Internet access needed: presently has 400 feet of Ethernet 10; planning multimedia with fast ethernet**			

Note that the items listed in bold are examples only. Be sure to tailor to your own library.

Figure 7–9 Technology Plan for Equipment Inventory

#	Description	Unit(s)	Unit(s)	Unit(s)
	Number of units			
	Purpose specify staff workstation, public use, OPAC, server, etc.			
1	**Value**			
2	**Year**			
3	**Type of computer**			
4	**Units of this type comp.**			
5	**RAM (memory)**			
6	**MHz (clock speed)**			
7	**Operating system**			
8	**Internal hard drive**			
9	**External hard drive**			
10	**Modem**			
11	**Monitor**			
12	**Printer**			
13	**CD-ROM type**			
14	**Units of CD-ROMs**			
15	**Other**			
16	**Other**			

INTEGRATED AUTOMATION SYSTEM

A very substantial piece of nearly any library's ongoing cost is devoted to its automation system—the system that provides catalog content, materials acquisition, book checkouts, and all the rest of the things that an integrated automation system can provide. This chapter cannot provide anything like an exhaustive treatment of issues surrounding an automated system—it can only touch on a few of the larger ones.

Some of the main questions to ask are featured in Figure 7–10. Bear in mind that many libraries serving less than 5,000 in

199

population will be looking at whether or not to obtain a first integrated library system rather than asking about upgrading or migrating.

Figure 7–10 Integrated Library System Questions

What system is currently in use?
How did we get it?
What are its strengths and weaknesses? (Get answers from all the stakeholders: board, administration, staff, and public.)
Is the vendor still developing the system or have they stopped development?
Is the vendor likely to stay in business?
What is the total cost of the automation system, including related telecommunications and staffing costs? (Be persistent, all related costs are not likely to be readily available.)
Does the library participate in a shared automation system? Could it do so? Would that be cost effective?
If the library is in a shared system, does it work as needed or does the library need to get into a different shared system or a stand-alone system?
Is there a plan for migration to a new system? What is it?
How much will the next migration cost? Is there enough budgeted for the migration?
Does the parent municipality require the library to include its upgrade costs in the municipality's capital improvement budget? Has the library done so? If not, what will it take to do so?
Does existing staff have the expertise to define the needs for the integrated library system upgrade? If not, how can the library obtain the necessary expertise?

ONLINE CATALOG

A proportion of library users are also Internet users who expect to find access to a library collection twenty-four hours a day, seven days a week. They expect to be able to order the items online from home and pick them up at the library at their convenience. They expect the library catalog to be graphically pleasing just like they find at Amazon.com.

Effective library planners will need to ask a variety of questions. Is your library's catalog online? If not, why not? If so, is it everything your users need and want? Can they search the catalog, request items, and expect to pick them up at their convenience? Does the catalog allow them to get notices of new items they will find useful? Can they get their overdue notices online if they want? Can they renew items and pay fines online? Sometimes the answers have to be no, not yet, because the library's automation vendor may not be able to do all these things. Even if it can, there may not be enough money in the library budget. Even if there is enough money, staff resistance and inertia may stand in the way. The library may not even have an automated library system yet.

WIRELESS OR WIRED

Most library buildings are wired to the Internet via a LAN. It is becoming increasingly common for hotels, airports, and conference centers to provide high-speed wireless access to the Internet, and a few libraries are getting on the bandwagon as well. There are substantial legal and privacy issues involved in providing wireless access, and not all libraries have the funding or the bandwidth capacity to deliver it. Library planners will need to determine if they want to deliver wireless only to library-supplied computers or to any personal computer or even PDA that users bring with them. The potential legal and technical problems are substantial, but libraries that want to be on the cutting edge and continue to supply value-added services to their users will want to strongly consider planning for wireless access within the library.

VIRTUAL REFERENCE

Any reference librarian will tell you that the Internet has radically changed reference work by diminishing many of the types of questions that library staff members used to handle. Many of the "ready reference" questions that we used to handle on the phone or at the reference desk can now be answered directly by the library user with an Internet connection and a search engine like Google. That leaves reference staff with the tough questions—the ones that take knowledge of full-text databases or the full range of print resources. That means that the raw statistical numbers of traditional reference queries are falling. It also means that many library reference staff are seeking new ways to answer the information needs of library users. One example is virtual reference.

Virtual reference is hard to describe unless you have experienced it. The library user is usually connected directly to the reference librarian in real time over the Internet using a Web-based dialog box that allows the user to interact with the librarian and clarify the question being asked. The reference librarian can then use available resources to either answer the question immediately or get back to the user in a timely fashion. The process relies on the Internet and (usually commercial) software. Depending on the software used and the resources of the library, the process can take place twenty-four hours a day and seven days a week. Some software packages allow libraries to share the queries and the reference librarian expertise across many time zones and throughout the country and the world.

Library planners will want to decide if this activity fits within the role and funding resources of the library.

WEB PAGES

In 1999 I found all the available Web pages for the top libraries in the HAPLR ratings and linked to them on the HAPLR Web page listing their scores. Less than half of the top 100 had available Web sites, and almost none of the smaller libraries had sites. Just four years later nearly all, even in the smallest population category, had a Web presence. No one has done an inventory, but it is probably fair to say that the majority of the 9,000 libraries in the country have some form of "Web presence" today, just as so many businesses and organizations do. Just how effective and efficient is that presence? That, of course, is another story; so, too, is the issue of keeping the library Web presence up to date.

Many library Web pages begin with an ambitious set of links to featured sources of information and a host of other links. Maintaining those links is a challenge since the average longevity before major changes of a link is usually measured in weeks or months rather than in years. Broken and redirected links become a major sources of frustration to users. Unless the initial enthusiasm for building a Web site is matched with continued commitment, the result can be frustrated users and a poor reflection on the library.

The American Library Association found itself in the midst of a firestorm of complaints in 2003 when it tried to redesign its extensive Web site. With thousands of links that were multiplying daily and becoming increasingly difficult to manage, it moved to a *database-driven site* that used dynamic links in an effort to keep the site up to date. In the process, it found itself in the company of the National Association of Counties, the Internal Revenue Service, and other managers of extensive Web sites with a high level of confusion and customer dissatisfaction. The links were too long to paste into browsers, most of the previous links became invalid, and the internal search engine misfired badly. Librarians and ALA Web site users throughout the nation complained mightily.

Let the ALA experience be a cautionary tale for libraries. Having an outside firm manage or redesign the Web site can lead to unforeseen and negative results; however, inertia and inaction are causing many library Web sites to suffer the same malady that ALA sought to heal. Effective library planners will look to the current library's Web site as a "work in progress" and seek to make it both more efficient and effective. You never get a second chance to make a good first impression, and for increasing numbers of library users, the library Web presence is that first impression. Only effective planning can make that first impression a good one.

Access and Facilities

The physical facility can be a source of infinite pride, infinite shame, or, more likely, something in between. The planning and development necessary for building or remodeling a library is beyond the scope of this book. Nevertheless, this section will indicate some of the general steps to take and issues to consider regarding buildings and how to assess the building elements even if there is no current need for a new or remodeled building.

WALK AROUND ASSESSMENT

There is a technique in management literature called "management by wandering around." Proponents assert that managers must spend a lot of time wandering around their firm or organization, making their presence known, asking pertinent questions and noting essential issues. Library planners should walk around (or drive around, if the system has branches) to look at the facilities and equipment with fresh eyes as if they were new users approaching the library for the first time.

An outdated and dilapidated building will be apparent to nearly all—except, of course, for retrogrades who insist on seeing cramped and outdated Carnegie-type structures as "quaint." However, encourage the team to look beyond the building itself. Are the shelves overcrowded with obviously outdated material? Is the physical arrangement of the materials unfathomable even to library professionals, not to mention the average user? Are there areas of the library where the lighting is a challenge even to the fully sighted? Can those in wheel chairs get around the entire library or are they consigned to only a part of the building, or worse, left waiting at the door?

Years ago, I interviewed for a job that, thankfully, I did not get. Walking around the building revealed a number of obvious problems that apparently the current library authorities did not see. In a community with tight parking, all the parking closest to the front door was reserved for library staff. The children's room shared space with the periodical storage area, which was simply roped off with a sign at about two-and-a-half feet high. In the space of a few minutes, several toddlers found themselves severely reprimanded by library staff or parents when they blithely ran under these adult size barriers while playing tag. A bit of walking around by effective planners could have done a world of good for the ambience, if not for the building design.

Look to the library signs. If you are on the staff or the board, you know where the building is, but does a newcomer? Municipal traffic personnel can usually place directional signs at nominal cost. You may know where the reference desk is (and what that means), but does the public? Can you find the administrative offices with ease, or do you need a tour guide?

Space Needs Assessment

There are four major phases of library building planning: space needs assessment, architectural development, contractor/building, and, unfortunately, second-guessing everything that went before! The first phase, space needs assessment, often falls to library staff or jointly to staff and outside consultants. That may or may not be a mistake, depending on the library's circumstances: the resources that the library can bring to bear on the building project, the depth of commitment that the community has to a new building, and the expertise of the staff in developing a building plan. A good space needs assessment can save many headaches later on by telling an architect or design engineer how big the various components to the library should be and what their relationship should be to one another. It indicates, for instance, where the workroom should be in relation to the circulation desk and the children's area, how many readers seats are needed in a quiet study area, or how big the meeting room should be, and so on.

We ought to be able to speak of a standard or average number of reader seats, square feet per capita, and the like in this country, but we cannot. The United States is one of the only countries in the industrialized world that does not keep track of the size of its public library buildings on a national level. The FSCS for libraries has promised such data in the near (2004 or 2005) future, but for now the data is available for only some individual states.

I have used 2001 Wisconsin library data to provide some rough estimates of the number of square feet per capita in the average library in Figure 7–11. Take care using the table; there are only a few libraries in Wisconsin in the over 50,000 population or 50,000 to 99,999 category. Averages on a national basis, when they are available, may vary from Wisconsin numbers. The table presents the data with two variations: municipal population and extended population. A single municipality usually establishes libraries in Wisconsin, as in many states. The library typically serves a wider extended population than just that of the establishing population, however. Take, for example, the "Cheeseville Memorial Library," whose building has 50,000 square feet. Its municipal population is 62,500, so the square feet per capita of municipal population is 0.8. Its service population is 83,300, so its number if square feet per capita of service population is 0.6.

Two additional cautions are in order when using the data in Figure 7–11. First, remember that these averages include brand new libraries as well as far older ones. The numbers also include buildings that are by no means adequate to the populations they serve. For planning purposes, the averages tend to be on the low end of the numbers that library planners should consider. Secondly, remember that when a building is being planned, it is important to project the future population rather than use the current population. A building plan should cover at least twenty years, so use the population estimates for the entire service population in that twenty years.

It is also important to remember that, especially in older buildings, as much as 33 percent of the building may be "unassignable." That means that the space is either mechanical, hallways, interior walls and supports, or other space that is not actually useable for library services.

The numbers in Figure 7–11 provide only a very rough beginning for space planning purposes. Many libraries will turn to a space needs consultant for further refinement. Help can sometimes be obtained from the state library agency, the library system, or other librarians in the area with experience in space needs assessment.

Figure 7–11 Square Feet per Capita in Wisconsin Libraries by Population Category (2001)

A Extended population category	B Number of libraries	C Square feet per capita municipal	D Square feet per capita extended
OVER 100,000	7	0.8	0.6
50,000 to 99,999	11	1.2	0.9
25,000 to 49,999	27	1.1	0.7
10,000 to 24,999	72	1.8	0.9
5,000 to 9,999	65	2.0	0.9
2,500 to 4,999	78	2.5	1.2
Under 2,500	110	2.9	1.8
State Total/Average	370	2.2	1.2

PUBLIC LIBRARY SPACE NEEDS

The CD included in this book contains interactive spreadsheets that allow library planners to plug in numbers and calculate their space needs. It also includes a "Capital Cost Calculator" that allows planners to obtain estimates about costs either for construction planning or development of impact fees. For more planning assistance, see *Public Library Space Needs: A Planning*

Outline by Anders C. Dahlgren (www.dpi.state.wi.us/dlcl/pld/pl space.html), available for download in PDF, MS Word, and MS Excel formats.

Public Library Space Needs: Worksheet

The sample table in Figure 7–12 is included as a spreadsheet on the CD in two formats—a traditional spreadsheet and one with a "Slider Bar." The latter form allows library planners to quickly calculate "what if" scenarios with various planning assumptions. Remember that the worksheet here is intended only for very preliminary estimates. Further work with a building consultant or an architect will refine and expand these numbers.

Figure 7–12. Public Library Space Needs Worksheet

Design criteria	Number	Factor	Calculation factor	Sq. ft needed
Primary population		Residents		
Extended population		Residents		
Total Design Population		Residents		
Book volumes		Volumes	10 volumes per square foot	
Current periodicals		Titles	Square foot per title	
Back issue periodicals (specify years retained, default is 3)	3	Titles	0.5 Square feet per title per yr.	
Nonprint material		Items	One square foot per item	
Public use computer workstations		Work-station	50 sq. ft. per workstation	
Reader seats		Seats	20 sq. ft per reader seat	
Staff workstations		Workstation	140 sq. ft. per workstation	
Meeting/program rooms		Persons	10 sq. ft. per person plus 100	
Conference/board room		Persons	35 sq ft. per conference seat	
Storytime room		Persons	15 sq. ft. per person plus 50	
Computer training lab		Persons	50 sq. ft. per workstation plus 80	
Subtotal without special or non-assignable				

Design criteria	Number	Factor	Calculation factor	Sq. ft. needed
Special use space		Not applicable	10 to 20% of subtotal	
Non-assignable space (mechanical, halls, etc.)		Not applicable	20 to 30% of subtotal	
Total square feet				
Square feet per capita				

READER SEATING CALCULATION

Library planners can use the worksheet in Figure 7–13 to look at the general reader seats needed. The parameters are based on Dahlgren's *Public Library Space Needs: A Planning Outline.* The recommended range of seating should be modified to meet local needs and conditions.

Figure 7–13 Reader Seating Calculation for a Library

Factor	This library now	Five yrs. from now
Population	75,000	100,000
Recommended low	150	225
Recommended high	225	375
Amount chosen	200	225
Population category	**Recommended range of reader seating**	
Under 5,000	20	50
5,000 to 9,999	50	70
10,000 to 24,999	70	125
25,000 to 49,999	125	150
50,000 to 99,999	150	225
100,000 to 249,999	225	375
250,000 to 499,999	375	500
Over 500,000	500	2,500

PUBLIC ACCESS WORKSTATION CALCULATIONS

Library planners who need guidance on how many computer workstations are needed for public use will have a hard time finding recommendations. Figure 7–14 will allow a library to compare its current and future needs for public access workstations. For libraries with a population of over 500,000 there is an average of 0.89 public terminals for every 10,000 library visitors. For the smallest population category, under 1,000, the average is almost 4.83 terminals for every user visit. The ratio of workstations to library visits increases as the population decreases. As Figure 7–15 demonstrates, there are substantial regional variations as well as population variations.

Figure 7–14 Public Access Workstations Comparisons in U.S.

Pop. category	Number of libraries	Public workstations	Sum of visits	Workstations per 10,000 user visits
a) 500,000 +	76	28,345	318,586,522	0.89
b) 250,000 to 499,999	95	13,145	130,993,583	1.00
c) 100,000 to 249,999	327	19,439	194,144,330	1.00
d) 50,000 to 99,999	541	15,000	159,400,085	0.94
e) 25,000 to 49,999	913	13,354	148,768,434	0.90
f) 10,000 to 24,999	1,767	15,137	144,755,346	1.05
g) 5,000 to 9,999	1,443	7,815	51,526,013	1.52
h) 2,500 to 4,999	1,305	4,770	22,182,676	2.15
i) 1,000 to 2,499	1,621	3,991	13,630,908	2.93
j) Under 1,000	1,040	1,802	3,729,954	4.83
Total/Average	9,128	122,798	1,187,717,851	1.03

Figure 7–15 Regional Variation in Public Access Terminals per 10,000 Visiys-

	Number of Libraries in Population category								
Popul category	Far West	Great Lakes	Mid-East	New England	Plains	Rocky Mountains	Southeast	Southwest	Grand total
a) 500 k	21	8	11	1	3	3	17	12	76
b) 250 k	17	8	9		14	2	38	7	95
c) 100 k	62	50	31	11	19	14	103	37	327
d) 50 k	57	105	87	41	27	17	170	37	541
e) 25 k	44	211	212	98	53	29	193	73	913
f) 10 k	80	423	401	246	126	70	266	154	1,766
g) 5 k	42	364	327	213	161	69	124	143	1,443
h) 2.5 k	32	316	207	233	227	75	78	137	1,305
i) 1 k	46	309	208	298	491	75	69	123	1,619
j) 0 k	77	84	85	161	507	40	39	47	1,040
Grand total	478	1,878	1,578	1,302	1,628	394	1,097	770	9,125

Public Access Terminals per 10,000 Annual User Visits								
Popul category	Far West	Great Lakes	Mid-East	New England	Plains	Rocky Mountains	Southeast	Southwest	Grand total
a) 500 k	0.86	1.19	1.07	2.13	0.92	0.58	1.05	0.92	0.99
b) 250 k	0.82	1.26	1.35		0.91	1.27	1.09	1.39	1.08
c) 100 k	0.79	1.08	1.45	0.81	1.06	0.57	1.34	1.62	1.17
d) 50 k	0.64	1.05	1.05	0.98	1.17	0.57	2.00	1.35	1.31
e) 25 k	0.76	0.90	1.13	0.99	1.67	0.86	2.24	2.14	1.38
f) 10 k	1.30	1.26	1.76	1.15	1.49	1.41	2.35	3.87	1.77
g) 5 k	1.20	1.89	2.56	1.82	1.89	2.68	3.55	5.05	2.51
h) 2.5 k	1.92	2.88	4.07	2.86	2.65	3.05	4.69	7.80	3.64
i) 1 k	3.84	4.62	4.98	4.89	4.38	4.36	6.27	7.25	4.88
j) 0 k	8.40	9.67	6.98	18.20	6.25	13.64	13.30	9.41	9.29
Grand total	2.49	2.49	2.80	4.51	4.03	3.63	3.05	5.20	3.46

Figure 7–16 Sample Planning Form for Workstations

Factor	At present	Five yrs from now
1. Population category	100,000 to 249,999	
2. Public workstations	50	
3. Annual library visits	100,000	
4. Workstations per 10,000 visits	0.50	
5. National average per 10,000 visits	1.00	
6. Regional (Mid-East) average per 10,000 visits	1.45	
7. This library as ratio to national average	50%	
8. This library as ratio to regional average	34%	

STAFF WORKSTATION CALCULATIONS FOR A LIBRARY

What about the number of workstations needed for staff? Since national comparison data are not available, Figure 7–17 allows a library to calculate its current and future needs for staff workstations using Wisconsin data to define possible benchmarks for comparison. In Wisconsin, libraries with over 100,000 population had 0.48 staff workstations for every 1,000 community residents and 0.90 workstations per full time equivalent employee. As with user workstations, the ratio of workstations to library staff members increases as the population decreases. I believes this to be true nationally as well.

Figure 7–17 Staff Computer Workstations in the U.S (2001)

Source: U.S. Federal State Cooperative Service

Pop. category	Number of libraries	Staff work-stations	Full time equivalent staff	Average work-stations per FTE staff
a) 500,000 +	76	25,277	34,921	0.72
b) 250,000 to 499,999	95	11,867	14,794	0.80
c) 100,000 to 249,999	327	18,661	22,117	0.84
d) 50,000 to 99,999	541	14,677	17,729	0.83
e) 25,000 to 49,999	913	12,743	16,789	0.76
f) 10,000 to 24,999	1,767	12,476	15,488	0.81
g) 5,000 to 9,999	1,443	5,185	6,110	0.85
h) 2,500 to 4,999	1,305	2,634	2,808	0.94
i) 1,000 to 2,499	1,621	1,929	2,003	0.96
j) Under 1,000	1,040	690	690	1.00
Total/Average	9,128	106,139	133,449	0.80

Figure 7-18 Staff Computer Workstations Planning Grid

Factor	This library now	Average for comparable libraries	Planned for 5 years from now
Staffing level in Full time Equivalents			
Workstations for staff			
Workstations per FTE employee			

ESTIMATING CAPITAL COSTS FOR BUILDING AND EQUIPMENT

Planners often need to use an estimated cost for new construction, remodeling costs, and so forth as demonstrated in Figure 7–19. The table was prepared for a community of about 20,000 population in Wisconsin and assumed equipment and other costs, but not site costs since they can vary quite widely. The 2001 national average was $143.10 for building costs and $207.70 with equipment, site, and other costs included. At the time of the comparison, a nearby library's cost for a 19,970 square foot building was $113.20. Equipment and other costs brought the total to $146.33, but that library had no site costs because it already owned the property.

This type of presentation can be useful for library boards, city councils, and other groups who want to consider potential costs for their library. The comparative data in Figure 7–19 is

211

expanded in Figure 7–20 to provide planners with somewhat more information for decision making.

Figure 7–19 Building Cost per Square Foot Comparisons—National
Source: *Library Journal*, December 2003

National	Fiscal 2001	Per sq. ft.
Number of buildings	80	
Square feet new buildings	1,924,548	
New building costs	$275,404,635	$143.10
New building equipment costs	$51,445,962	$26.73
New building site costs	$33,375,676	$17.34
New building other costs	$39,511,803	$20.53
Total new building costs	$399,738,076	$207.70
Nearby library, your state	Fiscal 2001	Per Sq Foot
Square feet new	19,970	
New building costs	$2,260,648	$113.20
New building equipment costs	$331,196	$16.58
New building site costs	$0	
New building other costs	$310,410	$15.54
Total new building	$2,922,224	$146.33

SPECIFIC LIBRARY COST ESTIMATES

Figure 7–20 shows a hypothetical table that library planners could modify to indicate capital cost projections for city councils, foundation groups, library boards, and other stakeholders. These projections assume the need for a 25,000 to 30,000 square foot building. Figure 7–20 also assumes that between 20,000 and 40,000 additional volumes need to be added to the library because it is currently substandard on volumes.

The table includes cost projections from low to moderate to high for comparative purposes. The calculations can be done on the capital cost calculator illustrate in Figure 7–21 and included as an MS-Excel spreadsheet on the CD-ROM. Note that the table assumes various bond interest rates to calculate annual payments.

Figure 7–20 Sample Building and Materials Cost Projection Options

Category	Low	Moderate	High
Building costs	$100.00	$143.00	$170.00
Equipment costs	$22.00	$27.00	$30.00
Site costs	$13.00	$17.00	$20.00
Other costs	$15.00	$21.00	$25.00
Combined	$150.00	$208.00	$245.00
Square feet needed	25,000	30,000	30,000
Building and furnishings costs	**$3,750,000**	**$6,240,000**	**$7,350,000**
Volume deficit	20,000	34,000	40,000
Unit Cost/volume	15.00	20.00	25.00
Volumes capital	**$300,000**	**$680,000**	**$1,000,000**
Combined amount	**$4,050,000**	**$6,920,000**	**$8,350,000**
Capital amortization period (in years)	10	10	10
Bond interest rate anticipated	6.000%	6.550%	7.200%
Annual payments	$550,265	$964,858	$1,199,867
Total principle and interest over 10 years	**$5,502,652**	**$9,648,581**	**$11,998,668**

CAPITAL COST CALCULATOR ON THE CD

The attached CD includes a handy tool for projecting capital costs. Planners will need to collect the needed data—population, tax base, square feet needed, interest rate for funds borrowed, term of the loan, and so forth—but once those numbers are plugged into the tool, planners may experiment with an infinite number of "what if" scenarios (Note that the CD also has instructions for how to change the parameters for each slider bar if they do not meet your needs).

Library planners often find themselves asked to estimate the costs of building a new library. Be careful, the answers depend on many factors and can be highly controversial. Make sure the library board and administration are truly ready to begin the discussion on building and capital costs. If they are, you may want to put the *Capital Cost Calculator* on a computer with projection capabilities so they can see it on a screen. It is then easy to demonstrate that there is no one "answer" to their question. Things depend on factors such as how the bids for various components come in and how large the building is (something that is usually not known for certain in the early stages of a program). The size

213

and length of the loan, along with the prevailing interest rates will greatly affect the results as well.

INSTRUCTIONS FOR THE CAPITAL COST CALCULATOR

These are the instructions for use of the interactive "Capital Cost Calculator" on the CD.

1. Enter your library's name in cell C1.

2. Enter the Population served in cell C2, and the total property tax base in cell C3.

Note: Property value assessments vary quite widely in the U.S. Some jurisdictions require property to be assessed at or near full market value while others allow assessment for tax purposes to be as little as 5 or 10 percent of market value. In cell E23, the national "average" is listed at $60,000 using full market value, but if your jurisdiction assesses at, say, 33 percent of market value, you will want to reset this value to 33 percent of $60,000 or $20,000 to get a proper comparison.

3. Move the slider bars back and forth to change the values. *Do not change any other values directly in their cells.* On the spreadsheet, you can either pull the tab along horizontally or press one of the left or right arrows to move it. Moving it will change the values in the cells in column D. If you want the value to be zero, move it all the way to the left. See Figure 7–21 for an illustration of the slider bar.

    —By moving the slider bar in column C from left to right, you can adjust building costs, equipment costs, site costs, and other costs in lines 6 to 9, column D the combined cost per square foot will total automatically. The National Averages in Column E will remain the same and your new rate compared to the national average will be automatically calculated as a percent in Column F.

    —By moving the slider bar in column C from left to right, you can change the number of square feet you need in line 11, Column D. The total cost for buildings and furnishings will be calculated in Column D, line 12.

—If you are adding volumes, use the slider bars to specify the number and estimated cost in lines 13 and 14 Combined building and volume costs will be calculated in line 16.

4. Next, specify the percent of the costs in line 16 to be financed by borrowing.

5. Now select the bond interest rate in line 18 and the amortization period for the loan in line 19. The annual payments as well as total principle and interest are calculated in lines 20 and 21.

6. The last four calculations provide context.

    —Tax capacity is used by planners, more affluent communities have higher amounts. A tax capacity of $60,000 per person is cited as "average." That would mean that the typical home with about 3 residents is worth a market value rate of about $180,000.

    —The building size is indicated in square feet per capita.

    —Payments per capita and per $1000 of market value are provided because these are the most commonly used measures for evaluating taxes.

Figure 7–21 Capital Cost Projection Slider Bar

Staffing and Personnel Issues

If the collection is the heart of a library, and circulation is its lifeblood, then the staff is its very soul. Just as with a physical body, when the soul leaves the body, the heart stops beating and circulation ceases. A plan made without a consideration of staffing issues is no plan at all. It is that simple. This section will motivate library planners to set goals and objectives that will get staff excited about the library's mission and service profile. Planners will want to consider fundamental issues such as ergonomic work stations, union rules (where applicable), and relations between the board and staff.

THE BALANCING ACT

Planners will want to consider the implications of the commonly used concept of "resources." The library's books, magazines, and databases are resources, of course. But we often speak of library staff as "human resources." Effective planning for staffing is a balancing act. Treating staff as resources has a tendency to make them feel like commodities, causing them to rebel. On the other hand, staff members *are* human resources and should be held accountable for inefficiency. In most libraries, 60 percent or more of the cost goes to salaries and benefits, so any long-range plan must address personnel issues. Remember that the most elegant and visionary plan will fail if the staff lacks the resources or motivation to make it work.

A look at the "Generally Accepted Accounting Principles" (GAAP) further illustrates the contradictions and the need for balance. Examine your municipal or library audit. The audit considers the books that library staff buys and the desks they sit at as assets. The staff, on the other hand, are carried on the cost or liability side of the ledger.

In many cases, the parent municipality will have developed personnel policies, procedures, salary scales, and fringe benefits for the library. Even when that is the case, there are likely to be areas of the library's policy manual that should be devoted to policies unique to library personnel. There is a distinction between creating a personnel policy manual and planning for personnel issues. The personnel policy manual outlines conditions of work, fringe benefits, and the rights and responsibilities of employer and employee. Planning, on the other hand, outlines how the staff will connect library users with library materials and services.

PERSONNEL COMPARISONS

The checklist on staffing in Chapter 9 will help identify issues to cover in planning. Be sure to check with legal counsel for issues relating to your state's labor laws and union requirements, if any. Examine the comparative data from Chapter 4 and the percentile comparisons in Appendix 2, as well. If some or all of the staffing measures or the output measures for the library differ substantially from the charts, further investigation will be in order.

For instance, a library with 95th percentile scores for total staff but a low (5th percentile) score for master degreed professionals would be highly atypical. A library with high percentile scores for interlibrary loan, visits, and reference but low scores for children's programs and general circulation may have decided to focus on a research library role.

Careful examination of the percentile comparisons may bring up a host of questions and planning issues. Planners will want to ask for and receive convincing answers for atypical results on staffing and output measures. They will want to assure that the profile that emerges is congruent with the roles and visions that the library planners have chosen. However, the percentile comparisons include only a few basic measures of staff utilization and productivity. Planners frequently have other questions and concerns along these lines. How long should it take to catalog and process an item? How many staff should be scheduled for peak hours and regular times? The Public Library Association has published an excellent manual that can help planners deal with such questions—Nelson, Altman, and Mayo's *Managing for Results* (see the Governance and Administration section in the bibliography). Chapter 2 of their book provides good information on managing staff resources. There are many useful survey and data collection forms in the book as well.

Reread the "Data Relevancy Test" (Figure 4–1) before asking staff to start (or continue) to fill out the forms recommended in *Managing for Results*, or indeed any others now in use. Know why you need the numbers and what you will do with them. Here is a pretty safe bet: in any of the 9,000 public libraries in the country you will find at least five examples of staff who are keeping track of something that is never used for any decision making purpose whatever. In addition, there will be at least as many examples of things that are not tracked that could be used in decision making.

Assuring that the right things are measured and that no measurement efforts are going to waste is a critical part of effective library planning.

TRAINING ISSUES

Pay close attention to the critical issue of staff training. In your long-range plan, consider how to obtain and finance the training needed to maintain a highly skilled staff. Too often city councils and even library board members view staff training as an easily eliminated expense. In the short term that may be true, but in the long term that approach leads to both reduced customer service quality and reduced staff morale. Effective planners will balance not only the books and the bytes but also the needs of the staff and library users.

Effective planners will also want to assure themselves that the library will make substantial efforts to identify all the types of training it needs. Some types of continuing education may be traditional: reference, children's storytelling, or cataloging workshops. Other types of training may become part of the planning because of previously identified goals: emergency training for tornado alerts or for heart defibrillators. Plans for encouraging diversity and providing service to users with special needs will carry with them an extensive curriculum. If surveys or library user focus groups have indicated that staff is either poorly trained in an area or insufficiently friendly and helpful, recommend that the plan include training in customer relations. Administration and staff should pay attention to ergonomic issues. Injuries and problems from the repetitive motion involved in the use of keyboards, mice, and related equipment can be avoided or reduced by attention to the equipment used and the work habits of the staff.

Whatever the current plans for continuing education look like, library planners should make extra efforts to assure that the staff has had a chance to voice its suggestions.

218

Other Service Issues

Planners need to address a myriad of library issues from home-land security and disaster preparedness to services to those with special needs to outreach by bookmobiles, branches, and other methods. This section deals with these issues along with planning and objectives relating to reference, youth services, public relations, and more.

SPECIAL NEEDS

Make sure your facilities are user friendly to the full array of potential users. The passage of the Americans with Disabilities Act (ADA) provided a major impetus to libraries and other agencies to improve the services provided to users with special needs; however, many actual and potential library users may not be able to access library resources and services without special considerations, including individuals in wheelchairs, those with visual or hearing impairments, as well as those with language differences, cultural or ethnic differences, or any other differences that make mainstream library services an issue. Plan to provide for the needs of these constituents as effectively and efficiently as possible.

The ADA requires facilities to be accessible to individuals in a wheelchair or those with other mobility problems. These goals and objectives relating to the physical facilities should also be included in any library planning. When considering building or remodeling programs, also consider ramps, elevators, Braille signs, and the width of aisles. Cirrillo and Danford have provided an excellent resource in *Library Buildings and the ADA*, published by the ALA. Library planners will want to review this title whether they are planning for a new building or looking anew at the existing facility.

Carefully consider accessibility needs for your library's computer workstations as well as the library's Web site. All too often careless design of the Web site or the online catalog make the library inaccessible to individuals using screen readers and other devices for the visually impaired. A review of both the catalog and the Web site using an accessability auditor like Bobby (http://bobby.cast.org/) will probably be in order.

219

Assistive devices for telephone access for the hearing impaired as well as hearing and visual augmentation devices are readily available. Should some of the library's workstations be provided with larger monitors, screen readers, and other assistive technology? Should some staff be trained in sign language or translation abilities for commonly used languages other than English? Plans should address these significant accessibility issues and indicate relative costs and target dates for implementation of needed programs, building redesign, and staff training.

REFERENCE

There are few areas of library that have been changed as radically by the emergence of the Internet and the Web as reference services. Many of the types of questions that were referred to as "ready reference" and relied on reference librarians with technical skills in using available print resources have been eclipsed by search engines that the public uses from home or by full-text databases that staff or the public can use at the library or at home. The remaining questions are tougher to answer and far more time consuming.

Look closely at virtual reference and examine the resources that need to be devoted to continued training for staff in full-text database skills, development of links for Web resources, and related issues.

CHILDREN'S SERVICES

Children make up a very substantial portion of the users of most public libraries. Library plans should provide guidance for these services, from summer reading programs to storytimes and specific materials collections for children. Professional recommendations such as those found in the ALA Planning Process are moving away from defining library roles, goals, and objectives to children or other age-specific groups, but library planners will need to determine whether or not to follow such advice.

In my opinion, libraries should continue to plan for their future by focusing intensively on children's materials and services. The times demand new responses. An interactive whiteboard with large motions, sounds, and color may be a good adjunct to the traditional storytime with a picture book. Considered the many other new technologies, from Internet for kids to electronic books to interactive leap books. The planners will need to ask strategic questions on the focus of children's activities, including "have we balanced the books and bytes?" Despite all those bells and whistles of new technologies, books still matter—just ask the Harry Potter readers.

BRANCH SERVICE

Dealing extensively with branches, bookmobiles, and other types of library outlets is beyond the scope of this book and my expertise. Only brief observations can be made.

The number of branch libraries in urban and suburban libraries exploded between the end of World War II and the beginning of the Reagan administration. The number appears to have leveled off since then and has even been declining in recent years. There have been many debates about the right number, location, and population served for public library branches, but objective information and professional guidance are sorely lacking.

Where do branch libraries belong? Approach this subject with great care in your planning process. In a lot of communities the cynical answer is that there should be at least one per aldermanic district; others will plan for a branch for every one, two, three, five, or ten mile radius in the community.

Many library directors will freely admit, off the record, of course, that they are "over-branched" but would never say so in public for fear of the political repercussions. Even in the type of budget crisis that enveloped most libraries in most states in 2003, few library boards were willing to consider closing branches that had outlived their usefulness or had never lived up to their anticipated potential. Instead of pruning a few so that the rest may thrive, the tendency is usually to starve all branches equally in a budget crisis. The unfortunate result is that all the branches end up dilapidated, with insufficient staff, outdated collections, and declining use rates. Communities with the need for a new or expanded headquarters building often find themselves under

221

great pressure to expand, or at least maintain, all existing branches, even the unproductive ones.

Library planners will want to look to other sources for help on these issues. Carefully chosen outside consultants may help a community find the right size and number of branches for the future. Christine Koontz's *Library Facilities Siting and Location Handbook* will also be of value.

Disaster Preparations

Effective library planners will consider what to do if a disaster strikes the library or its users. Police, fire, and emergency personnel can and should be enlisted to train staff in library emergency procedures. What should be done if there is a bank robber known to be in the vicinity of the library? How should the staff handle an apparent heart attack, drug overdose, or domestic violence incident? How can or should the public be confined to the building when a tornado is known to be heading towards town? These and similar questions should be considered by planners.

Plan for a business continuity or recovery plan including a method to get the library back into operation as quickly as possible following a major disaster. Critical phone numbers, records, and library documents should be stored and accessible off-premises in anticipation of a disaster hitting the entire library operation. The need for such plans has taken on new urgency since 9/11. Many municipalities have taken on the responsibility for business continuity planning, and library planners should tie library planning to these wider plans.

Conclusion

This chapter has provided:

- a recommended grouping of goals, objectives, and tasks by
  - electronic services,
  - collection development,
  - technology,

- access and facilities,

- staffing and personnel, and

- other service issues.

• a discussion of each of the activity areas with suggestions for how to plan effectively in each. The charts and spreadsheets indicated are available on the accompanying CD-ROM.

Chapter 8

Planning for New Organizational Options

Chapter Contents

Overview
Are Wider Library Units Wiser?
  Wider and Wiser
  Special Districts
  Legal basis for Wider Units
  Planning for Wider Units
  Why Go Wider?
Would a District Help?
Model District Law Proposal
Joint or Multi-jurisdictional Library Planning
  Joint Library Planning Checklist
Conclusion

List of Figures

Figure 8–1 Types of Library Jurisdictions
Figure 8–2 District Compared to Multi-jurisdictional Library
Figure 8–3 Joint Library Planning Checklist
Figure 8–4 Steps in Establishing a Joint Public Library
Figure 8–5 Outline of a Sample Plan for a Joint or District
       Library

Overview

Use this chapter if you are giving consideration to a new form of governance for your library. Most of the time, planners will recognize their current form of governance as the best possible for their circumstances. Still it is possible that a new form of governance and taxation may be preferable, and strategic plans should consider these new forms. This chapter asks planners to consider multi-jurisdictional, joint library, and library district organizational structures.

Are Wider Library Units Wiser?

This section was originally published in the June/July 2002 issue of *American Libraries*. It examines many of the issues involved in determining the form of library organization that best suits your library's circumstances.

WIDER AND WISER

What form of organization delivers the best library service? For many years library leaders have told us that wider units of service will produce better results. After an examination of some of the issues using national data, my findings suggest that, in most cases, wider units of library service are, indeed, wiser. Library planners will want to consider the issues carefully and consult the accompanying planning checklist and outline of a model district library law as they choose the road their library is to travel.

Special district libraries are the fastest-growing type of library organization even though only nineteen states have laws that permit them. In other states, multi-jurisdictional libraries can be established by various means, including joint-powers agreements between municipalities or counties.

Congressman Tip O'Neill was famous for asserting that "all politics is local." The same can be said about libraries. In the United States, libraries developed in a local and decentralized pattern rather than in the more centralized model of European libraries. In this country educational functions, including libraries, are generally state and local prerogatives. Andrew

Carnegie's early-twentieth-century endowments of 1,679 libraries in 1,412 communities led to a sudden proliferation of libraries in many communities. At that critical juncture in the nation's growth, the Carnegie grants encouraged local rather than district, regional, or state library development. The sheer number of small libraries, mostly municipal, is still an important factor in state and regional planning activities. If wider units had become the norm, these activities might have taken a different direction.

Although the most common form of library organization in the United States is a municipal library, such facilities serve only about one-third of the population; county libraries, district libraries, or other types of libraries serve the other two-thirds. These other forms (with the exception of the nonprofit or agency form) can be considered "wider units of service."

Federal data allows for a comparison of libraries by a variety of organizational structures. The accompanying table (Figure 8–1) outlines the situation in each state. The FSCS, an endeavor of the U.S. Department of Education and state library agencies, has been collecting and compiling data on the nation's libraries since 1988. The data used here comes from the annual reports filed with state library agencies by some 9,000 libraries as reported to FSCS during 2001, the latest year available at the time of writing.

All but twelve states have county, city-county, or parish libraries. The lower per capita rate found for these types of libraries may be more apparent than real. The per capita revenue in such organizations is spread across residents, usually in rural areas, that are completely unserved, or taxed at a lower rate, in other areas. This distorts per-capita funding measures for county libraries when compared to municipal libraries.

In some states, notably Illinois and New York, library district boundaries may be drawn along lines that do not correspond to existing municipal boundaries. In other states, the multi-jurisdictional libraries are formed along county or municipal lines. Many district libraries have taxing authority and elected boards. In some states, districts can expand territory by a process similar to municipal annexation, usually with voter approval.

Many multi-jurisdictional libraries are multicounty organizations; in other cases such arrangements encompass one or more municipalities. Multi-jurisdictional libraries, unlike district libraries, do not usually have either elected boards or taxing authority. Ohio has a large number of multi-jurisdictional libraries.

Many multi-jurisdictional libraries, lacking any taxing authority, suffer from the "Where does the buck stop?" syndrome. In these cases the library board must go to two or more independent municipalities to ask for operating and capital funds. The low bidder most often wins the budget battle, but the library loses. In Wisconsin, where no library-district legislation exists, joint libraries operate on 50 percent less funding per capita than their municipal counterparts. Some would argue that the "Where does the buck stop?" syndrome is to blame.

SPECIAL DISTRICTS

At nearly 300, Illinois has the largest number of special district libraries ; but as a percent of libraries in the state, Kentucky bests the Illinois tally at 90 percent to Illinois' 48 percent. Another state with significant numbers of special districts is Delaware with 53 percent. Colorado, Nevada, Michigan, Washington, Idaho, and Arizona all have more than 25 percent district libraries. Ten other states have at least one district library.

Special district libraries on average spend over 25 percent more per resident than municipal libraries do. One might thereby conclude that that form of governance results in better support. It is possible, however, that the majority of the extra spending is for services for which municipal libraries are not charged; for example, parent municipalities often do not charge municipal libraries indirect costs for maintenance, accounting, payroll services, and so forth. Such indirect costs must usually be accounted for in wider-unit operations. A 1999 study by Keith Lance of the Colorado Library Research Service (available online at www.lrs.org/documents/fastfacts/156plfund.pdf) does an excellent job of demonstrating this correlation and noting the variability of the spending data. Additional research on this point is sorely needed.

There is less variation between materials spending than there is for total spending when comparing special district and municipal libraries. In the same manner, the variation in total spending observed when comparing municipal and multi-jurisdictional operations is greatly lessened when we compare only materials spending.

School district libraries spend almost twice as much per capita as the average municipal library. Public libraries in school-district configurations have a higher rate of materials expenditures. In school-district libraries, the materials spending and library-visitor rates are not as much higher as the materials spending rates would appear to suggest.

Ohio, with 11.2 million residents, has 250 library units (but 350 branch libraries); while Iowa, with 3 million residents, has 530 library units (and 26 branches). Both states average more spending per capita than the national average; but while Iowa residents borrow 50 percent more items than the national average, Ohio residents borrow 100 percent more. Do wider units affect the outcome? It appears so, but more study is needed. Both New York and Illinois have large numbers of both district and municipal libraries. Researchers should investigate the comparative outcomes in each state.

Legal basis for Wider Units

Many states allow for joint-powers-agreement libraries even when no district legislation has been enacted. A joint public library is usually administered by a library board consisting of a specified number of members representative of the populations of the participating municipalities. The joint library board usually has the same powers as those set forth in state statutes for a municipal library board. Usually the head of the municipal governing body of each participating municipality appoints board members.

A joint public library might be created by any two or more municipalities or by a county and one or more municipalities by appropriate agreement of their governing bodies.

Planning for Wider Units

An extensive planning checklist is available in Figure 8–3. It should help communities determine whether such a combination will be the best way to provide effective public library service and help guide library planners in making good decisions. Library planners are advised to seek advice from state library agencies and regional library staff before embarking on such plans.

Why Go Wider?

While far more research is needed to provide definitive answers, I have some suggestions on why wider units are wiser.

Economies of scale come into play. With very small units, a disproportionate amount of time is spent on the administrative, budgeting, technical service, acquisitions, and political end of things. Seven libraries, each serving a thousand customers, need seven monthly board meetings, seven annual budgets, seven annual audits, and so forth. One wider unit serving 7,000 needs just one monthly board meeting, one budget, one acquisitions department, and so on. The same number of total staff can be focused on customer service rather than going toward administrative overhead. If the organization gets too large, secondary layers of management and bureaucracy can develop, but that is not inevitable. Good managers and alert boards avoid this pitfall.

In some cases—and this is where the research need is so critical—it may be more the form of organization than size that matters most. Consider the districts in New York State. Many New York districts serve a number of jurisdictions; they are classified as wider units. But beyond simply serving wider units, these districts go to the voters directly for their budgets, and they do so annually. Anecdotes abound about the extraordinarily high level of customer service that happens in the month before the annual budget referendum in one New York library.

In other states, districts with taxing authority must seek a referendum only periodically to expand the authorized mill rate. In still other states, elected boards are given taxing authority.

Impact fees allow communities to assess up-front costs on new homes as they are built in a community. They are intended to allow communities to levy a fee to offset the impact that a new household has on the ability of a library to sustain its service level. Such impact fees are far more workable in larger units of service. See Chapter 8 and Appendix 3.

The University of Wisconsin, Madison's Doug Zweizig, among others, has made the case that the formation of special districts for libraries runs a major public-policy risk. Popular items like parks and libraries in "a la carte" districts can soak up public funds. That leaves less for important but nonattractive government functions like accounting or road building. The converse of this argument is that too often local government officials use the very popularity of library services to the library's own detriment. City mayors have used this strategy in local budget battles: Threatening to close a branch library causes city council members to rally to the defense of their branches and voila—the budget is restored. Meanwhile other less-popular city services are protected from scrutiny.

When the ship is sailing smoothly, perhaps good manners are in order and the "nod and wink" strategy may apply. But when a budget-cutting iceberg like the present economic downturn threatens, it is our professional duty to fight for space on the lifeboats. If a district can be that lifeboat, then it may be time for some to get aboard. But only nineteen states have provided for library-district legislation. ALA should provide model legislation for the formation of library districts.

Are wider units of library service wiser units? The data seem to point to a guarded answer of yes, but the final word must await a great deal more research on the issue. As Frost noted in "The Road Not Taken," "Two roads diverged in a wood, and I—/I took the one less traveled by,/And that has made all the difference."

We cannot compare how well a library may have fared had its planners chosen a different road in the past. We can only compare the results for the roads taken by other libraries in different areas of the country, hoping that the comparisons will help library planners choose wisely in the future.

Figure 8–1 Types of Library Jurisdictions

8,614 libraries with available data

Type of library organization	States with this type	Number of states with this library type	Percent of all U.S. libraries	Percent of U.S. pop. served	Per capita average operating expend.
Municipal	ALL BUT: GA, HI, MD, PA, WY	46	54.6%	34.2%	$23.69
County/parish	ALL BUT: CT, DC, HI, ID, IL, MA, ME, NH, PA, RI, VT, WA	39	11.4%	33.9%	$19.10
Non-profit/agency	AK, CO, CT, ID, MA, ME, MN, MO, NC, NH, NJ. NM, NY, OH, OR, RI, TX, VT	18	9.8%	3.1%	$27.82
Special district	AL, AZ, CA, CO, DE, FL, ID, IL, KS, KY, LA, MI, MT, NV, NY, OR, TX, VT, WA	19	8.6%	8.5%	$29.65
Multi-jurisdictional	AK, AL, AR, CA, CO, FL, GA, IN, KS, KY, LA, MN, MO, MS, MT, NC, ND, NH, NJ, NM, OK, SD, TX, VA, VT, WI, WV	29	5.6%	9.9%	$23.52
School district	ID, MI, NY, OH, OR, WI, WV	7	3.6%	2.7%	$42.20
City/county	FL, LA, MN, MO, MS, ND, TX, UT, WI	9	0.6%	2.0%	$14.70
Miscellaneous	AR, CO, HI, IA, IL, IN, KS, MN, MO, NE, NM, NY, PA, TN, TX, VA	15	0.4%	1.3%	$18.45
Indian or tribal	AK, AZ, NM, NY, WI	5	0.3%	0.1%	$39.83
Unclassified	PA	1	5.3%	4.4%	$13.17
Totals		--	100.0%	100.0%	$24.16

Brief Observations on U.S. Library Types

In the over-500,000 population category, only fifteen of seventy-two libraries are municipal; the rest are county or multi-jurisdictional. Municipal libraries become the predominant type only for libraries serving under-100,000 populations.

School district libraries are found in only seven states, but where they occur, they have the highest rate of spending per capita. County or parish libraries appear to have lower levels of per capita spending than municipal libraries; but the fact that the

funding is spread over more population than their municipal counterparts probably lessens the apparent gap.

Special district libraries spend more per capita overall than
municipal libraries, but the variations are diminished when we
observe materials spending or the outputs of such agencies.

The only type of library in Maryland, except for the Enoch
Pratt in Baltimore, is the county library. In the FSCS data set, all
the Pennsylvania libraries are listed as "other types of libraries."

Would a District Help?

The purpose of this section is to help communities determine
whether a district library will be the best way to provide effective
public library service. The information found here should help
library planners in making the right decisions for their library.
Please note that a district library is not the same as a joint
library. For information on districts, see the next chapter.

There is a need for model district library legislation, as I
have noted several times.[1] I reviewed legislation in California, Illinois, Idaho, Michigan, New York, and Texas. I looked at district
library laws in Colorado and Arizona, though less carefully. While
the draft of the legislation here is not a "model," it did draw from
the examples of many other pieces of state legislation.

Figure 8–2 District Compared to Multi-jurisdictional Library

Area of concern	District	Multi-jurisdictional
Ownership of building	District owns building	A variety of options, most often one or the other of the constituent communities owns building (the library board cannot usually own property in most states.)
Board appointment	Various methods, ideally the public at large elects the board	Varies by contract, state law, and local custom
Decision on operating budget	The library district board	The constituent municipalities must agree, either consecutively or concurrently, or in some manner outlined in contract. There is usually a contractual method for resolving impasses, but it is often dissolution of the partnership.
Decision on capital budget	The library district board, sometimes in consultation with local community	Same as above, except that the contract often does not specify how to resolve capital budget impasses.
Basis of organization	State law and bylaws passed by the district board	State law and contracts negotiated between the constituent municipalities

Model District Law Proposal

As noted only nineteen states have district legislation currently on the books. My ideal district library legislation would have the following characteristics.

1. The board should consist of nine elected board members with taxing authority for library services in the district.

2. The district may be formed only along current municipal lines but may be formed by either petition of the electorate or two-thirds vote of the governing bodies of the municipalities concerned. (Note that some states allow districts to deviate from existing municipal boundaries. I judges that to be problematic for a variety of reasons.)

3. A library forming the district must be at least five years old.

4. The boundaries of the municipalities included must be contiguous.

5. The district must contain at least 4,000 residents.

6. The law should allow for anticipation tax loans (as in Idaho) to use anticipated district taxes to cover known and planned start up costs for initiating a district (such as a transition to independent auditing and personnel administration, and so on).

7. The law should provide that a county board may only create a countywide library district with the consent of *each* municipality acting individually rather than by a plurality in a countywide referendum (This provision will vary by state circumstance since some county governments have a different relation to local units than do others. Where strong local municipal home rule is the norm, this provision will probably apply or the legislation won't pass).

8. There is a problem that may be created if a city or village annexes territory in a township that is in a library district, especially if the territory annexed contains a main or branch library of the district. This has led to problems in Illinois as cities annexed areas containing branches of district libraries. There does not appear to be any method to prevent this outcome.

9. The districts, unlike many municipal libraries, should have the power to sue and be sued. Municipal libraries are creatures of their municipality. Not so for districts.

10. The legislation should provide an orderly method for the merger of two or more districts into a single district. Such a merger should only be by action of the respective district boards rather than by municipality-by-municipality referendum.

11. The planning committee should be given the option of preparing a plan for the ballot that allows for formation of district library board members that are elected either "at large" or by "aldermanic-like wards."

12. Each district should be allowed to set by referendum its own maximum mill rate rather than fixing the maximum in state law. The planning committee should be given the option of preparing a plan for the ballot that allows for the use of a fixed

235

percent sales tax to supplement or supplant the mill rate (Both sales and property tax rates and millage taxes are conditional on state law, of course)

13. A petition referendum (as opposed to municipal board action only) should be permitted both for the formation of a district and for the increase of the maximum millage rate allowed.

14. The district must go back to referendum to increase the maximum mill rate authority of the district board.

15. The district board should be required to have an annual public hearing on the budget proposed by the district board.

District Planning Issues

While there is a substantial difference between a district and a joint library, many of the planning elements are the same. The planning checklist in the next chapter will be *mostly* relevant to district planning issues as well. The contract considerations section of the joint library chapter will not be relevant to a district library because the district is developed by legal action rather than a contract between two or more parties. Some of the steps in forming a joint library will be similar to those for a joint library, depending on the state legislation that must be followed, so check through that section as well. The format that a plan for a district must take is likely to be heavily dependent on state law, of course, but the sample outline of a plan in the next chapter should be useful as a guide.

Joint or Multi-jurisdictional Library Planning

Could a multi-jurisdiction library be the best way to provide effective public library service for your community? Consult the information and checklists found here to guide your decision making. Please note that a joint library is not the same as a district library. For information on districts, see the previous section. The statements made here will not be true for every state. Check with your library's attorney or with consultants at the regional or state level to confirm the legality of any issue discussed here.

The formation of a library district or a multi-jurisdictional library is not possible in all states. See Figure 8–2, which indicates the types of library organizations in the U.S. Even where it is possible to form a district or joint library, it is not a transformation to be considered lightly. Seek advice from state library agencies and regional library staff before embarking on such plans. The names for such forms of libraries vary quite widely throughout the country—often they are called "districts" or "joint libraries." Other names are used as well. Here the term "joint library" will be used.

There are significant obstacles to establishing joint libraries. This section will deals with the legality and desirability of forming joint public libraries and help provide for effective implementation of joint library agreements.

Seek technical assistance from your public library system and contact your state library agency in order to clarify the legal, governance, and funding consequences of a combined program.

Joint Library—Legal Basis

Some states permit any two or more municipalities or a county and one or more municipalities located in whole or in part in the county to form a joint public library. Such library agreements must usually contain provisions necessary to establish a library board and perform the duties of such a board under state law for other types of structures.

A joint public library is usually administered by a library board consisting of a state specified number of members representative of the populations of the participating municipalities. The joint library board usually has the same powers as set forth in state statutes for a municipal library board. Usually the head of the municipal governing body of each participating municipality appoints board members.

Municipalities may own and operate physical facilities jointly or individually. The respective share of operating costs is usually determined at the time the joint library agreement is written. Costs may be apportioned based on populations served or some other factor such as level of use. Each municipality participating in a joint library agreement levies a tax to support its share of costs. Most municipal services are based on the proportionate share of equalized property values rather than on use rates or population formulas. This is probably the most advisable basis for distribution of costs.

One municipal party to the joint library agreement should agree to provide municipal administrative services such as serving as the depository of tax funds, personnel administration, and bill paying. It is my opinion that public funds should only be handled by municipal agencies, not a library board or a separate private agency. Some state laws may provide otherwise.

JOINT LIBRARY PLANNING CHECKLIST

Figure 8–3. Joint Library Planning Checklist

Yes	No	Planning
		There has been an assessment of the impact the proposed merger will have on the funding and usage patterns of neighboring libraries.
		All parties have reviewed any existing planning documents and there is agreement on established priorities.
		A preliminary study of the feasibility and suitability of the joint library program for the community has been conducted, including the review of alternatives to establishing a combined library.
		Concerned community groups have examined the proposed joint library and are aware of the range of services and costs involved.
		The municipal governing boards that will fund the program have defined their responsibilities in a formal agreement drawn up during the planning phase.
		Counsels for the participating municipalities, the public library system, and the state library agency have reviewed the agreement noted above.
		If a town is merging with an existing library, has the county board been consulted?
Yes	No	Legal Issues
		The library will be established in accordance with relevant state laws.
		A legally appointed and constituted public library board will govern the operation of the public library program.
		The method and number of appointments to the board by each municipality has been determined and there is an agreed upon method in the contract for changing the number of appointments if the relative funding levels of the parties changes enough to warrant such a change.

		The public library board will have exclusive control of the expenditure of all moneys collected, donated, or appropriated for the public library fund. One of the constituent municipalities will have custody (in many states library boards, even joint ones cannot handle public funds directly but must do so through a municipality).
		The public library board will employ a library director who is qualified and maintains the appropriate level of certification under the provisions stated in state law (if any).
		Is there a clear definition of how legal counsel will be provided? There should be provision for allocating indirect costs if legal advice is received through one of the participating municipalities.
Yes	**No**	**Contractual**
		General procedures for operating the combined library have been discussed, and all parties agree on principal elements such as hours of operation, responsibility for expenses, access to resources and activities, user rights and responsibilities, and authority for daily decision making.
		The public library will be a member of the regional public library system (if any) and actively participate in its programs of service, including reciprocal borrower's privileges and interlibrary loans.
		The public library board will follow statutory requirements regarding fiscal year, audits, budgeting process, and annual reports to the municipal governing authority and the state library agency.
		The proposed contract clearly spells out a defined process, timetable and notice requirements for any dissolution.
Yes	**No**	**Building**
		The building that will house the proposed combined public library is in compliance with the provisions of Title II of the Americans with Disabilities Act (ADA).
		The building provides adequate space to implement the full range of library services consistent with the library's comprehensive long-range plan, and appropriate State Public Library Standards (if any).
		The contract clearly identifies who owns the building, land, equipment and other tangible assets. Clear provision is made in the contract for dispersal of all tangible assets in the case of dissolution of the agreement.
Yes	**No**	**Financial**
		Improving service, rather than saving money, is the overriding concern in planning a combined library.
		The agreement will provide for a library in compliance with necessary state statutes for funding.
		The contract clearly specifies the respective liabilities for legal claims and judgments made against the library, especially as regards the amounts beyond any insurance coverage obtained by the library.

		There is a clearly established contractual method for determining the total amount of annual operating and capital budgets, including provisions for what happens if one municipality agrees to a library board proposal and the other party or parties do not. The contract clearly identifies needed deadlines, timetables, and procedures.
Yes	**No**	**Personnel**
		The contract defines for which employment purposes the staff are to be considered employees of the library or one or the other of the constituent municipalities. Human resource professionals and legal counsel should be consulted so that employee as well as employer rights and privileges are properly considered.[2]
		Does the contract define the share of state and federal retirement costs attributable to each participating municipality?
		Does the contract define the shares of unfunded pension liability (if any) attributable to each participating municipality?
		Is there a clear delineation regarding the personnel policy for the library staff? This should include grievance policies, severance conditions, and necessary requirements regarding state and federal laws for equal employment, ADA requirements, and so forth.

Contract Considerations

Parties involved in a combined library have long-term interests that must be protected by a carefully written contract supported by written policies that cover operational matters. The library board adopts and maintains policies, but all parties should review the initial policies. A committee made up of members of the public library board, and the municipal governing bodies should outline the content of the basic contract and an attorney should put it into legal form. This agreement is essential to the long-term success of a joint library, so it is important to take the necessary time to do it right. Drafts should be sent to the library system administrator and the Division for Libraries Technology and Community Learning for comment.

There can be a temptation to place more in the basic contract than is necessary. The contract should deal with the fundamentals of governance, staffing, funding, ownership, and termination of the agreement. Other matters can be handled through policies. The answers to two questions will help to determine whether a point should be a part of the contract or of a policy manual:

- Is this of overriding importance?

- Is this likely to be changed during the time frame of the agreement?

An answer of yes to the first and no to the second suggests the matter is a good candidate to be placed in the contract.

The successful operation of a joint library depends on doing a number of things right. Below are items that must be dealt with in order to set up and manage the combined library properly.

Contract Categories

- *Governance.* The contract should list the parties entering into the agreement and cite the statutory authority for entering into an agreement of this sort. Ordinarily the parties to the agreement should be the library board and the municipal governing bodies involved. It is essential to understand that the city board or city council may not act on behalf of the library board unless authorized by the library board to do so. The agreement should also cite the statutes under which the parties will operate the library.

- *Staffing.* Appropriately certified public library personnel must be employed. The agreement should state the intent of all participant municipalities to fund the agreement. It should specify retirement and disability compensation issues. The intention to meet statutory staffing requirements should be stated in the agreement.

- *Funding.* It is important to determine and put into the contract the financial responsibilities of each party, including both capital and operational costs as well as ongoing maintenance and grounds upkeep for the present and future facilities. Distribution of costs based on respective shares of equalized value will ordinarily be preferable to shares based on population, use, or other considerations. This is so because equalized valuation is the basis on which nearly all other municipal services are based. In states with other sources of revenue such as sales or income taxes, the same principle of allocating

241

respective costs applies. A given community will often want to share costs on a use basis or population basis if that amounts to less than it would pay on a pure tax ratio basis. The battle to agree on these elements is often a foreshadowing of disagreements over funding to come in future years.

- *Budget setting.* When two or more municipalities must determine the annual budget for a joint library, there is always the danger of a deadlock. Even if the proportions paid by each municipality are set by contract, there still remains the question of total budget in a given year. The contract should clearly specify a method for resolving differences between municipalities on an annual budget. Some joint library contracts call for a budget summit as a joint meeting of the participating municipalities. Others specify that if agreement cannot be reached, the budget reverts to the prior year's level. Other agreements specify that a joint subcommittee be appointed to resolve the budget. Since it is important to meet the requirements of all communities that a budget be set in a timely manner, the contracts should specify deadline dates that assure completion of the budget within the calendars of all parties to the joint agreement.

- *Ownership of assets.* The agreement should clarify the ownership of assets brought into the shared library (such as equipment, collection, etc.) and how ownership will be determined in the event of termination of the combined library agreement.

- *Physical plant.* The agreement should state the requirements that must be met by the party providing the physical facility for the combined library. This can include the library's location in the building, public access to the library, maintenance, and more. There should be a clear statement regarding the cost sharing arrangements for the building maintenance. In some instances, one municipality owns the building and leases it back to the joint library, often for a nominal fee.

- *Termination of the agreement.* The agreement should state the conditions related to termination of the agreement. Some agreements state that dissolution requires just a few months notice by either party. Given the magnitude of the impact this could have on library users and/or remaining parties to a library agreement, a longer time frame should usually be included. Some contracts in the state call for eighteen months notice prior to the dissolution. Others specify an annual month in which notice must be given. Consider a rolling two or three year contract that can be continuously renewed.

Figure 8–4 Steps in Establishing a Joint Public Library

These steps will vary depending upon the legal structures in each state. Be sure to check that a district or joint library is permissible in your state.

1. Ask a library planning committee representative of all municipalities involved to formulate a plan or joint library agreement which addresses the following:

    - The names of the municipalities that will be members of the joint public library

    - The statutory authority under which the joint library will be established

    - The size of the joint library board and proportionate distribution of the members among the participating municipalities

    - The method by which a school district administrator, or representative shall be appointed (in states that require such appointment)

    - The initial terms of office which will be assigned to each board member

    - The designated municipality to be responsible for paying bills and custody of library funds

- The disposition of existing and future assets of the joint library in case of dissolution of the joint library

- The method by which annual budgets will be formulated and costs apportioned among the participating municipalities

2. If the proposed joint library territory lies in two or more counties that are not in the same system, designate the system in which the joint library will participate (in Wisconsin).

3. Submit the proposed plan to the governing bodies of each participating municipality for approval.

4. Submit the proposed plan to county board of supervisors for approval (if appropriate for your state).

5. Submit the proposed plan to the state library agency for an opinion regarding the desirability and feasibility of the plan.

6. Draw up legal joint library agreement incorporating provisions of plan.

7. Submit the final plan and joint library agreement to municipalities for action and for appointment of library board members.

Figure 8–5 Outline of a Sample Plan for a Joint or District Library

Name of proposed district	
Current budget of library	
Proposed first year budget of library [List participant amounts individually]	
Names of proposed participant municipalities	
Statutory authority for district	
Municipality designated as legal custodian of funds	
System of which joint library will be a member	
Grade level certification of director (if required by state law)	
Number of proposed trustees for joint library [List participant amounts individually]	

Executive Summary
Mission Statement

Committee Membership
List members of the planning committee that developed this document.

Brief History of Library Development
Provide a history of the library (or libraries) that is the basis of the proposed joint library.

Current Library Services
List current circulation, attendance, collection and other input and output data for the current library operation.

Current Funding of Library Services
Provide a three to five year summary of past funding for the library.

Proposed Revenue Collection Formula
Indicate the specific formula that will be used for allocating all elements of the joint library budget. Include data on how operating budget will be apportioned, but also indicate how present and future capital budgets, building maintenance budgets and employee fringe benefit costs will be apportioned.

Proposed Resolution for Budget Impasse
Provide a specific methodology that is proposed for resolving disagreements between the municipalities on operating and capital budgets.

Provide Impact Statement
Indicate the impact that the proposed merger is projected to have on funding and usage patterns in the county and the region. Include letters or reports from the system and the county on feasibility.

Relations with Other Libraries

Funding formulas (if any)

Often regional or county funding programs for nonresident borrowing or interlibrary loan will be disrupted by newly formed districts. The impacts should be outlined here.

Regional Library System Opinion on Feasibility (if any)
County Opinion on Feasibility (if appropriate)

Tax Base-All Municipalities

Provide a current summary of the tax base (Property Valuations) for the participants in the proposed joint library over the last several years, if appropriate. If the tax revenue source will be income or sales tax, as is the case in a few states, indicate the appropriate numbers for fiscal capacity of the proposed district.

Standards For Libraries

Provide a listing of how the current and projected joint library compare to the numerical requirements for state and county library standards-if there are no state standards, it is possible to use the percentile comparisons in this book as benchmarks.

State Standards (if any)
County or regional standards (if any)

Buildings

Describe the building in which the joint or district library will be housed. Include relevant data regarding square feet, collection capacity, parking, and so forth. Also indicate who will own the building and how physical assets will be distributed in the event of dissolution.

Contracts, Bylaws, etc.

Attach copies of proposed bylaws and contracts. Indicate whether they have been reviewed by the relevant municipalities, county board, and the library division.

Conclusion

This chapter has provided:

- a caution to library planners to use this chapter only if they are giving consideration to a new form of governance for their library. Most of the time, effective library planners will recognize that their current form of governance as the best possible for their circumstances;

- a consideration of multi-jurisdictional, joint library, and library district forms of organizational structures;

- guidance for those considering such major changes in operations.

Note

1. Hennen, Thomas J., Jr. 2002. "Are Wider Units Wiser?" *American Libraries* 33, no. 6 (June/July): 65–68.

Chapter 9
Using the Planning Checklist and Revising Policies

Chapter Contents

Overview
Planning Issues Checklist
  Governance
  Planning
  Output Measures
  Funding
  Access and Public Relations
  Staffing
  Continuing Education
  Technology and Electronic Access
  Special Needs
  Collection
  Reference Services
  Facilities
Revising Library Policies
  Role of the Board, Staff and the Governing Body in Policy
    Development
  Personnel Policy Issues
  Library Use Policies
  Challenged Materials
  Internet Use
  Privacy of Records
  Distinction Between Policies and Procedures
  Policy Manual Inventory
Conclusion

List of Figures

Figure 9–1 Governance Checklist
Figure 9–2 Planning Checklist
Figure 9–3 Output Measures Checklist
Figure 9–4 Funding Checklist
Figure 9–5 Access and Public Relations Checklist
Figure 9–6 Staffing Checklist
Figure 9–7 Continuing Education Checklists
Figure 9–8 Technology and Electronic Access Checklist
Figure 9–9 Special Needs Checklist
Figure 9–10 Collection Checklist
Figure 9–11 Reference Services Checklist
Figure 9–12 Facilities Checklist
Figure 9–13 Test for Good Policies
Figure 9–14 Steps in Policy Creation
Figure 9–15 Policy Manual Inventory

Overview

This chapter uses checklists that library planners can employ to evaluate actions that they should undertake to develop and maintain an adequate and effective service profile. The list has been compiled from standards checklists from a number of states including Kansas, North Carolina, Iowa, Rhode Island, and Wisconsin. The chapter also considers the need for making changes to the library's policies while making plans.

The long-range plan should address those areas in which the answer to the checklist question is no. A library lacking a collection development policy, for instance, should be planning to develop one. It will often be helpful to have the entire library board review the answers to the checklist. Have a discussion with staff and board on the ways in which any shortcomings of the library discovered through the checklists can be resolved.

The planning committee must remember that it cannot unilaterally alter library policies. Unless it is only an advisory body, policy adoption is the prerogative of the library board. If a library's policies do not support its mission and goals then it is time to change either the policies or change the mission and goals. As a result, a thorough review of library policies is a critical part of any long-range planning process.

This policymaking section:

- explains the role of the board, staff, and governing body in policymaking,

- urges planners to highlight the distinction between policies and procedures,

- provides an overview of critical issues for library use policies,

- highlights the importance of personnel policies,

- provides a test for good policies,

- outlines the steps in policy creation,

- distinguishes between policies and procedures, and

- provides a comprehensive inventory of the types of policies that libraries should have.

Planning Issues Checklist

GOVERNANCE

Figure 9–1 Governance Checklist

Issue	Yes	No	Comments
1. The library provides free access to tax supported service.			
2. The library board is legally constituted.			
3. Library is established in accordance with state laws.			
4. The library board has complete authority, within legal limits, over the library's budget and over all gifts, bequests, and donations.			
5. The library is in compliance with federal laws.			
6. The library board is provided with information about state library laws and with other state and federal laws that affect library operations, such as open meetings, minimum wage, unemployment compensation, criminal theft of library materials, and confidentiality of library records.			
7. The library has determined whether its board and financial staff should be bonded.			
8. The library has a written ethics, conflict of interest, and financial disclosure policy for all board members and key staff.			
9. The library board follows statutory requirements as to fiscal year, audits, and budgeting, and makes annual and other reports to its funding authority(ies), the regional library system, and to the state.			
10. The library board (or other authority) hires and evaluates the director.			
11. The board has written bylaws that are periodically revised.			
12. The library board adopts written policies for operations, collection development, and personnel, and reviews them at least every three years. All three policies are available for public inspection.			
13. The library policies are periodically reviewed for conformance with federal, state, and local laws and court decisions.			
14. The board meets regularly (usually monthly) and in accordance with open meeting laws.			

Issue	Yes	No	Comments
15. The library trustees are provided continuing education and training opportunities.			
16. The library is a member of the regional system (where applicable).			
17. The director is paid for at least the minimum numbers of hours/week specified by state law (if any).			
18. The director prepares written financial and statistical reports for each board meeting.			
19. There is an orientation for new library trustees.			
20. The library board is continuously informed of pending legislation.			
21. The library director is responsible for personnel administration (where applicable, this means that the director hires, fires, and evaluates staff while the board sets overall policy).			
22. The director informs the board of necessary legal issues that will influence policy changes.			
23. The library director develops operating procedures while the board sets policies.			

PLANNING

Figure 9–2 Planning Checklist

Issue	Yes	No	Comments
1. The library engages in periodic long-range planning that includes staff and community input.			
2. If the library belongs to a regional system, it participates in planning with that system.			
3. The plan shows goals to be achieved over a specified period (usually 3 to 5 years) and specific, annual actions to achieve the goals.			
4. The plan is reviewed and updated annually by the library board; an of the library's progress toward the plan's goals, objectives, and timetable is included in the review.			
5. The long range plan includes a mission statement that has been revised recently.			
6. The library engages in periodic community studies as part of the planning effort.			
7. The library has specific and measurable goals and objectives in a written format.			

OUTPUT MEASURES

Figure 9–3 Output Measures Checklist

Issue	Yes	No	Comments
1. The library keeps its borrowers' registrations up to date. Registration records must be updated at least every 3 years.			
2. The library annually calculates its output measures as defined in *Output Measures for Public Libraries* (van House et al., 1987).			
3. The library provides programs at no cost for persons of all ages and abilities.			
4. Planning for library programs is based on community analysis, demographic assessments, and expressed community needs.			

FUNDING

Figure 9–4 Funding Checklist

Issue	Yes	No	Comments
1. The library is supported by municipal funds or library levy (except in rare cases, grants, donations and endowments serve only to supplement library support).			
2. The community provides sufficient financial support to implement the library's long range plans.			
3. The administration prepares a written annual budget for library board adoption and governing body approval.			
4. The library board reviews and adopts an annual budget which has been developed by the library director with input from the library staff. The budget reflects board-approved priorities for the library. The library board and the library director present the budget to their funding authority(ies).			
5. The library director and the board present the annual operating and capital budgets to the governing authority.			
6. The library follows fiscal procedures that are consistent with state and federal laws as well as applicable auditing requirements.			

7. The library staff provides the board and governing body with information on available grant and other funding sources.		
8. If required by state or local law, the library board approves bills for payment.		

ACCESS AND PUBLIC RELATIONS

Figure 9–5 Access and Public Relations Checklist

Issue	*Yes*	*No*	*Comments*
1. The library's budget and plan include periodic activities to enhance publicity and public relations.			
2. The library designates a staff member to coordinate public relations activities.			
3. The library plans for adequate print and graphics for directional signs within and outside the library.			
4. The library budget provides for printing materials for library materials and activities promotion.			
5. If available, the library uses nonprint media such as radio and TV to promote the library.			
6. The library cooperates in regional or state publicity programs (if available).			
7. Publicity and marketing activities include contact with schools, other education agencies, social service agencies, and so forth.			
8. The library develops a mailing list of key community leaders, interest groups, and agencies and regularly sends them promotional materials.			
9. If possible, the publicity and marketing efforts of the library is made available in alternate formats for those with disabilities.			

STAFFING

Figure 9–6 Staffing Checklist

Issue	Yes	No	Comments
a) The library has a qualified staff that meets applicable state or local standards.			
b) The library has adopted personnel policies outlining the conditions and requirements of employment of library staff; these policies are consistent with state and federal regulations, are reviewed at least every three years, and are made available to all staff members. Policies are consistent with especially the Fair Labor Standards Act and the Americans with Disabilities Act, and equal opportunity requirements.			
c) If a collective bargaining agreement exists, the manual is consistent with and addresses any issues not covered in the collective bargaining agreement.			
d) The library has a written personnel classification plan.			
e) The library board (or appropriate authority) determines salaries and benefits that are comparable to other positions in the community.			
f) The library has written position descriptions for each position in the library, and they are periodically reviewed.			
g) The library meets service targets for staffing as measured in full-time equivalents per capita (if such state requirements exist, otherwise the library uses available national comparisons).			
h) The staff receives periodic emergency training regarding evacuation, fires, first aid, problem patrons and related activities.			
i) Employee performance is evaluated annually.			

Continuing Education

Figure 9–7 Continuing Education Checklist

Issue	Yes	No	Comments
1. The library has a specific, written budget for continuing education that is consistent in funding level with other area libraries.			
2. The library provides continuing education for its board, director, and staff at all levels by spending a percentage of its total payroll costs on direct costs of staff development and training. Specify the percentage. Some states recommend between 1 and 2% of the operating budget.			
3. The library supports the continuing education of the library board.			
4. The library supports the continuing education of the library director.			
5. The library supports the continuing education of the library staff.			
6. The library has a planned orientation program for all new employees and board members.			

TECHNOLOGY AND ELECTRONIC ACCESS

Figure 9–8 Technology and Electronic Access Checklist

Issue	*Yes*	*No*	*Comments*
1. The library has a technology plan that specifies current and future technology needs and their potential costs. The plan is reviewed at least every three years.			
2. The library's catalog is available over the Internet with the use of a Web browser. It is available 24 hours a day, 7 days a week.			
3. The library has a dedicated connection to the Internet that is available to most if not all library workstations.			
4. The library provides a minimum of one public workstation per every 35 visits per day (or an alternate state, regionally, or locally defined standard).			
5. The staff are trained in assisting the public in the use of available electronic and nonprint resources.			
6. The library allocates funds for materials and electronic resources purchasing consistent with its long range plan.			
7. The library has staff or contract support for its technology.			
8. The library has a written policy regarding both staff and public acceptable use of electronic resources.			
9. The library participates in regional or state technology & resource sharing plans (if any).			
10. The library provides CD-ROM or online full text databases as outlined in a written plan.			
11. The library has a Web page.			
12. Links on the library Web page are maintained for accuracy and current viability by staff or contract.			
13. The library provides access to its bibliographic database on line for use by users at home or in their businesses.			
14. The library has equipment to provide access to alternate formats for the public such as CD players, VCRs, etc.			
15. The library has converted its bibliographic records into machine-readable form using the MARC standard.			
16. The library collects and submits statistics on the use of its databases and electronic resources to the appropriate regional and state authorities.			
17. The library budgets sufficient sums for repair, maintenance, and replacement of all equipment on a scheduled basis.			

SPECIAL NEEDS

Figure 9–9 Special Needs Checklist

Issue	Yes	No	Comments
1. The library identifies the needs of special population groups of all ages in its service area and develops goals and objectives for implementing services to special populations.			
2. The library tries to reach all users by using services to the homebound, institutionalized, imprisoned, and so forth.			
3. The library has staff trained to help users with special needs and disabilities and appropriate assistive devices (Assistive technology is any item or piece of equipment that is used to increase, maintain, or improve the functional capabilities of individuals with disabilities. It ranges from low tech items such as magnifying glasses to specialized high-tech items like screen readers.). The library pursues use of assistive technology commensurate with its size and resources.			
4. The library provides access to its collections and services for patrons unable to travel to the library (for example, homebound services, deposit collections, programs held outside the library, bookmobile service, service to hospitals, jails, or institutions).			
5. The collection development policy recognizes the needs for formats for those with disabilities or special needs, such as books on cassette, braille, and so forth.			
6. The library staff is familiar with procedures and policies for their regional library for the blind and physically handicapped and how to enroll users in the program as needed.			
7. The library provides access to literacy, English as a second language, and related materials.			
8. The library provides assistive technology to allow access to those with disabilities to its databases and catalog.			
9. The library Web page is accessible to the visually impaired.			

259

10. Aisles between book stacks are 36 in. wide and free of obstacles. The ends of aisles allow ample room to turn a wheelchair (Buildings that have not been renovated since 1990 may not meet all ADA regulations, but every effort should be made to provide reasonable accommodations for people with disabilities.).			
11. The library has designated a staff member in the library to serve as a specialist in the area of services for individuals with disabilities.			
12. The library offers transcription or sign language interpreters for library events with advance notice. It publicizes events to all groups in the community.			
13. The library has designated at least one computer as an accessible workstation and labels it as such. It provides: • A workstation that can easily be adjusted to different heights • A mouse that can be used by left- or right-handed people • A monitor at least 19 in. wide • Screen enlargement software. Screen reading software and a sound card or speech synthesizer • Adaptive keyboard (with large keys, a different alphabetic arrangement, etc.)			
14. The staff periodically receives diversity, disability, and language training.			

COLLECTION

Figure 9–10 Collection Checklist

Issue	Yes	No	Comments
1. The library has a written collection development policy that is reviewed by the board on a periodic basis.			
2. The library allocates funds for purchasing materials in all appropriate formats based on its collection development policy, the library's plan, current use, and the role(s) the library has chosen.			
3. The library participates in interlibrary loan, using the data for collection development and not allowing interlibrary loan to supplant its own collection development.			

4. The library participates in regional or state planning for coordinated collection development (where available).			
5. The library board adopts policies consistent with the principles set forth in the American Library Association Library Bill of Rights and all official ALA interpretations.			
6. The library includes bibliographic records in the required format for any available regional or state databases. The records are maintained and updated by competent staff.			
7. The library weeds (removes from its collection) outdated and unneeded items on a regular basis, according to established benchmarks and reports the activity to the board on a regular (usually annual) basis.			
8. The library meets state, regional, or locally established standards for print materials.			
9. The library meets any state, regional, or locally established standards for periodicals.			
10. The library meets any state, regional, or locally established standards for audio materials.			
11. library meets any state, regional, or locally established standards for video materials.			
12. The library meets any state, regional, or locally established standards for reference materials.			
13. If there are no state, regional, or locally established standards for materials listed above, the library has a plan to develop such standards and benchmarks locally.			
14. The library has an interlibrary loan fill rate. The library determines the number of ILL transactions successfully completed in proportion to the total number of transactions.			
15. The entire collection of the library is cataloged according to defined bibliographic standards.			

REFERENCE SERVICES

Figure 9–11 Reference Services Checklist

Issue	Yes	No	Comments
1. The library provides reference and readers' advisory services to persons of all ages and literacy levels.			
2. The library cooperates with other types of libraries and with other agencies in the local area to provide information services to all residents. Questions that cannot be answered locally are forwarded to the library's regional reference center, if applicable.			
3. The library determines the reference transactions per capita-the average number of reference questions asked by members of the community during the year. Reference transactions per capita are calculated by dividing the total number of reference questions by the jurisdiction population.			
4. Reference staff are provided during all open hours for library users of all ages and abilities.			
5. The library participates in any available regional or state reference referral and resource sharing.			
6. At least every three years, the library determines the reference fill rate-the number of reference transactions successfully completed in proportion to the total number of reference transactions.			
7. The library keeps and reports reference statistics as required by the regional or state authorities.			
8. The library provides training in the use of electronic and other reference sources to the public.			
9. The library prepares bibliographies and other resources for the use of the public in accessing its collections and services.			

FACILITIES

Figure 9–12 Facilities Checklist

Issue	Yes	No	Comments
1. At least every five years the library director, with input from the staff, completes and shares with the board a written space needs assessment document.			
2. Library hours are fixed, posted, and visible.			
3. A book return is provided for returning library materials when the library is closed.			
4. The library has sufficient incoming telephone lines to accommodate staff and user needs.			
5. All library services are available all hours that the library is open.			
6. An accessible library facility is available to all residents of the service area-within a 15 minute drive in urban areas or a 30 minute drive in rural areas (local state and regional conditions will vary).			
7. Directional signs on major streets indicate where the library is located.			
8. The outside of the building is well-lit and identified with appropriate signs of high visibility. The signs include service hours.			
9. Interior lighting is evenly distributed and glare is avoided.			
10. The library has proper temperature and humidity control throughout the year for the comfort of the public and staff and for protection of library materials.			
11. The library has public meeting space available for its programming and for use by other community groups.			
12. Open hours are based on surveys and assessment of actual and potential user needs.			
13. The library is open at least as many hours as required by state or regional standards (if any) or it is open as many hours as set forth in the library's long-range plan based on assessment of peer library operations.			

14. The library is listed in the phone book, with variations on its name as appropriate.			
15. The library provides a photocopier for patron use.			
16. The library has adequate space to provide the services outlined in its long-range plan.			
17. The library board assesses and prepares a written statement of the library's space needs at least once every five years.			
18. The library meets all applicable Americans with Disabilities Act requirements or, if not, has outlined its deficiencies and prepared an action plan for meeting them.			
19. The library provides directional signs for the visually impaired (see http://wwe.access-boar.gov/bfdg.htm).			
20. The accessible features (entrances, water fountains, etc.) display the International Symbol of Accessibility.			
21. Adequate public parking is essential for the success of a library facility. Available public parking represents at least one parking space for every 200 square feet of gross square footage of the facility. See local codes for variations on these requirements.			
22. The building is wired to support current and future technology expected for the library.			
23. There is adequate, well-lit, and safe parking for library users and the required number of handicapped stalls have been provided and marked.			
24. The entrance is clearly visible, well-lit and includes visible signs.			
25. Emergency facilities and exits are clearly marked and provided according to applicable local codes.			
26. Lighting complies with standards issued by the Illuminating Engineering Society of America (or applicable state or local requirements).			
27. The library provides for return of materials when the library is closed and the book drops are fire proofed.			
28. The library provides a public meeting room (or rooms) that are fully accessible.			

Revising Library Policies

ROLE OF THE BOARD, STAFF AND THE GOVERNING BODY IN POLICY DEVELOPMENT

It is not possible to make universal statements about how policy is developed in all libraries because state laws and the legal authority of the policymakers vary widely. Nevertheless, this section contains general recommendations that are usually true. Check with legal counsel that is familiar with library law in your state to be sure.

In most library settings it is the library board that determines both the personnel and public policies for the library, but this is not always the case. In some cases the library board is an advisory one. If the library director reports to a city manager or the mayor directly, it may be necessary to have policies approved by the city or city council after having been recommended by the library board.

PERSONNEL POLICY ISSUES

Library board policy should make it clear to staff that if they have complaints about the director, policies, or materials they should discuss the situation with their supervisor or the director first. If that does not resolve the issue, the staff should be encouraged to follow the library's grievance or complaint procedure provided for in the personnel policy.

If the board desires staff input it should get such input through the director whenever possible. Some library boards obtain library staff input on the director's performance as part of a formal evaluation process. Except in unusual circumstances, communication between the library board and library staff about library business should be carried on through the library director. Anything else undermines the director's authority. This point is spelled out in a good personnel policy so that it is clear to board and staff alike.

Even in cases where the library board has the statutory authority for personnel policy, the practice for the library may be

265

to follow the general personnel policies of the parent municipality rather than set up an entirely separate personnel policy.

State laws vary regarding the authority of the library board for personnel policy. The most common situation is to have the library board responsible for hiring the director. The board sets the compensation level and personnel policies for the director and all library staff. The director in turn, is responsible for hiring, firing and discipline of the staff policies as set by the board. In most cases, the library director recommends personnel policy changes, but can implement only policies officially approved by the board.

LIBRARY USE POLICIES

Every public library should have a collection development policy, and this and other policies should support the ideals of freedom of expression and inquiry and reflect the library's mission and goals.

Only a few of the more critical policy issues will be considered regarding library use policies:

- Challenged materials,

- Internet use, and

- Privacy of records.

These issues are among the more difficult library use problems that the board must face.

CHALLENGED MATERIALS

The library's challenged materials policy should specify that all board deliberations will be made at open meetings and that an official spokesperson that will give out all information on a challenge, especially to the media.

Periodic "fire drills" are a good way to rehearse the steps in their challenged materials procedure before a complaint makes its way to the board. The staff should also have frequent reminders and rehearsals of the steps required when a library user initiates a challenge to a library item. It is critically important that board and staff alike understand that due process must be followed if a library user has a complaint. Staff or board members who offer opinions as individuals before the challenged materials process is executed do a great disservice to the library, the library user, and themselves.

Collection development policies should contain statements on:

- Purpose and scope of the collection,

- Staff responsibility for selection,

- Use of professional selection tools,

- Types of materials to be added to the collection,

- Basis and method of withdrawing and disposing of materials,

- Acceptance of gift materials (apply the same standards as for selection), and

- Endorsement of the ALA Bill of Rights and Freedom to Read Statements (or a similar statement on intellectual freedom).

INTERNET USE

Modern library policies require constant attention to the Internet Use section of the library policy manual. At the very least, libraries will need policies on:

- CIPA (Children's Internet Protection Act): Upheld by the U.S. Supreme Court in 2003, it requires libraries that receive federal e-rate grants to provide filters.

- Filters: The policy should indicate if filters are used and where. If they are used, libraries should consider a policy regarding turning off the filter if adults request it (pursuant to the Supreme Court ruling in the CIPA case).

- Acceptable Use:

  - Chat: Some libraries limit or prohibit so-called chat room use on their workstations, though this is often hard to enforce.

- E-mail: Some libraries limit or prohibit use of Internet for this purpose, but this is becoming less common.

- Time Limits: Length of time for use of workstations is often specified.

- Commercial Use: Use of workstations for commercial purposes is often prohibited.

- Hacking: Willful damage or virus spreading is prohibited.

- Copyright: Users are warned against illegal copying of files on the Internet workstations in the library.

- Threats: Internet use policies usually note that the library workstations cannot be used to send threats or engage in other types of illegal activities.

- Content Disclaimer: Whether or not a library filters any or all of its workstations, most libraries include wording in their policies regarding the possibility that users may be offended by some content.

- Damage Disclaimer: Most libraries will explicitly note that they assume no responsibility for any damages, direct or indirect, arising from the use of its on-line resources.

PRIVACY OF RECORDS

Library users have the right to confidentiality and privacy; however, Internet users should be advised that because security is technologically difficult to achieve, electronic transactions and files could become public. Furthermore the Federal PATRIOT Act requires disclosure of records based on a court order and prohibits library staff from notifying the individual being investigated. Most observers indicate that the PATRIOT Act is not in contradiction to most state privacy of records laws because most states allow records to be disclosed based on a court order.

State laws also vary when it comes to privacy of records for children. Some states have specifically provided for children's privacy, others have not. Age limits vary by state. Some states allow for parents to have access to children's circulation records for certain purposes. Library planners will need to consider the state in which they are operating and its particular privacy laws before attempting to consider policies for these issues.

Some questions to ask about library privacy are:

- Does the staff understand the provisions of PATRIOT Act and what to do if asked to disclose records by a law enforcement official?

- Does the board understand the provisions of PATRIOT Act and what to do if asked to disclose records by a law enforcement official?

- Do you tell library users about the provisions of the PATRIOT Act?

- Are there variations on privacy provisions when it comes to children?

- Does the library have a policy on the retention of library records that is consistent with state and federal law?

- Does the automated circulation system provide sufficient safeguards on user privacy to agree with any privacy statements in the library's policy manual?

- Is there provision for staff training on issues of library user privacy as well as response to law enforcement officials and the press?

Figure 9–13 Test for Good Policies

Question	Yes	No
1. Do they fit with the overall vision, mission, and goals of the library?		
2. Are they reasonable and can they be applied consistent?		
3. Are they clear and understandable to the public and staff?		
4. Are they nondiscriminatory and applied equally to all users?		
5. Are they communicated clearly to staff (especially new staff)?		
6. Are they communicated clearly to board members (especially new ones)?		
7. Are they communicated clearly to the public by appropriate means?		
8. Do they comply with all applicable state and federal laws?		
9. Do they include the date when the policy was adopted *and* last reviewed by the board?		

Figure 9–14 Steps in Policy Creation

1. The staff and/or director define the need for policies or revisions. The initial suggestion for the policy may also come from the board or the public, but the administration should refine the description of the issues.
2. The director develops recommendations based on staff and public input. The recommendations are presented to the board.
3. The director seeks legal opinions on policy recommendations when appropriate.
4. The library board considers all policies in properly noticed public meetings.
5. The board considers, discusses, revises (if necessary), and approves policies.
6. The director makes the staff and public aware of policies by appropriate means. This will often include policy manuals for the staff, notices in the library for the public, and in some cases publicity releases.
7. The board reviews policies on a regular cycle so all policies are reviewed at least every three to five years.
8. The director and/or staff develop appropriate procedures to implement the policies adopted by the board and communicate them to the staff and the public.
9. The board and the director routinely discuss the distinction between policy creation and implementation through procedures.

Distinction between policies and procedures

Most libraries have a written procedure manual as well as a written policy manual. Procedure manuals are especially useful to new staff. Policy manuals are especially useful to both board and staff members. Policy manuals cover the broad matters for the staff of the public. Procedure manuals outline the steps necessary to accomplish various tasks.

Dealing with how the meeting room is to be used by the public is a policy issue. Setting up the scheduling, cleaning and monitoring of the meeting room is a procedural matter. In some libraries the distinction between policy and procedure and the role of board and staff in each are not clear. Effective planners will bring the distinctions to the fore during the planning process.

The board should delegate the development of procedures and day to day operations to the director. Discourage micromanagement of such activities; this is a diversion of the board's time from more critical issues.

POLICY MANUAL INVENTORY

Figure 9–15 Policy Manual Inventory

Policy Area	Yes	No	Incomplete	Date of policy	Comments
1. Mission and Goal Statements					
2. Statement on Who May Use the Library					
3. Patron Responsibilities and Conduct					
4. Services of the Library					
5. Responsibilities and Authority of the Library Board					
6. Conflict of Interest-Board					
7. Programming in the Library					
8. Public Relations					
9. Equipment Use Policy					
10. Internet Use Policy					
11. Meeting Room Policy					
12. Displays and Exhibits Policy					
13. Public Notice Bulletin Board Policy					
14. Disasters Policy					
15. Privacy of Records					
16. Volunteers and Friends					
17. Circulation Services					
• Borrower Eligibility and Procedures					
• Borrowers' Responsibilities					
• Confidentiality of Records					
• Equipment Use					
• Fines and fees					
• Loan Periods					
• Lost/Damaged Materials					
• Nonresident Fees					
• Registration					
• Renewals and Reserves					

18. Interlibrary Loan Services					
• Fees (if allowed by law)					
• Participation in Regional/State Networks					
• Protocols/Procedures					
• Reference Services					
• Homework Assignments					
• In-person vs. Telephone Questions					
• Online Searches					
• Reference Interviews					
19. Collection Development					
• Community/Clientele Descriptions					
• Evaluation of Collection					
• Purpose of Collection					
• Selection Criteria/Procedures					
• Statement Concerning Intellectual Freedom					
• Withdrawal of Materials					
20. Personnel					
• Salary Schedules					
• Benefits					
• Appointment					
• Disciplinary Procedures					
• Grievance Procedures					
• Insurance					
• Job Descriptions					
• Leaves					
- Disability					
- Family					
- Jury					
- Leaves of Absence					
- Military					
- Sick Leave					

273

• Organization Chart					
• Performance Evaluation					
• Personnel Records					
• Position Classification					
• Probationary Periods					
• Promotions/Demotions					
• Recruitment					
• Resignation and Dismissals					
• Retirement					
• Retirement Plan					
• Staff Development/Training					
• Travel Expenses					
• Vacancies					
• Vacations					
• Worker's Compensation					
21. Form: Statement of Concern About Library Resources					
22. Form: Internet Use Agreement					
23. Library Bill of Rights					
24. The Freedom to Read Statement					
25. Revision of Library Policies					

Conclusion

This chapter has provided:

- coverage of the use of the planning checklist as well as recommendations for policymaking;

- checklists that library planners should employ to evaluate actions that should undertake to develop and maintain an adequate and effective service profile. The checklist was compiled from standards checklists from a number of states but should be appropriate for nearly every state. The long-range plan should address deficiencies indicated here;

- the suggestion that the library board review the answers to the checklist. Have a discussion with staff and board on the ways in which any shortcomings of the library on the deficient items can be resolved;

- an explanation of the role of the board, staff, and governing body in policymaking;

- an overview of the critical issues for Library Use and Personnel Policies;

- a test for good policies and noted the key steps in policy formation;

- a checklist is that allows a comprehensive inventory of the types of policies that libraries should have. Those interested in further information on developing policies should consult Nelson and Garcia's *Creating Policies for Results*.

## Chapter 10

Writing and Implementing the Plan

Chapter Contents

Overview
Steps in the Planning Process
Writing the Plan
Implementing the Plan
Conclusion

List of Figures

Overview

As noted in Chapter 1, a single person should be assigned the task of writing the drafts and final plan. Often that person will be the director or someone assigned by the director to do the planning document. If the library has an existing plan, it will need to be reviewed by the planning committee. The director or lead planner will also need to assure that the background data needed for the committee's deliberations will be available for distribution at the appropriate points during the planning cycle.

This chapter provides two key tables. Figure 10–1 is a summary of all the steps in the planning process with short tips on what planners should expect and references to appropriate chapters and figures. The second table, Figure 10–2 is the suggested outline of the plan suggested in Chapter 1 but this time with commentary from the various chapters of the book and references to key figures.

Effective library planning never stops, and it is always a challenge. This chapter considers some of the strategies and questions that can be used to assure that the plan is properly implemented.

Steps in the Planning Process

Figure 10–1, Steps in the Planning Process, is provided as a blueprint of the steps in a planning process. The library director, writer, or key facilitator will find the table useful for managing the planning process on a day to day and week to week basis.

Figure 10–1 Steps in the Planning Process

Task	Description	Chapter	Figure	Target date	Actual date
1. Conduct self-assess-ment	Conduct the Library Planning Self-Assessment. Use results to begin planning the elements of the plan that need development or revision.	1	1		
2. Review tasks checklist	Review the "Preliminary Tasks Checklist"	1	2		
	a. Obtain board approval; get endorsement by governing board, union, and library related groups such as the Friends of the Library or the Library Foundation.	1			
	b. Develop a budget for the process. Get approval for the budget by the library board, governing body, foundation, or whatever group is paying the bill for the planning process.	1	3		
	c. Set deadlines for the entire project-usually 3 to 12 months.	1			
	d. Determine whether or not you will need a consultant or added staff resources to do the plan-ning process. If so, develop a Request for Proposal or contact possible consultants, facilita-tors, or temporary help. For engaging a consultant, consider using "Typical Request for Pro-posal for Library Consultant."				

	e. Determine who will be the lead writer for the plan. Decide who will develop the necessary data for the planning committee's consideration.	1			
	f. With library board approval, decide on the composition of the planning committee (if it is to include individuals beyond the library board itself). Try to get representatives from the full range of library stakeholders. Review the Stakeholder section in Chapter 2, as well as Figure 2-3, "Involving Stakeholders in the Planning Process."	1			
3. Review Library Planning Matrix	Review the "Library Planning Matrix" for ideas on how much effort is involved for various activities. This will help in defining level of effort in the step below.	1	4		
4. Determine level of effort	The director and board determine the level of effort involved with the project: intensive, moderate, or basic (see "Defining the Level of Effort").	1			
5. Review and evaluate the previous plan (if any)	Examine the previous plan (if any) and evaluate the results in a written form. Where goals have gone unmet and objectives unfilled, list reasons.				
6. Schedule meetings	Consultant or administration will need to develop the schedules for all planning committee efforts.	1			
7. Publicize meetings	Part of developing a plan is publicizing its development. Plan to put out press releases and invite the media to all meetings.	1			

8. Develop mailing materials and agendas	Effective planning committees will receive an agenda and decision documents well in advance of each meeting so the documents can be carefully considered.	1			
9. Review planning issues checklist	The board and administrator can use the Planning Issues Checklist to develop additional areas that need work for a planning cycle. For instance, if trustees and staff are not bonded and a review indicates that they should be, this should be included in the planning.	2	2-12		
10. Include overview questions	Ask the planning committee, the board, and the staff key essay questions at the start of the process. Compile the responses and consider strategy based on the written replies.	2			
11. Review policy manual Inventory	The results of the policy manual inventory should be used to recommend policy changes that are consistent with the plan being drafted. Review the steps in policy creation as well as the "Test for Good Policies."	9	9-13		
12. Present demographic and statistical data	Develop charts, tables, and graphs on the key data for decision makers. Planners will need to be made aware of key issues such as population growth trends, circulation patterns, tax base changes, and so forth. The consultant, director, or assigned staff member will develop these data.	4			

13. Review budget options	The consultant or the director will work with the library's auditors, municipal finance personnel, and the board to assure that the library's budget, financial records, and so forth are in good order. The entire planning committee need not be involved, perhaps a subcommittee will be in order.	6			
14. Review governance options	Assemble and evaluate information on governance options in your state.	6	6-1		
15. Review finance options	Assemble and evaluate information on finance options in your state.	6			
16. Review impact fees	Evaluate options for impact fees in your area.	6; Appendix 3			
17. Identify added elements-surveys, etc.	Planning committee will determine added information it needs for decision making.	4			
18. Build consensus	Consider the types of activities that will be needed to develop consensus on the elements of the plan.	3	3-1 through 9		
19. Decide on mission, vision, core values, roles	There is a section on each in Chapter 2, while Chapter 3 provides planners with the neeeded consensus building tools.	2, 3	3-1 through 9		

20. Establish goals and objectives	Goals and objectives are the heart of any strategic plan. Effective planners will spend most of the planning committee discussions developing them. Libraries in states with standards should use them in developing objectives. All libraries should consider using the percentile comparisons and the Metrics Worksheet to develop measurable objectives	5	5-1 through 4		
21. Revise board bylaws	Effective planners will recommend that the board's bylaws be up to date and consistent with local, state, and federal law.	6	6-3		
22. Draft plans	The single author decided upon at the beginning of the process (Chapter 1) writes a draft of the plan in the format provided in Figure 10-2, and uses the elements of the planning process discussed throughout this book. This draft is clearly marked DRAFT so that planning committee participants, the staff, the library board, the governing body, and all stakeholders recognize that it is scheduled for revision.	1	10-2		
23. Build consensus	The draft is presented to the planning committee for further amendments. Feedback from the other stakeholder groups is incorporated considered by the planning committee. Depending on the degree of consensus on the plan, various consensus building tools will be used.	3	3-1 through 9		
24. Hold public hearing	Depending on the library and municipality's circumstances, it is usually a very good idea to hold a public hearing on the plan. Check with legal counsel on the statutory requirements for a public hearing in your state and follow the advice given very carefully.				

25. Revise plan	Based on data from the public hearing it may be necessary to revise the plan yet again. Use the consensus building techniques in step 23 again, as necessary.	3	3-1 through 9		
26. Board and govern- ing body adopt plan	Present a copy of the finished plan to the library board for its formal adoption of the entire plan. Depending on local political circumstances, it is usually a good idea to present the plan to the city council (or other govern- ing body). This is especially true if the plan has recommendations for significant spending (on a building or a new circulation sys- tem, for instance.)				
27. Publish plan	In step 2b, you established a budget that included the costs for printing and dissemination of the plan to all the appropriate stake- holders.				
28. Set evalua- tion sched- ule	Based on the parameters you built into the plan, set up a pro- posed schedule of evaluation of the elements of the plan. Do this at least on an annual basis.				

Writing the Plan

Figure 10–2 provides an outline of a library strategic plan. For each section of the plan there is a brief description and reference to appropriate chapters and figures in this book.

1. How were the program goals and objectives established?

2. Was the process effective? How could it be improved?

3. What is the status of the library's progress toward achiev- ing its current goals?

4. Will the goals be achieved according to the timelines spec- ified in the program implementation? If not, why not?

5. Does the staff have adequate resources to achieve the library's goals?

6. How should priorities be changed to put more focus on achieving the goals?

7. How should timelines be changed (be careful about making these changes—know why efforts are behind schedule before timelines are changed)?

8. How should goals be changed, added or removed? Why?

9. How does the library usually decide on what new services are needed?

10. What training is needed for staff to deliver current services? New services?

11. How are employees trained about delivering services?

12. What is required of library users? Are the requirements reasonable?

13. What do library users consider to be strengths of the library? Weaknesses?

14. What do staff members consider to be strengths? Weaknesses?

15. What typical complaints are heard from library users? Staff members? Elected officials or other key stakeholders? How do these complaints relate to the plan?

16. What does staff recommend to improve the library service program?

17. What do others recommend to improve the library?

18. Are there products or services that are no longer needed?

Figure 10–2 Plan Outline with Chapter and Table References

Plan area	Comments	Chapter	Figure (if any)
A. Executive Summary	This section is presented first but written last. It covers the essential highpoints of the entire plan.		
B. Planning Framework			
1. Process Description	Tell the reader how the entire process and plan were put together and why.	1, 2	
2. Stakeholders	The reader needs to know who the library's stakeholders are and how they were represented or consulted with in the planning process.	2	2-3
3. Problems and Opportunities	List the library's strengths, weaknesses, opportunities and threats, along with a strategy for dealing with them.	2	2-4
4. Vision Statement	This provides the reader with a description of an ideal for the library and its place in the community.	2	
5. Mission Statement	This deals with what a library does in the community.	2	
6. Core Values	List key values that have affected the development of the plan.	2	
7. Role Selection	The Public Library Association has defined 13 service responses or roles. List the ones the library has chosen (note that the goals and objectives section can be organized by service response or by functional area). The goals and objectives section of this table is organized by functional area.	2	2-5
8. State standards (if any)	Forty-one states have library standards. Planners should look to the requirements for their library in state standards. In states lacking any standards or in states lacking solid numerical standards see the "Pursuing Percentile Comparsions" section of Chapter 5 and the Metrics Worksheet (Figure 5-4).	5	5-2 through 4

9. Timeline for Key Activities	If there are key activities in the plan, a section that highlights them is useful. Key activities might include an automation upgrade, building program, or comprehensive salary and position review.	2	
C. Goals and Objectives	Review tests for good goals and objectives.	2	2-6 and 2-7
1. Collection Development	Review the current collection development policy and make recommendations for revisions that are consistent with the goals and objectives developed with the plan.	7, 9	9-10 and 9-11
2. Electronic Services	Electronic resource statistics are difficult to find, use, and compare. Effective planners will need to take extra care on this section of the plan.	7, 9	
3. Access and Facilities	Develop a building plan, possibly as a separate document from the long range plan but referenced in the plan.	7, 9	7-19, 7-20, 9-12
4. Staffing and Personnel	Review personnel policies along with a review of all other policies. This will often require careful coordination with the municipal personnel office and/or the staff union.	7, 9	7-17, 7-18, 9-6
5. Technical and Automation Services	Planning for automation and technology is critical for effective library services. Technology plans like building plans are often separate documents but should be referenced in the strategic plan.	7, 9	
6. Other services	These other services will include reference, special needs, children's service, branch operations, disaster preparations, and so forth.	7, 9	
D. Demographics and statistical comparisons	Review the "Data Relevancy Test" and how to display data graphically.	4	4-1
1. Population and tax base comparisons and projections	Data on population and tax base are useful for planners, municipal officials and the library board as they approach their budget duties.	Chapter 4 & Appendix 5	Section 4 of Appendix 5
2. Circulation and library use comparisons	The director, facilitator, or consultant will provide current and historical library circulation and use data in order to give planners an idea of the scope of current library activities.	Chapter 4 & Appendix 5	Section 4 of Appendix 5

3. Comparison to state standards	If there are state standards, the consultant, director or facilitator should list how the library compares to them. If not, the library may wish to use the Metrics Worksheet and the percentile measures provided in Appendix 2.	Chapter 4, Appendix 2, Appendix 5	4-2 and Section 4 of Appendix 5
4. Other comparative data	Chapter 4 provides quite a few data sources for planners to consider in developing their library plan. Library staff or a consultant will be in a good position to detail the appropriate types of demographic data for each library. Planners should suggest added statistics and demographic data but only to the degree that the data will enhance the plan.	Chapter 4 & Appendix 5	4-7
E. Budget data	Assess data for past 2 to 3 years and project into future as appropriate.	Chapter 2, 4 & Appendix 5	2-9, 2-10, 4-12
1. Indicate capital improvement plan (if any)	The capital improvement plan will ordinarily list projects and funding for the next 5 to 10 years. Unless the library is an independent taxing district, the capital improvement plan will usually be part of the budget plan for the municipality as a whole.	2	2-10
F. Relevant Appendix materials	The committee will develop added materials such as surveys, focus groups, and so forth. The plan writer will include summaries and reports from such added material	Chapter 4, Appendix 4, and Appendix 5	
1. Survey results	Suggestions on surveys are included in Chapter 3.	3	3-8, 39
2. Focus group results			
3. Publicity items	Notable press coverage of the planning process should be included with the plan.		
4. Other			

Implementing the Plan

It is all too easy to let a long range plan become yet another report, sitting on a shelf, gathering dust. If all the goals are achieved it was probably because the plan was not ambitious enough to really challenge the library and its staff. If few of the key objectives were accomplished, it is probably because the objectives were too ambitious, unrealistic, or too costly. It could also be that the board, administration, or staff were not committed to carrying out the plan.

As you monitor the current plan, keep in mind that much can be learned from monitoring and evaluation in order to improve future planning activities. Periodic reports by department or by the director on progress towards achieving goals are critical. If the goals and objectives are being achieved, the library board should recognize the achievements and spread the word widely to the public and city council, county board, or other municipal authority.

A plan is not a law. Changing it is not a crime. Failing to monitor a plan and failing to provide recognition for its successes and failures, while not a crime, is certainly a mistake on the part of the board and administration of the library.

Feedback and communication between the board, administration, and library staff on the successes and failures of initiatives in the plan is crucial for ongoing growth of the library and its activities. Often the library planning team is dismissed after the planning effort is over, but it can be very useful for them to meet again periodically (annually or semiannually) to address problems with plan implementation. The planning committee, in conjunction with the board and administration, will want to:

- Assess the outcomes of the current plan to assure that library users are getting the benefits that the plan envisioned,

- Examine what needs to be done to increase the efficiency of service delivery for the goals and objectives listed in the plan (which should be included in a revised plan or in the next new plan), and

- Verify that the library is doing what it set out to do in the plan's goals and objectives (midcourse corrections help the organization stay on target).

When reviewing the plan, library boards should ask themselves some important questions.

- Should the deadlines be changed? Find out why the activities are behind schedule. If the original plans were unrealistic, they need to be altered.

- Do staff members have enough resources to achieve the goals? If not, it is up to the board to come up with the money, equipment, facilities, training, and so forth that are needed to do the job.

- Have staff members been given the opportunity to address the implementation of goals and objectives? If goals are going unmet, the most likely individuals to recommend improvements are those charged with carrying them out.

- Are the goals and objectives unrealistic because of changed financial or technological circumstances?

- Does the board need to change budget priorities in order to put more focus on achieving the goals in the plan? If not, perhaps some of the goals and objectives in the current plan need to be changed.

- Have we distinguished between inputs, process, outputs, and outcomes? Inputs include funding, equipment, staff training programs, and the like. Process refers to how library programs are carried out—storytime promotion, library user self-check activities, turnaround time on book processes, and so forth. Outputs are the things we count— library visits, circulation numbers, and number of videos cataloged, for instance. Outcomes are the impacts on our library users—increased knowledge about the world, improved job prospects, and a greater appreciation for culture. We can set new priorities for inputs by reordering budget priorities. Administrators can attempt to improve the processes involved so as to increase efficiency. Outputs can be more carefully measured and more consistently defined and assessed. But confusing any of the four with another in the evaluation of the plan will result in trouble.

Conclusion

This chapter has provided:

- some of the strategies and questions that can be used to assure that the plan is properly implemented;

- questions the library board, administrator, staff, and all stakeholders need to ask continuously to assure that the plan they established is properly carried out.

It is my sincere hope that this book will help those who cherish the library to continuously challenge its stewards to make that library the best it can possibly be. Remember, effective planning does not start when someone calls for a plan, and it does not stop when the planning committee presents its report. It is an ongoing process.

Appendix 1

HAPLR Rating Information

HAPLR Scorecards

Practically every time you pick up a magazine or newspaper there is another rating system for universities, places to work, hospitals, mutual funds, you name it. But there were none for libraries. Worse than that, the *Money* magazine listing of best places to live covered libraries by measuring only books per capita. I was certain that a more comprehensive tool was needed, so I devised the HAPLR rating system.

The HAPLR Index is the first of its kind for libraries in the United States. The standards and performance measures developed in the U.K. (www.lic.gov.uk/publications/policyreports/building/index.html) is not quite the same thing as the HAPLR Index, but close. The closest thing to the HAPLR Index is Germany s "BIX The Library Index," a project sponsored by the Bertelsmann Foundation. The BIX Index uses some data from the official "German Library Statistics" (http://bix-bibliotheksindex.de). The first results were published in Spring of 2000. A further description of the project may be found at: www.bertelsmann-stiftung .de/de/index.jsp (available in German only).

Ratings in the U.S.

The HAPLR ratings (http://haplr-index.com) use data published by FSCS and obtained from 9,000 libraries through 50 state agencies, the District of Columbia, and a number or outlying territories to create comparative rankings in broad population categories. Nationwide public library statistics are collected and disseminated annually through the FSCS (http://nces.ed.gov/surveys/public.html#contents). The HAPLR ratings have received newspaper, magazine, and television coverage all over the country.

The fifth edition of the HAPLR Index was featured in the October 2003 issue of *American Libraries* magazine; the first edition was in the January 1999 issue. All editions are based on the same data from the Federal-State Cooperative Service (FSCS).

The HAPLR Index includes fifteen factors. The focus is on circulation, staffing, materials, reference service, and funding levels. The Index does not include data on audio and video collections or interlibrary loan, among other items that could have been calculated from the FSCS data.

Why No Internet or Electronic Measures?

Perhaps most prominently absent from the data are any measures of electronic use or Internet service. While such measures would have been desirable, the FSCS data simply are simply not sufficient for such comparisons at this time. Internet, electronic services and audiovisual services are excluded because there is not enough data reported by enough libraries to make comparisons meaningful. What remains are traditional data for print services, book checkouts, reference service, funding, and staffing.

The FSCS data have only been collected on a consistent national basis since 1988. Since then, the data have been refined to be more consistent and to include more information. That trend is likely to accelerate, making the additional comparisons of Internet use, electronic services, and nonprint services possible soon.

294

Population Factors to Consider

The population served often extends beyond the population of the community that established it and provides its initial support. Left to their own devices, libraries would undoubtedly claim wider service territories that, when added together, would far exceed the total population. The FSCS data system had no choice but to ask states to make some rather arbitrary assignments of population.

Depending on the demographic makeup of the state, there will be inconsistencies in population assignment. Consolidated county and regional library systems are more prevalent in some states and regions than in others, skewing some population data. Take the author's home state and the fifteen largest communities there. One community is assigned one additional person for every 100 city residents, while another is assigned seventy-five persons for every 100 city residents. The former community, with fewer additional residents assigned, will fare better than the latter community in any per capita comparison.

Mixing Inputs and Outputs

Some have criticized the HAPLR Index for including both input and output measures in the same rating system. They note that inputs like how much money is spent on materials or how many periodicals the library owns are different from outputs such as circulation per capita or turnover rate. Combining the two makes it possible to have a library with good inputs and poor outputs score moderately well. Conversely, a library shortchanged by its community on funding that manages, through good management, to provide excellent service outcomes may rank more poorly than a library in a rich community with only moderately good management and output measures. I hope to evolve the index to get closer to answering the "are you getting what you paid for" type of question. At this point, it appears to me that 70 to 80 percent of the output is traceable to good input levels. The rest is probably traceable to good management or other factors that may not be measurable. The author hopes to do further investigation on the correlation of input and output some day soon.

What the Rating Numbers Mean

The HAPLR Index is similar to an ACT or SAT score with a theoretical minimum of one and a maximum of 1,000. Most libraries scored between 260 and 730, so scores above and below those numbers are remarkable. A library above the 75th percentile for expenditure per capita will get a higher score on this measure than one below the 25th percentile.

Expenditure per capita is weighted more heavily than percent of budget devoted to materials. In the HAPLR Index, each library is compared to all others in its population category on each of the fifteen measures. The combined score is then transformed into an index score so that all can be easily compared with a single number.

How to order HAPLR Ratings

Reports are available online at http://haplr-index.com/order.html. Reports may also be ordered by mail at:

> haplr-index.com
> 6014 Spring Street
> Racine, WI 53406

All reports are copyrighted, but purchasing one for your library gives you the right to reproduce any reasonable number of copies for distribution, providing that copyright notice is included. All reports include:

- A library's HAPLR score, rank of all comparably sized libraries and percentile scores.

- A graphic comparison of the percentile ranking of your library for the fifteen input and output measures.

- A detailed report on the library's score on each of the fifteen factors and the library's rank among like sized libraries.

- Comparisons to the five closest sized libraries in the state and nation.

How HAPLR Scores are Calculated

For those who would like to know how the HAPLR scores are generated, here is a step-by-step description. Readers with an aversion to mathematics or intensely technical information can safely skip this section and go on to the next appendix.

All fifteen measures are calculated for each of 72 libraries in the over 500,000-population group in 2000. Each library is then ranked on each of the fifteen measures. Measures and their related weights are:

Figure 1 HAPLR Element Weighting

Type	Measure	Weight
Inputs	Expenditure per capita	3
	Percent budget to materials	2
	Materials expenditure per capita	2
	FTE staff per 1,000 population	2
	Periodicals per 1000 residents	1
	Volumes per capita	1
Outputs	Cost per circulation (rated low to high)	3
	Visits per capita	3
	Collection turnover	2
	Circulation per full-time equivalent staff hour	2
	Circulation per capita	2
	Reference per capita	2
	Circulation per hour	2
	Visits per open hour	1
	Circulation per visit	1

- There are 72 libraries in over 500,000-population category (100K).

- Expenditure per capita rank is 22, the weight is 3.

- Expenditure per capita score is (72–22=50) times 3 = 150.

- Volumes per capita rank is 12, weight is 1.

- Volumes per capita score is (72–12=60) times 1 = 60.

Take special note that cost per circulation is rated low to high, assuming that lowest cost is best; therefore, the calculation for this factor differs. It is the rank times weighting rather than the number of libraries minus the rank that is used.

- Cost per circulation rank is 10, weight is 3.

- Cost per circulation score is 10 times 3 = 30.

- The above scores plus the remaining 12 items total 1,073 for a given library.

- There are 29 weighted points, so divide that 1,073 score by 29 to get a weighted average score for all measures of 37.0.

- Divided weighted score of 37.0 by the 72 libraries in population group (this number varies, of course by the number of libraries in the population category). Multiply by 1000 to get the index rating.

- 37.0 divided by 72 equals 0.513889.

- Multiply the resulting number (0.513889) by 1000 to get 514 as the index number for the library.

- Arrange all 72 libraries in the grouping by index score to get a ranking for each library on the index score. *Repeat the process for each of the ten population categories.*

In the relevant year for the calculation above, there were 8,946 library entities included in the Federal State Cooperative Service database. Library systems with multiple branches are counted as a single entity. The population categories used are those used by the FSCS for other comparisons, with one exception. The FSCS data includes another category of libraries over one million population, but that would have provided too few libraries for purposes of the Index.

Figure 2. U.S. Public Libraries by Population Size

Pop. category	Number of libraries
a) 500,000 and over	76
b) 250,000 to 499,999	95
c) 100,000 to 249,999	327
d) 50,000 to 99,999	541
e) 25,000 to 49,999	913
f) 10,000 to 24,999	1,767
g) 5,000 to 9,999	1,443
h) 2,500 to 4,999	1,305
i) 1,000 to 2,499	1,621
j) Under 1,000	1,040
Total/Average	9,128

Figure 3 Sample HAPLR Scorecard (For a full sample and other types of reports, see: haplr-index.com.)

Hennen's American Public Library Rating Index ©

Anywhereville Library

June 8, 2003

Number of Libraries in this Population Category: *877*

HALPR Score for this Library	791
Rank of Libraries in this population category	50
Percentile	94%

Appendix 2

Percentile Tables By Population

All tables in this section can be found on the CD-ROM. Each of the ten tables that follow provides data on the same thirty-eight measures of library service, from revenue by source to output measures. The measures are divided into categories from 95th to 5th percentile as well as averages for each group.

The number of libraries in each population category varies widely, so the percentile comparisons will vary as well. The percentile measures here demonstrate what percent of libraries are above or below a particular amount. For instance, a library close to the 95th percentile on a measure rates higher than 95 percent of all libraries in that category. In the larger population categories like the over 500,000 population category (500 K) that is only a handful of libraries. In the larger population categories like the 2,500 to 4,999 population category (2.5 K) the 95th percentile represents many more libraries.

Figure 1 Number of Libraries by Population Category in the U.S.

Population category	Number of libraries
a) 500k	76
b) 250 K	95
c) 100K	329
d) 50K	541
e) 25K	911
f) 10K	1,764
g) 5K	1,441
h) 2.5 K	1,300
i) 1K	1,587
j) 0K	958
Grand total	9,002

301

Figure 2 Percentile Details for 500,000+ Population Libraries

Category	Title	Measure	This library	95th %ile	75th %ile	50th %ile	25th %ile	5th %ile
a) Staff	Master-degreed librarian	Per 1000 pop.		0.25	0.16	0.11	0.08	0.05
	Nondegreed professional	Per 1000 pop.		0.26	0.18	0.13	0.09	0.05
	Other staff	Per 1000 pop.		0.63	0.42	0.30	0.23	0.14
	Total staff	Per 1000 pop.		0.94	0.61	0.45	0.32	0.20
b) Revenue	Local govt.	Per capita		$48.74	$33.16	$23.93	$17.08	$9.29
	State govt.	Per capita		$24.82	$2.67	$1.77	$0.53	$0.00
	Federal govt.	Per capita		$0.63	$0.14	$0.05	$0.00	$0.00
	Other income	Per capita		$12.10	$2.98	$1.78	$0.95	$0.32
	Total income	Per capita		$68.69	$41.03	$28.68	$20.83	$12.23
c) Expend.	Salaries	Per capita		$36.88	$19.36	$13.34	$10.00	$5.73
	Benefits	Per capita		$9.04	$5.15	$3.40	$2.44	$1.03
	Personnel costs	Per capita		$45.60	$24.24	$17.22	$12.41	$7.56
	Materials collection	Per capita		$13.15	$6.02	$4.02	$3.07	$2.00
	Other operating	Per capita		$18.25	$7.57	$5.32	$3.92	$1.82
	Total expenditure	Per capita		$65.76	$38.72	$27.30	$19.98	$11.35
	Capital expenditure	Per capita		$8.61	$3.21	$0.73	$0.26	$0.00
d) Materials	Book volumes	Per capita		5.4	2.8	2.2	1.6	1.2
	Audio	Per 1000 pop.		492.5	156.2	90.1	61.2	31.0
	Video	Per 1000 pop.		170.7	87.3	61.9	41.0	22.3
	Subscriptions	Per 1000 pop.		18.7	7.9	4.6	3.5	1.4

Category	Title	Measure	This library	95th %ile	75th %ile	50th %ile	25th %ile	5th %ile
e) Hours	Total hours	All		161,642	76,176	60,649	50,529	29,535
	Hours open	Per bldg., per wk.		65	53	47	41	35
f) Outputs	Visits	Per capita		7.9	5.1	4.0	3.0	2.1
	Reference	Per capita		2.8	2.1	1.4	0.8	0.5
	Total circulation	Per capita		17.5	9.2	5.3	3.8	2.3
	Interlibrary loan IN	Per 1000 pop.		71.4	14.7	7.1	2.3	0.2
	Interlibrary loan OUT	Per 1000 pop.		42.5	10.4	4.4	1.9	0.3
	Children's circulation	Per capita		6.4	2.9	1.9	1.4	0.8
	Children's prog. attend.	Per 1000 pop.		344.7	199.7	123.8	92.1	54.9
	Electronic materials expend.	Per capita		$1.08	$0.47	$0.26	$0.10	$0.00
	Electronic access items	Per capita		$2.25	$0.92	$0.59	$0.34	$0.00
	Electronic materials	Per 1000 pop.		22.2	5.2	2.0	0.5	0.0
	Collection turnover			6.0	4.2	2.5	2.0	0.7
	Circulation per FTE staff hr.			13.8	8.9	6.7	4.8	2.3
	Reference per capita	Per capita		2.8	2.1	1.4	0.8	0.5
	Circulation per hour	Per hour		188.2	112.3	82.7	61.2	30.6
	Visits per hour	Per hour		110.9	72.7	57.2	42.3	33.0
	Annual electronic access	Per capita		3.3	1.6	0.9	0.4	0.1
	Circulation per visit	Per visit		2.9	1.9	1.4	1.1	0.8

- There are seventy-six libraries in this population category.

- See Chapter 5 for information on how to use the data presented here. The data here are from 2001 annual reports filed with the FSCS in 2002.

- It is *critical* to note that the population used for this table is the "Legal Service Area" population assigned by the state library agency and the Federal State Cooperative Service, not the census population of the community in which the library is located. For consistency when using this table, use the Legal Service Area population for your library. To get your library's Legal Service Area either contact your state library agency, or visit one of the two Web sites below:

http://nces.ed.gov/surveys/libraries/publicpeer

www.haplr-index.com/AverageStatewideScores.html

Figure 3 Percentile Details for 250,000 to 499,999 Population Libraries

Category	Title	Measure	This library	95th %ile	75th %ile	50th %ile	25th %ile	5th %ile
a) Staff	Master-degreed librarian	Per 1000 pop.		0.21	0.14	0.10	0.07	0.03
	Nondegreed professional	Per 1000 pop.		0.26	0.17	0.12	0.08	0.04
	Other staff	Per 1000 pop.		0.60	0.37	0.27	0.20	0.12
	Total staff	Per 1000 pop.		0.82	0.52	0.40	0.30	0.19
b) Revenue	Local govt.	Per capita		$42.63	$30.47	$20.61	$14.52	$6.44
	State govt.	Per capita		$8.22	$2.33	$1.28	$0.56	$0.00
	Federal govt.	Per capita		$0.68	$0.17	$0.05	$0.00	$0.00
	Other income	Per capita		$6.91	$2.48	$1.51	$0.55	$0.04
	Total income	Per capita		$59.40	$35.56	$24.28	$17.88	$11.03
c) Expend.	Salaries	Per capita		$25.78	$15.97	$11.55	$8.35	$5.63
	Benefits	Per capita		$6.80	$3.80	$3.03	$1.94	$1.23
	Personnel costs	Per capita		$32.30	$20.41	$14.41	$10.67	$6.97
	Materials collection	Per capita		$8.76	$4.78	$3.53	$2.65	$1.33
	Other operating	Per capita		$12.66	$7.23	$4.59	$3.27	$2.23
	Total expenditure	Per capita		$53.07	$32.76	$22.94	$17.30	$10.86
	Capital expenditure	Per capita		$18.76	$3.80	$0.58	$0.00	$0.00
d) Materials	Book volumes	Per capita		5.1	2.7	2.0	1.5	0.9
	Audio	Per 1000 pop.		300.7	136.0	72.4	44.7	18.3

Category	Title	Measure	This library	95th %ile	75th %ile	50th %ile	25th %ile	5th %ile
	Video	Per 1000 pop.		196.9	83.9	55.4	35.5	13.2
	Subscriptions	Per 1000 pop.		12.7	6.3	4.7	3.4	1.7
e) Hours	Total hours	All		54,392	36,212	29,653	19,127	11,637
	Hours open	Per bldg., per wk.		66	54	48	42	34
f) Outputs	Visits	Per capita		6.5	5.2	3.8	2.9	1.3
	Reference	Per capita		2.6	1.3	0.9	0.6	0.2
	Total circulation	Per capita		13.1	7.9	5.9	4.1	1.9
	Interlibrary loan IN	Per 1000 pop.		159.7	26.3	10.6	3.4	0.8
	Interlibrary loan OUT	Per 1000 pop.		149.8	16.0	8.2	4.2	1.6
	Children's circulation	Per capita		4.8	2.8	2.0	1.3	0.4
	Children's prog. attend.	Per 1000 pop.		351.9	205.9	134.3	89.4	40.0
	Electronic materials expend.	Per capita		$0.95	$0.40	$0.20	$0.04	$0.00
	Electronic access items	Per capita		$2.10	$0.74	$0.42	$0.15	$0.00
	Electronic materials	Per 1000 pop.		18.8	5.4	2.2	0.2	-
	Collection turnover			5.0	4.0	2.9	2.0	1.0
	Circulation per FTE staff hr.			11.4	8.8	6.9	5.4	2.9
	Reference per capita	Per capita		2.6	1.3	0.9	0.6	0.2
	Circulation per hour	Per hour		140.5	105.0	70.3	47.4	27.5
	Visits per hour	Per hour		87.9	59.8	48.8	30.3	17.8
	Annual electronic access	Per capita		3.1	1.0	0.6	0.3	0.1
	Circulation per visit	Per visit		2.8	1.9	1.6	1.2	0.9

- There are ninety-five libraries in this population category.

- See Chapter 5 for information on how to use the data presented here. The data here are from 2001 annual reports filed with the FSCS in 2002.

- It is *critical* to note that the population used for this table is the "Legal Service Area" population assigned by the state library agency and the Federal State Cooperative Service, not the census population of the community in which the library is located. For consistency when using this table, use the Legal Service Area population for your library. To get your library's Legal Service Area either contact your state library agency, or visit one of the two Web sites below:

  http://nces.ed.gov/surveys/libraries/publicpeer

  www.haplr-index.com/AverageStatewideScores.html

Figure 4 Percentile Details for 100,000 to 249,999 Population Libraries

Category	Title	Measure	This library	95th %ile	75th %ile	50th %ile	25th %ile	5th %ile
a) Staff	Master-degreed librarian	Per 1000 pop.		0.24	0.14	0.08	0.05	0.02
	Nondegreed professional	Per 1000 pop.		0.25	0.17	0.11	0.07	0.03
	Other staff	Per 1000 pop.		0.69	0.40	0.29	0.19	0.11
	Total staff	Per 1000 pop.		0.88	0.54	0.40	0.27	0.16
b) Revenue	Local govt.	Per capita		$45.25	$30.72	$17.30	$10.42	$4.47
	State govt.	Per capita		$8.38	$3.53	$1.54	$0.26	$0.00
	Federal govt.	Per capita		$0.93	$0.15	$0.01	$0.00	$0.00
	Other income	Per capita		$5.15	$2.28	$0.83	$0.31	$0.00
	Total income	Per capita		$57.79	$36.26	$21.43	$14.36	$8.27
c) Expend.	Salaries	Per capita		$27.23	$17.30	$11.38	$7.01	$3.90
	Benefits	Per capita		$7.78	$4.61	$2.33	$1.64	$0.58
	Personnel costs	Per capita		$33.46	$22.46	$13.16	$8.14	$4.68
	Materials collection	Per capita		$7.61	$4.21	$3.27	$2.06	$0.91
	Other operating	Per capita		$12.27	$6.26	$3.69	$2.49	$1.02
	Total expenditure	Per capita		$51.59	$33.85	$20.15	$13.28	$8.20
	Capital expenditure	Per capita		$15.91	$2.22	$0.49	$0.00	$0.00
d) Materials	Book volumes	Per capita		3.9	2.8	2.1	1.6	0.9
	Audio	Per 1000 pop.		287.4	140.7	83.7	39.2	12.6

Category	Title	Measure	This library	95th %ile	75th %ile	50th %ile	25th %ile	5th %ile
	Video	Per 1000 pop.		176.7	100.1	65.1	38.4	13.0
	Subscriptions	Per 1000 pop.		11.5	6.1	4.2	3.1	1.2
e) Hours	Total hours	All		23,049	13,453	8,632	5,974	3,185
	Hours open	Per bldg., per wk.		68	58	48	37	28
f) Outputs	Visits	Per capita		7.5	4.6	3.3	2.2	1.2
	Reference	Per capita		2.2	1.1	0.6	0.4	0.1
	Total circulation	Per capita		13.0	7.6	5.0	3.2	1.2
	Interlibrary loan IN	Per 1000 pop.		267.4	36.7	11.4	2.6	0.0
	Interlibrary loan OUT	Per 1000 pop.		253.6	27.3	11.4	4.6	0.5
	Children circulation	Per capita		5.3	2.9	1.5	1.1	0.4
	Children prog. attend	Per 1000 pop.		400.7	212.4	117.7	68.1	10.6
	Electronic materials expend.	Per capita		$0.72	$0.23	$0.08	$0.00	$0.00
	Electronic access items	Per capita		$1.74	$0.86	$0.51	$0.19	$0.00
	Electronic materials	Per 1000 pop.		27.3	4.9	1.0	0.2	-
	Collection turnover			5.8	3.6	2.7	1.6	0.9
	Circulation per FTE staff hr.			12.8	8.0	6.5	4.6	2.3
	Reference per capita	Per capita		2.2	1.1	0.6	0.4	0.1
	Circulation per hour	Per hour		251.3	102.6	60.5	34.5	15.2
	Visits per hour	Per hour		130.9	66.4	45.3	21.0	9.6
	Annual electronic access	Per capita		2.5	0.9	0.5	0.3	0.1
	Circulation per visit	Per visit		2.8	2.0	1.5	1.2	0.7

- There are 329 libraries in this population category.

- See Chapter 5 for information on how to use the data presented here. The data here are from 2001 annual reports filed with the FSCS in 2002.

- It is *critical* to note that the population used for this table is the "Legal Service Area" population assigned by the state library agency and the Federal State Cooperative Service, not the census population of the community in which the library is located. For consistency when using this table, use the Legal Service Area population for your library. To get your library's Legal Service Area contact your state library agency, or visit one of the two Web sites below:

  http://nces.ed.gov/surveys/libraries/publicpeer

  www.haplr-index.com/AverageStatewideScores.html

Figure 5 Percentile Details for 50,000 to 99,999 Population Libraries

Category	Title	Measure	This library	95th %ile	75th %ile	50th %ile	25th %ile	5th %ile
a) Staff	Master-degreed librarian	Per 1000 pop.		0.28	0.15	0.08	0.04	0.01
	Nondegreed professional	Per 1000 pop.		0.32	0.20	0.13	0.07	0.02
	Other staff	Per 1000 pop.		0.79	0.41	0.27	0.18	0.07
	Total staff	Per 1000 pop.		1.09	0.59	0.40	0.27	0.14
b) Revenue	Local govt.	Per capita		$59.37	$27.90	$16.28	$8.68	$1.75
	State govt.	Per capita		$26.45	$3.74	$1.72	$0.69	$0.00
	Federal govt.	Per capita		$0.68	$0.18	$0.00	$0.00	$0.00
	Other income	Per capita		$6.87	$2.81	$1.46	$0.57	$0.00
	Total income	Per capita		$69.52	$36.51	$22.23	$13.84	$6.08
c) Expend.	Salaries	Per capita		$34.30	$18.19	$10.70	$6.35	$2.98
	Benefits	Per capita		$8.16	$4.24	$2.37	$1.42	$0.20
	Personnel costs	Per capita		$42.50	$22.45	$12.78	$7.90	$3.62
	Materials collection	Per capita		$9.58	$4.66	$3.18	$1.86	$0.66
	Other operating	Per capita		$13.78	$6.78	$3.97	$2.38	$0.99
	Total expenditure	Per capita		$60.80	$33.66	$20.53	$13.09	$5.87

Category	Title	Measure	This library	95th %ile	75th %ile	50th %ile	25th %ile	5th %ile
	Capital expenditure	Per capita		$9.69	$1.80	$0.33	$0.00	$0.00
d) Materials	Book volumes	Per capita		4.9	3.1	2.3	1.7	1.0
	Audio	Per 1000 pop.		311.0	142.6	76.9	37.1	11.0
	Video	Per 1000 pop.		253.3	121.6	65.7	34.2	8.8
	Subscriptions	Per 1000 pop.		13.2	6.8	4.7	3.2	1.5
e) Hours	Total hours	All		17,274	9,948	6,310	3,466	2,635
	Hours open	Per bldg., per wk.		69	60	47	37	25
f) Outputs	Visits	Per capita		9.5	5.4	3.8	2.3	1.0
	Reference	Per capita		2.3	1.0	0.5	0.3	0.1
	Total circulation	Per capita		16.0	8.9	5.1	3.2	1.4
	Interlibrary loan IN	Per 1000 pop.		437.9	53.1	11.2	2.3	-
	Interlibrary loan OUT	Per 1000 pop.		290.5	45.3	14.4	5.5	0.9
	Children's circulation	Per capita		6.0	3.1	1.8	1.0	0.4
	Children's prog. attend	Per 1000 pop.		470.4	229.5	135.7	81.7	30.4
	Electronic materials expend.	Per capita		$0.96	$0.26	$0.07	$0.00	$0.00
	Electronic access items	Per capita		$2.56	$1.09	$0.52	$0.16	$0.00
	Electronic materials	Per 1000 pop.		51.1	6.1	1.6	0.3	-
	Collection turnover			5.0	3.4	2.4	1.6	0.7
	Circulation per FTE staff hr.			12.0	8.4	6.3	4.6	2.6
	Reference per capita	Per capita		2.3	1.0	0.5	0.3	0.1
	Circulation per hour	Per hour		219.3	111.9	58.1	28.6	12.3
	Visits per hour	Per hour		137.4	74.5	43.5	20.6	7.9
	Annual electronic access	Per capita		3.9	1.1	0.5	0.3	0.1
	Circulation per visit	Per visit		3.2	1.9	1.5	1.1	0.6

- There are 541 libraries in this population category.

- See Chapter 5 for information on how to use the data presented here. The data here are from 2001 annual reports filed with the FSCS in 2002.

- It is *critical* to note that the population used for this table is the "Legal Service Area" population assigned by the state library agency and the Federal State Cooperative Service, not the census population of the community in which the library is located. For consistency when using this table, use the Legal Service Area population for your library. To get your library's Legal Service Area contact your state library agency, or visit one of the two Web sites below:

  http://nces.ed.gov/surveys/libraries/publicpeer

  www.haplr-index.com/AverageStatewideScores.html

Figure 6 Percentile Details for 25,000 to 49,999 Population Libraries

Category	Title	Measure	This library	95th %ile	75th %ile	50th %ile	25th %ile	5th %ile
a) Staff	Master-degreed librarian	Per 1000 pop.		0.35	0.17	0.09	0.04	-
	Nondegreed professional	Per 1000 pop.		0.43	0.25	0.16	0.09	0.03
	Other staff	Per 1000 pop.		0.85	0.44	0.29	0.18	0.05
	Total staff	Per 1000 pop.		1.15	0.67	0.45	0.31	0.14
b) Revenue	Local govt.	Per capita		$71.38	$31.40	$18.80	$8.59	$0.56
	State govt.	Per capita		$28.00	$3.11	$1.26	$0.31	$0.00
	Federal govt.	Per capita		$0.71	$0.06	$0.00	$0.00	$0.00
	Other income	Per capita		$8.75	$3.38	$1.66	$0.63	$0.00
	Total income	Per capita		$81.40	$39.74	$24.63	$14.73	$5.64
c) Expend.	Salaries	Per capita		$39.97	$18.83	$11.99	$6.92	$3.03
	Benefits	Per capita		$9.27	$4.21	$2.45	$1.22	$0.12
	Personnel costs	Per capita		$48.62	$22.66	$14.57	$8.46	$3.66
	Materials collection	Per capita		$9.91	$5.43	$3.41	$1.88	$0.66
	Other operating	Per capita		$15.40	$7.46	$4.56	$2.61	$1.07
	Total expenditure	Per capita		$72.94	$35.41	$23.03	$13.56	$5.30

Category	Title	Measure	This Library	95th %ile	75th %ile	50th %ile	25th %ile	5th %ile
	Capital expenditure	Per capita		$20.61	$2.01	$0.34	$0.00	$0.00
d) Materials	Book volumes	Per capita		5.6	3.6	2.7	1.8	0.9
	Audio	Per 1000 pop.		333.7	163.5	91.1	43.4	10.4
	Video	Per 1000 pop.		262.0	144.6	82.9	42.5	9.4
	Subscriptions	Per 1000 pop.		16.2	9.2	6.3	3.8	1.6
e) Hours	Total hours	All		11,211	5,434	3,432	3,000	2,288
	Hours open	Per bldg., per wk.		69	63	55	42	26
f) Outputs	Visits	Per capita		11.0	6.0	4.2	2.4	0.8
	Reference	Per capita		2.2	1.0	0.5	0.3	0.1
	Total circulation	Per capita		15.7	9.1	5.8	3.1	1.3
	Interlibrary loan IN	Per 1000 pop.		598.9	131.0	21.2	2.3	-
	Interlibrary loan OUT	Per 1000 pop.		605.6	111.6	29.9	9.7	1.9
	Children circulation	Per capita		6.1	3.4	2.1	1.1	0.4
	Children prog. attend	Per 1000 pop.		502.2	265.8	159.5	91.8	24.1
	Electronic materials expend.	Per capita		$1.01	$0.25	$0.06	$0.00	$0.00
	Electronic access items	Per capita		$2.68	$1.17	$0.58	$0.13	$0.00
	Electronic materials	Per 1000 pop.		30.0	6.4	1.4	0.3	-
	Collection turnover			4.9	3.1	2.1	1.4	0.8
	Circulation per FTE staff hr.			12.2	7.8	6.0	4.4	2.4
	Reference per capita	Per capita		2.2	1.0	0.5	0.3	0.1
	Circulation per hour	Per hour		154.8	81.4	47.6	25.1	9.7
	Visits per hour	Per hour		101.2	57.2	37.0	17.3	5.8
	Annual electronic access	Per capita		3.1	1.1	0.5	0.3	0.1
	Circulation per visit	Per visit		3.1	1.9	1.4	1.1	0.6

- There are 911 libraries in this population category.

- See Chapter 5 for information on how to use the data presented here. The data here are from 2001 annual reports filed with the FSCS in 2002.

- It is *critical* to note that the population used for this table is the "Legal Service Area" population assigned by the state library agency and the Federal State Cooperative Service, not the census population of the community in which the library is located. For consistency when using this table, use the Legal Service Area population for your library. To get your library's Legal Service Area contact your state library agency, or visit one of the two Web sites below:

http://nces.ed.gov/surveys/libraries/publicpeer

www.haplr-index.com/AverageStatewideScores.html

Figure 7 Percentile Details for 10,000 to 24,999 Population Libraries

Category	Title	Measure	This library	95th %ile	75th %ile	50th %ile	25th %ile	5th %ile
a) Staff	Master-degreed librarian	Per 1000 pop.		0.35	0.16	0.07	-	-
	Nondegreed professional	Per 1000 pop.		0.50	0.29	0.18	0.09	0.05
	Other staff	Per 1000 pop.		0.82	0.47	0.29	0.16	0.02
	Total staff	Per 1000 pop.		1.18	0.69	0.48	0.32	0.14
b) Revenue	Local govt.	Per capita		$61.98	$30.44	$17.89	$8.38	$0.87
	State govt.	Per capita		$17.28	$2.37	$1.02	$0.25	$0.00
	Federal govt.	Per capita		$0.83	$0.00	$0.00	$0.00	$0.00
	Other income	Per capita		$10.66	$3.86	$1.79	$0.72	$0.00
	Total income	Per capita		$74.77	$38.27	$23.96	$13.94	$5.73
c) Expend.	Salaries	Per capita		$37.03	$18.71	$11.88	$6.92	$3.47
	Benefits	Per capita		$8.66	$4.04	$2.28	$0.89	$0.00
	Personnel costs	Per capita		$44.13	$22.06	$14.43	$8.28	$3.96
	Materials collection	Per capita		$10.67	$5.20	$3.31	$1.82	$0.66
	Other operating	Per capita		$15.48	$7.53	$4.66	$2.72	$1.14
	Total expenditure	Per capita		$65.08	$34.33	$21.91	$12.72	$5.53

Category	Title	Measure	This library	95th %ile	75th %ile	50th %ile	25th %ile	5th %ile
	Capital expenditure	Per capita		$14.96	$1.62	$0.25	$0.00	$0.00
d) Materials	Book volumes	Per capita		6.7	4.3	3.1	2.2	1.1
	Audio	Per 1000 pop.		342.4	165.3	94.2	48.5	14.0
	Video	Per 1000 pop.		301.6	152.2	97.4	51.0	10.3
	Subscriptions	Per 1000 pop.		19.3	11.9	8.1	4.9	1.8
e) Hours	Total hours	All		5,720	3,328	2,886	2,456	1,929
	Hours open	Per bldg., per wk.		66	59	51	42	25
f) Outputs	Visits	Per capita		12.2	6.7	4.4	2.4	0.8
	Reference	Per capita		2.3	0.9	0.5	0.2	0.0
	Total circulation	Per capita		16.0	9.6	6.2	3.6	1.3
	Interlibrary loan IN	Per 1000 pop.		761.1	177.1	28.3	1.8	-
	Interlibrary loan OUT	Per 1000 pop.		775.5	180.3	48.7	14.1	1.6
	Children's circulation	Per capita		6.5	3.7	2.2	1.2	0.4
	Children's prog. attend.	Per 1000 pop.		708.2	326.1	189.2	101.6	20.0
	Electronic materials expend.	Per capita		$0.82	$0.14	$0.01	$0.00	$0.00
	Electronic access items	Per capita		$3.02	$1.33	$0.47	$0.07	$0.00
	Electronic materials	Per 1000 pop.		27.2	6.1	1.9	0.3	-
	Collection turnover			4.3	2.7	1.9	1.3	0.6
	Circulation per FTE staff hr.			12.9	8.3	6.0	4.4	2.5
	Reference per capita	Per capita		2.3	0.9	0.5	0.2	0.0
	Circulation per hour	Per hour		86.4	50.3	31.0	18.5	7.7
	Visits per hour	Per hour		66.9	36.1	21.6	12.0	4.8
	Annual electronic access	Per capita		3.4	1.1	0.5	0.3	0.1
	Circulation per visit	Per visit		3.6	1.9	1.4	1.1	0.6

- There are 1,764 libraries in this population category.

- See Chapter 5 for information on how to use the data presented here. The data here are from 2001 annual reports filed with the FSCS in 2002.

- It is *critical* to note that the population used for this table is the "Legal Service Area" population assigned by the state library agency and the Federal State Cooperative Service, not the census population of the community in which the library is located. For consistency when using this table, use the Legal Service Area population for your library. To get your library's Legal Service Area contact your state library agency, or visit one of the two Web sites below:

  http://nces.ed.gov/surveys/libraries/publicpeer

  www.haplr-index.com/AverageStatewideScores.html

Figure 8 Percentile Details for 5,000 to 9,999 Population Libraries

Category	Title	Measure	This library	95th %ile	75th %ile	50th %ile	25th %ile	5th %ile
a) Staff	Master-degreed librarian	Per 1000 pop.		0.34	0.14	-	-	-
	Nondegreed professional	Per 1000 pop.		0.64	0.35	0.19	0.13	0.09
	Other staff	Per 1000 pop.		0.85	0.45	0.26	0.11	-
	Total staff	Per 1000 pop.		1.28	0.74	0.51	0.35	0.16
b) Revenue	Local govt.	Per capita		$55.99	$27.21	$16.39	$7.65	$0.87
	State govt.	Per capita		$8.65	$2.20	$0.83	$0.17	$0.00
	Federal govt.	Per capita		$0.95	$0.00	$0.00	$0.00	$0.00
	Other income	Per capita		$13.06	$4.43	$2.02	$0.75	$0.00
	Total income	Per capita		$70.67	$35.83	$22.56	$13.46	$6.37
c) Expend.	Salaries	Per capita		$36.32	$17.98	$12.29	$8.31	$4.72
	Benefits	Per capita		$7.80	$3.77	$1.92	$0.79	$0.00
	Personnel costs	Per capita		$42.07	$21.66	$14.54	$9.71	$5.52
	Materials collection	Per capita		$10.37	$5.44	$3.19	$1.82	$0.65
	Other operating	Per capita		$16.27	$7.98	$5.15	$3.15	$1.23

Category	Title	Measure	This library	95th %ile	75th %ile	50th %ile	25th %ile	5th %ile
	Total expenditure	Per capita		$62.81	$31.41	$20.26	$12.38	$5.63
	Capital expenditure	Per capita		$13.57	$1.74	$0.05	$0.00	$0.00
d) Materials	Book volumes	Per capita		7.8	5.4	3.9	2.9	1.7
	Audio	Per 1000 pop.		385.5	170.8	100.8	51.8	12.2
	Video	Per 1000 pop.		389.3	194.4	114.8	56.8	7.0
	Subscriptions	Per 1000 pop.		24.8	15.2	10.6	6.3	1.6
e) Hours	Total hours	All		3,536	2,786	2,392	2,023	1,436
	Hours open	Per bldg., per wk.		60	52	44	36	23
f) Outputs	Visits	Per capita		12.3	6.1	4.0	2.3	0.9
	Reference	Per capita		2.4	0.8	0.4	0.2	0.0
	Total circulation	Per capita		17.0	9.6	6.1	3.6	1.4
	Interlibrary loan IN	Per 1000 pop.		852.9	167.8	26.0	1.6	-
	Interlibrary loan OUT	Per 1000 pop.		878.7	184.2	55.6	17.8	1.2
	Children's circulation	Per capita		6.9	3.6	2.3	1.2	0.4
	Children's prog. attend.	Per 1000 pop.		740.7	358.3	193.1	87.2	10.6
	Electronic materials expend.	Per capita		$0.68	$0.07	$0.00	$0.00	$0.00
	Electronic access items	Per capita		$3.12	$1.04	$0.29	$0.01	$0.00
	Electronic materials	Per 1000 pop.		27.8	8.3	2.9	0.2	-
	Collection turnover			3.3	2.1	1.6	1.1	0.5
	Circulation per FTE staff hr.			12.7	7.9	5.7	4.1	2.2
	Reference per capita	Per capita		2.4	0.8	0.4	0.2	0.0
	Circulation per hour	Per hour		46.2	26.4	18.3	11.7	5.2
	Visits per hour	Per hour		33.9	17.8	11.7	7.3	3.2
	Annual electronic access	Per capita		2.9	1.1	0.5	0.3	0.1
	Circulation per visit	Per visit		4.0	2.1	1.5	1.1	0.7

315

- There are 1,441 libraries in this population category.

- See Chapter 5 for information on how to use the data presented here. The data here are from 2001 annual reports filed with the FSCS in 2002.

- It is *critical* to note that the population used for this table is the "Legal Service Area" population assigned by the state library agency and the Federal State Cooperative Service, not the census population of the community in which the library is located. For consistency when using this table, use the Legal Service Area population for your library. To get your library's Legal Service Area contact your state library agency, or visit one of the two Web sites below:

  http://nces.ed.gov/surveys/libraries/publicpeer

  www.haplr-index.com/AverageStatewideScores.html

Figure 9 Percentile Details for 2,500 to 4,999 Population Libraries

Category	Title	Measure	This library	95th %ile	75th %ile	50th %ile	25th %ile	5th %ile
a) Staff	Master-degreed librarian	Per 1000 pop.		0.29	-	-	-	-
	Nondegreed professional	Per 1000 pop.		0.77	0.42	0.28	0.20	0.11
	Other staff	Per 1000 pop.		0.79	0.37	0.18	0.03	-
	Total staff	Per 1000 pop.		1.23	0.76	0.53	0.35	0.16
b) Revenue	Local govt.	Per capita		$49.04	$25.21	$15.20	$8.13	$1.46
	State govt.	Per capita		$6.33	$1.48	$0.62	$0.04	$0.00
	Federal govt.	Per capita		$1.30	$0.00	$0.00	$0.00	$0.00
	Other income	Per capita		$14.85	$5.04	$2.14	$0.66	$0.00
	Total income	Per capita		$61.71	$31.73	$21.15	$13.02	$5.64
c) Expend.	Salaries	Per capita		$37.97	$19.89	$14.64	$10.96	$7.18
	Benefits	Per capita		$8.28	$3.93	$2.17	$0.96	$0.00
	Personnel costs	Per capita		$43.38	$23.45	$17.10	$12.20	$7.87
	Materials collection	Per capita		$9.30	$5.18	$3.27	$1.93	$0.62
	Other operating	Per capita		$18.32	$9.67	$6.22	$3.81	$1.91
	Total expenditure			$54.08	$28.71	$19.19	$12.06	$4.89

Category	Title	Measure	This library	95th %ile	75th %ile	50th %ile	25th %ile	5th %ile
	Capital expenditure	Per capita		$16.26	$1.73	$0.00	$0.00	$0.00
d) Materials	Book volumes	Per capita		10.4	6.7	5.1	3.6	2.2
	Audio	Per 1000 pop.		415.5	190.2	106.7	48.1	7.5
	Video	Per 1000 pop.		517.7	236.6	139.6	60.9	4.2
	Subscriptions	Per 1000 pop.		33.6	20.1	13.2	7.4	1.6
e) Hours	Total hours	All		2,808	2,288	1,884	1,517	1,021
	Hours open	Per bldg., per wk.		52	43	36	29	18
f) Outputs	Visits	Per capita		11.7	5.6	3.7	2.2	0.8
	Reference	Per capita		2.7	0.9	0.4	0.2	0.0
	Total circulation	Per capita		17.4	9.2	6.1	3.6	1.4
	Interlibrary loan IN	Per 1000 pop.		787.5	94.2	19.6	0.2	-
	Interlibrary loan OUT	Per 1000 pop.		741.1	164.4	62.2	18.9	0.6
	Children's circulation	Per capita		7.2	3.6	2.1	1.2	0.4
	Children's prog. attend.	Per 1000 pop.		861.2	349.6	178.4	68.2	6.5
	Electronic materials expend.	Per capita		$0.36	$0.02	$0.00	$0.00	$0.00
	Electronic access items	Per capita		$3.34	$0.77	$0.15	$0.00	$0.00
	Electronic materials	Per 1000 pop.		34.9	10.0	3.1	-	-
	Collection turnover			2.8	1.7	1.2	0.8	0.4
	Circulation per FTE staff hr.			12.8	7.9	5.6	3.8	1.9
	Reference per capita	Per capita		2.7	0.9	0.4	0.2	0.0
	Circulation per hour	Per hour		30.2	17.1	11.7	7.5	3.3
	Visits per hour	Per hour		20.0	10.5	6.9	4.5	2.0
	Annual electronic access	Per capita		2.9	1.1	0.6	0.3	0.0
	Circulation per visit	Per visit		3.8	2.1	1.6	1.2	0.7

- There are 1,300 libraries in this population category.

- See Chapter 5 for information on how to use the data presented here. The data here are from 2001 annual reports filed with the FSCS in 2002.

- It is *critical* to note that the population used for this table is the "Legal Service Area" population assigned by the state library agency and the Federal State Cooperative Service, not the census population of the community in which the library is located. For consistency when using this table, use the Legal Service Area population for your library. To get your library's Legal Service Area contact your state library agency, or visit one of the two Web sites below:

  http://nces.ed.gov/surveys/libraries/publicpeer

  www.haplr-index.com/AverageStatewideScores.html

Figure 10 Percentile Details for 1,000 to 2,499 Population Libraries

Category	Title	Measure	This library	95th %ile	75th %ile	50th %ile	25th %ile	5th %ile
a) Staff	Master-degreed librarian	Per 1000 pop.		0.36	-	-	-	-
	Nondegreed professional	Per 1000 pop.		1.04	0.60	0.43	0.30	0.09
	Other staff	Per 1000 pop.		0.92	0.30	0.06	-	-
	Total staff	Per 1000 pop.		1.57	0.89	0.58	0.39	0.18
b) Revenue	Local govt.	Per capita		$45.35	$23.06	$15.11	$8.06	$1.64
	State govt.	Per capita		$5.63	$1.52	$0.82	$0.08	$0.00
	Federal govt.	Per capita		$2.30	$0.00	$0.00	$0.00	$0.00
	Other income	Per capita		$24.61	$6.44	$2.27	$0.63	$0.00
	Total income	Per capita		$65.70	$32.29	$21.13	$13.60	$5.45
c) Expend.	Salaries	Per capita		$66.90	$29.92	$21.84	$16.13	$7.89
	Benefits	Per capita		$17.31	$5.69	$2.75	$1.37	$0.00
	Personnel costs	Per capita		$79.05	$35.15	$25.04	$18.04	$8.67
	Materials collection	Per capita		$11.08	$5.76	$3.75	$2.09	$0.65
	Other operating	Per capita		$35.24	$17.47	$9.82	$5.73	$2.03
	Total expenditure			$58.40	$30.05	$19.70	$12.61	$5.12

Category	Title	Measure	This library	95th %ile	75th %ile	50th %ile	25th %ile	5th %ile
	Capital expenditure	Per capita		$16.36	$1.73	$0.00	$0.00	$0.00
d) Materials	Book volumes	Per capita		15.4	9.9	7.3	5.2	3.2
	Audio	Per 1000 pop.		469.0	202.2	105.1	45.1	1.6
	Video	Per 1000 pop.		680.2	340.9	203.0	84.4	5.4
	Subscriptions	Per 1000 pop.		50.4	31.4	19.1	9.7	0.4
e) Hours	Total hours	All		2,368	1,800	1,352	1,040	572
	Hours open	Per bldg., per wk.		45	34	26	20	11
f) Outputs	Visits	Per capita		12.1	6.3	4.0	2.4	0.8
	Reference	Per capita		2.7	1.0	0.5	0.2	0.0
	Total circulation	Per capita		20.0	10.4	6.6	3.8	1.2
	Interlibrary loan IN	Per 1000 pop.		490.3	70.5	11.8	-	-
	Interlibrary loan OUT	Per 1000 pop.		682.9	182.1	68.2	17.5	-
	Children's circulation	Per capita		8.1	4.1	2.3	1.3	0.4
	Children's prog. attend	Per 1000 pop.		1,199.3	434.1	190.1	67.2	4.3
	Electronic materials expend.	Per capita		$0.42	$0.01	$0.00	$0.00	$0.00
	Electronic access items	Per capita		$4.69	$0.67	$0.12	$0.00	$0.00
	Electronic materials	Per 1000 pop.		45.1	16.3	5.4	-	-
	Collection turnover			2.3	1.3	0.9	0.6	0.2
	Circulation per FTE staff hr.			13.2	7.6	5.2	3.5	1.5
	Reference per capita	Per capita		2.7	1.0	0.5	0.2	0.0
	Circulation per hour	Per hour		21.1	11.9	7.9	5.0	2.1
	Visits per hour	Per hour		12.1	7.2	4.8	3.2	1.4
	Annual electronic access	Per capita		3.5	1.3	0.7	0.3	-
	Circulation per visit	Per visit		4.4	2.1	1.6	1.1	0.7

319

- There are 1,587 libraries in this population category.

- See Chapter 5 for information on how to use the data presented here. The data here are from 2001 annual reports filed with the FSCS in 2002.

- It is *critical* to note that the population used for this table is the "Legal Service Area" population assigned by the state library agency and the Federal State Cooperative Service, not the census population of the community in which the library is located. For consistency when using this table, use the Legal Service Area population for your library. To get your library's Legal Service Area contact your state library agency, or visit one of the two Web sites below:

http://nces.ed.gov/surveys/libraries/publicpeer

www.haplr-index.com/AverageStatewideScores.html

Figure 11 Percentile Details for Under-1,000 Population Libraries

Category	Title	Measure	This library	95th %ile	75th %ile	50th %ile	25th %ile	5th %ile
a) Staff	Master-degreed librarian	Per 1000 pop.		0.36	-	-	-	-
	Nondegreed professional	Per 1000 pop.		1.04	0.60	0.43	0.30	0.09
	Other staff	Per 1000 pop.		0.92	0.30	0.06	-	-
	Total staff	Per 1000 pop.		1.57	0.89	0.58	0.39	0.18
b) Revenue	Local govt.	Per capita		$45.35	$23.06	$15.11	$8.06	$1.64
	State govt.	Per capita		$5.63	$1.52	$0.82	$0.08	$0.00
	Federal govt.	Per capita		$2.30	$0.00	$0.00	$0.00	$0.00
	Other income	Per capita		$24.61	$6.44	$2.27	$0.63	$0.00
	Total income	Per capita		$65.70	$32.29	$21.13	$13.60	$5.45
c) Expend.	Salaries	Per capita		$66.90	$29.92	$21.84	$16.13	$7.89
	Benefits	Per capita		$17.31	$5.69	$2.75	$1.37	$0.00
	Personnel costs	Per capita		$79.05	$35.15	$25.04	$18.04	$8.67
	Materials collection	Per capita		$11.08	$5.76	$3.75	$2.09	$0.65
	Other operating	Per capita		$35.24	$17.47	$9.82	$5.73	$2.03
	Total expenditure			$58.40	$30.05	$19.70	$12.61	$5.12

Category	Title	Measure	This library	95th %ile	75th %ile	50th %ile	25th %ile	5th %ile
	Capital expenditure	Per capita		$16.36	$1.73	$0.00	$0.00	$0.00
d) Materials	Book volumes	Per capita		15.4	9.9	7.3	5.2	3.2
	Audio	Per 1000 pop.		469.0	202.2	105.1	45.1	1.6
	Video	Per 1000 pop.		680.2	340.9	203.0	84.4	5.4
	Subscriptions	Per 1000 pop.		50.4	31.4	19.1	9.7	0.4
e) Hours	Total hours	All		2,368	1,800	1,352	1,040	572
	Hours open	Per bldg., per wk.		45	34	26	20	11
f) Outputs	Visits	Per capita		12.1	6.3	4.0	2.4	0.8
	Reference	Per capita		2.7	1.0	0.5	0.2	0.0
	Total circulation	Per capita		20.0	10.4	6.6	3.8	1.2
	Interlibrary loan IN	Per 1000 pop.		490.3	70.5	11.8	-	-
	Interlibrary loan OUT	Per 1000 pop.		682.9	182.1	68.2	17.5	-
	Children's circulation	Per capita		8.1	4.1	2.3	1.3	0.4
	Children's prog. attend.	Per 1000 pop.		1,199.3	434.1	190.1	67.2	4.3
	Electronic materials expend.	Per capita		$0.42	$0.01	$0.00	$0.00	$0.00
	Electronic access items	Per capita		$4.69	$0.67	$0.12	$0.00	$0.00
	Electronic materials	Per 1000 pop.		45.1	16.3	5.4	-	-
	Collection turnover			2.3	1.3	0.9	0.6	0.2
	Circulation per FTE staff hr.			13.2	7.6	5.2	3.5	1.5
	Reference per capita	Per capita		2.7	1.0	0.5	0.2	0.0
	Circulation per hour	Per hour		21.1	11.9	7.9	5.0	2.1
	Visits per hour	Per hour		12.1	7.2	4.8	3.2	1.4
	Annual electronic access	Per capita		3.5	1.3	0.7	0.3	-
	Circulation per visit	Per visit		4.4	2.1	1.6	1.1	0.7

- There are 958 libraries in this population category.

- See Chapter 5 for information on how to use the data presented here. The data here are from 2001 annual reports filed with the FSCS in 2002.

- It is *critical* to note that the population used for this table is the "Legal Service Area" population assigned by the state library agency and the Federal State Cooperative Service, not the census population of the community in which the library is located. For consistency when using this table, use the Legal Service Area population for your library. To get your library's Legal Service Area contact your state library agency, or visit one of the two Web sites below:

  http://nces.ed.gov/surveys/libraries/publicpeer

  www.haplr-index.com/AverageStatewideScores.html

Appendix 3
Sample Impact Fee Statement

Executive Summary and Fee Statement

In most states impact fees cannot be used to close existing deficits. The fees can only be used to maintain standards levels that are based on the effect of new residents. Anywhereville meets or exceeds all current state standards for library service, but new residents will strain that capacity.[1]

The assumptions used in this report lead to a recommended impact fee assessment of $526 per household.

This needs assessment addresses only the library and the needs associated with serving the area until 2015 based on the development pattern discussed in the next section. If development occurs that is not currently anticipated, this needs assessment should be revised. One city-wide fee was calculated because one library serves the entire city. The planners projected residential development through the year 2015 with assistance from the city and preliminary plat maps and descriptions of proposed development in the area. Development outside the city limits but within the library's service territory is not considered in this report because the city does not have the ability to impose impact fees outside its boundaries.

We estimated a city population for 2015 using the regional average of 2.88 persons per housing unit. Due to the high use of the library by noncity residents, a "nonresident population" was established using current circulation information. The facility needed to serve the total resident and nonresident population was determined. We estimated costs with the assistance of the director of the library. The costs were apportioned and the city impact fee calculated. The fees were established based on 2002 expenses, budgets, and cost estimates. In order to keep pace with inflation, the fees will need to be adjusted on a yearly basis, using an appropriate cost index.

Chapter 1—Introduction—Impact Fee

COMMUNITY PROFILE

The City of Anywhereville is located in southeastern Somewhere County. The city was incorporated in 1905. The city itself had a population of approximately 6,162. [*Continue your community profile here with demographic and historic information appropriate to a summary. The profile should average about one to two pages.*]

LIBRARY PROFILE

The library is a member of the Somewhere County Federated Library System and serves not only the residents of the city but also residents in the surrounding area. Anywhereville is a city of approximately 5,800 people with a library service area of 17,500. The immediate area that the library serves includes the Town of Anywhereville, and parts of the Towns of Alpha, Beta, and Gamma. The library is also available to all residents of Nearby and Veryclose Counties. It provides substantial services to the Towns of Omega and Epsilon in Nearby County. The original library was located in one of the city churches and then moved to one room of what is now the fire station. In 1957, it became the F. & J. Carnegie Public Library when the family donated a former two-story residence (less than 2,000 sq. ft.) for that purpose. Before the most recent expansion in 1996, a needs assessment survey indicated that the library needed to consist of 24,000 sq. ft., but the city board cut the size to 12,200 because of a lack of funds. In April of 1996, the library moved into its present facility of 12,200 sq. ft. The library meets the standards for its population at present.

SCOPE

Historically, the city has not levied an impact fee on new development; therefore, presently the City does not have a method of financing costs associated with the library expansion needed to serve the growing population. Libraries in areas where other impact fees exist will, of course, want to change this statement. This report and needs assessment was prepared by the Somewhere County Federated Library System to assist the city in developing a library impact fee ordinance that conforms to the requirements of Chapter 66.55 of the State Statutes. Substantial development is anticipated in the city, and the cost of expanding the library to adequately serve the new development will exceed the ability of current residents to pay for this service.

RELATED REPORTS

Several documents were utilized in the preparation of this report; these include Library 2004 Annual Report, *State Library Building Project Handbook* by the Wisconsin Department of Public Instruction, *State Public Library Standards (2003)*, and *Library Space Needs A Planning Outline* by State Library Agency.

Chapter 2—Community Growth

RECENT HISTORY

From 1990 to 2000, the population within the city increased by 26.4 percent. Building permits added 35 to 100 new households each year. The recent annexations and expansion of sewer water lines to the new subdivisions in the area are likely to increase that rate of growth. Planners assume a growth rate of at least 90 households per year through 2015.

DEVELOPMENT

Commercial development as planned plats indicated below will not affect population calculations.

PRELIMINARY PLAT BREAKDOWNS

[*Include the plat table indicating projected developments. This is usually available from the local planning and zoning agency. Contact them directly.*]

RESIDENTIAL EQUIVALENT UNITS

Impact fees are not assessed on a per person basis, so the population was converted to residential equivalent units (REUs) by dividing the population by the regional average of 2.88 persons per housing unit. One housing unit is equal to one REU; therefore, the 637 additional units platted calculated to an additional population of 1,835, giving a projected population of 2,935 + 1,835 4,770. This growth is realistic compared to the growth in the last few years. [*Fill in your locally appropriate numbers here*].

CITY POPULATION PROJECTIONS

The Regional Planning Commission projects the 2020 population for the South Central Area at 38,300 for the intermediated growth rate. For purposes of this report, it is assumed that about 7,000 of those residents would be in the service territories of either the Big Bear or Somewhere Libraries and that the remaining 25,000 would be in the Anywhereville Community Library service area.

[*Place a local population projection table here. This should be available from either your local planning agency, regional development commission or the state population planning agency.*]

There are a large number of noncity residents that use the library, so an estimate of the nonresidents population must be made to adequately size the library and its collection. The table below shows current circulation information.

CIRCULATION

[*Include locally appropriate library circulation numbers in this section.*]

Circulation data was used to estimate the nonresident population using the basic assumptions that on average the proportion of circulation to population is the same for residents and nonresidents and that the proportion of residents to nonresidents will remain the same.

Using the first assumption, the 2002 resident circulation was 18,897 for a population of 2,935 persons, a ratio of approximately 6.4, therefore with a nonresident circulation of 26,257, the nonresident population is estimated to have been 4,078 in 2000. Using the second assumption, if the 2005 resident population is estimated to be 4,770 and 58 percent of the circulation goes to nonresidents, then the nonresident population is estimated to be 6,628.

Therefore, the current design population is 2,935 + 4,078 or 7,013 persons. This is the number that must be used when evaluating current deficiencies. The design population for the year 2005 is 4,770 + 6,628 = 11,398. This number should be used when determining necessary improvements.

[Put current local circulation table here]

Chapter 3—Library Background

LIBRARY BUILDING NARRATIVE

[The narrative provided is intended to be illustrative only. Your library's narrative will vary.]

The original spaciousness of the library has gradually disappeared as more materials have been added to the library collection. The limit may have been reached. Books fill all of the shelves, and some books that the librarians would rather have kept had to be discarded to make space. No room is available for proper display of the video or audiocassettes.

There is a definite lack of study rooms, which are often requested by library patrons. Not only is meeting room space limited to twenty-six chairs, but also many groups who want to use it are turned away because it is heavily booked. Storage space is very limited.

County (or State, if applicable) minimum standards and the more expansive State materials standards indicate that the collection needs to grow to accommodate an expanding population of users, but there is no shelf space.

SEATING

[*Note that numbers in this section are left blank, to be filled in locally. Statements are simply samples; tailor to your own circumstances.*]

____tables have been reduced to ___ and ___ study chairs have dropped to ___. There are ___ lounge chairs and a round table for newspapers.

STAFF SPACE

Staff space is at bare minimum. A _____ foot area includes the director's office, the desk of the children's librarian, the cataloging and processing areas, and the staff/work table. Staff work area is very congested. Shelves have gotten to the point of overflow, so the staff has put many items in storage and sold many others. There are ____ staff members all trying to share the same work area. The present circulation desk is ___ square feet and is inadequate to function efficiently.

REFERENCE

The reference collection is housed on ___ linear feet of eight-foot-high shelving. Every shelf is used and filled to capacity. The reference area lacks sufficient seating and computer workstation access for any patrons using that section.

CHILDREN'S DEPARTMENT

The children's department is next to the circulation desk without any visual or sound barriers. When classes from school come to work at the library, the area is overcrowded and becomes too noisy for other library users.

JUVENILE

The young adult books are in a corner of the children's space. The collection is housed on ___ linear feet of shelf space in one bookcase at the end of a row of juvenile books. Young adult paperbacks are placed along the tops of the low juvenile shelving.

ADULT FICTION

The entire collection is housed on ___ linear feet of shelving. Every shelf, including top and bottom are used, and books are lined up on top of the seven-foot shelves. Current fiction is on low shelves below the level of convenient inspection for adults. Adult paperbacks are shelved on ___ linear feet of eight-foot-high wall shelving.

ADULT NONFICTION

The nonfiction collection takes up ___ linear feet of shelving. Over-sized books are on ___ linear feet of shelving.

PERIODICALS

The library has ___ current magazines and ___ newspapers. The magazines are on eight-foot-high periodical shelving.

VIDEO MATERIAL

There is limited space for popular AV materials, many of which are in storage.

BUDGET

Items that will be affected by growth include expenses such as library maintenance, supplies, postage, children's programming, telephone expenses, equipment repair, and material costs for periodicals, adult materials, and children's materials.

NEEDS ASSESSMENT

There are design standards recommended by the State Library Agency regarding collection size and space needed for libraries. The appendix contains the standards and a calculation for the existing and future population needs. Table ____ is a summary of the space needs at present and in 2012.

IMPACT FEE CALCULATION

The future gross area needed was calculated based on the projected population of 25,000, which includes the total resident and nonresident users. The space included in the cost estimates for the impact fee was calculated by taking the space needed in 2012 and subtracting the existing (2000) space and (2000) deficiencies. The impact fee was calculated by dividing the total project cost by the number of applicable REUs for the city.

The library fee was determined to be $526 per Residential unit. [Note that impact fees are frequently scaled by the type of unit more for single family homes on large lots, less for condominium units, still less for apartments of various sizes.] This sample plan includes just one impact per residential unit, but gradations are frequently more appropriate.

State statutes specifically prohibit application of the impact fee to eliminate existing deficiencies. *[Assure that this point is true in your state and cite the specific statute if possible.]* For that reason, the space needed to serve the existing population was determined. Table___ is a summary of the calculations for needed space. The size of the collection needed to serve the population was calculated and used to determine the needed space. The cost of increasing the collection size and items the library will need to properly serve the additional population is included below and was compiled with the assistance of the library director.

Calculation for Additional Building and Equipment Costs for Impact Fee

The most recent state survey found that for libraries in the 10,000 to 25,000 population range the average square footage was 0.92. This included quite a few inadequately sized facilities, of course, so a range of 1 to 1.5 square feet per capita is realistic. *[Use appropriate state data for your state. This information should be available by population size from your state library agency.*]

Using the building specifications in the appendix, we calculated that 40,208 square feet are needed for an extended service population of 25,000. That is about 1.6 square feet per capita. Some of the space needed is fixed and not population sensitive, such as administrative and mechanical space. This needs assessment determined that a figure of 1.2 square feet per capita was appropriate for impact fee calculation. Assuming 2.88 residents per home, each household will add 3.45 square feet to the needed facility. Current construction costs would indicate between $100 and $150 for library building and equipment costs.

Building costs for Impact Fee: $150 per square foot.

Materials costs for Impact Fee: $25 per item.

PUBLIC LIBRARY STANDARDS COMPARED TO ANYWHEREVILLE ACTUAL TECHNOLOGY STANDARD

Some assume that electronic resources and the Internet are reducing the space requirements in libraries, but the opposite is true. Computer workstations take up more cubic feet of space than books and magazines by far. The library is studying its use of electronic resources and data from this report are expected to help in planning efforts. In addition to the numerical items below, the state recommends a minimum for computer workstations at one for each thirty-five visitors per day. At the current rate of 412 visits, the library requires at least thirteen public access computer workstations exactly the number now available. Planning for expansion and peak loads should add at least another fifteen workstations. That in turn would require another 1,500 or so square feet of floor space.

NUMERICAL STANDARDS COMPARISON

Calculations are provided here based on State library standards for service area population and then assuming two different populations for Anywhereville 25,000 and 16,000.

Current state library projections put the service population at about 16,000 today. For building and long range planning purposes, it is important to consider the impacts of population growth.

A population served of closer to 25,000 is likely in the next twenty years. The dramatic difference in the size of the facilities, collection, and staff depending on the population size serves to amply demonstrate the impact of development on the library service pattern.

[Place chart of library comparison to state standards here.]

Statutory References—Impact fees

[Reprint the state's impact fee statute here or at least provide statutory references.]

Model Impact Fee Ordinance

WHEREAS the City Board of the City of Anywhereville imposes impact fees in accordance with State Stat. /_____ pursuant to Anywhereville Municipal Code /____; and

WHEREAS a separate impact fund for public library improvements exists pursuant to Anywhereville Municipal Code /____(6) which consists of impact fees collected by the City for the purpose of paying the capital costs of public library improvements; and

WHEREAS Anywhereville Municipal Code /____ authorizes the use of monies collected per its terms for capital costs for new, expanded or improved public facilities which are related to the effects of general population growth in the City of Anywhereville; and

WHEREAS the City of Anywhereville has experienced such population growth within its system and has made necessary improvements to the City's public library system pursuant to Exhibit A, attached hereto and made a part hereof by reference, in conformance with the Public Facilities Needs Assessment; and

WHEREAS the capital costs for the expenditures shown on said exhibit were paid by the City of Anywhereville Public Library System from various accounts as listed in said Exhibit A, and properly consist of public library system improvements capital costs:

NOW, THEREFORE, BE IT RESOLVED by the City Board of the City of Anywhereville, that, pursuant to the above, $_____ shall be transferred from the City of Anywhereville Public Library Improvements Impact Fee Fund to the City of Anywhereville Public Library System Operating Account and $_____ shall be transferred from the City of Anywhereville Public Library Improvements Impact Fee Fund to the City of Anywhereville Public Library System Fundraising Account to reimburse the library system for the capital costs for public library improvements expended through _____, having made the findings as follows:

These expenditures for these items bear a rational relationship to the need for new, expanded or improved public library facilities created by land development within the City of Anywhereville and the attendant population growth; and

The costs of these capital improvements do not exceed the proportionate share of the capital costs to serve land development compared to existing uses of land within the City; and these costs are actual and not estimated capital cost items; and

There are no special charges or offsets against these expenditures, and there are no federal or state contributions of any nature toward the acquisition of these capital assets; and

These capital costs were not incurred for the purpose of addressing existing deficiencies; and the City finds that it is in the best interest of the public library system of the City of Anywhereville to reimburse the public library system accounts for these capital costs.

Note

1. In most cases impact fees cover only the capital costs of a library rather than the ongoing operating costs. Note, however, that usually for purposes of impact fee calculations and distributions, books and tangible library materials are considered to be capital assets. Note also that new audit and accounting standards in GASB 34 indicate that library books should be counted as capital assets in this context.

St. Joseph County Public Library Long-Range Plan

A Vision for the Beginnings of a New Century
2000–2004

> South Bend, Indiana
> Approved by the St. Joseph County Public Library Board
> December 13, 1999

- *Bruce Bancroft*, Attorney, Barnes and Thornburg

- *Pete Mullen*, owner of Eckler-Lahey Lumber Co. and President of St. Joseph County Chamber of Commerce

- *Charlotte Pfeifer*, Common Council Member, South Bend, 2nd District, and Professor at IUSB

- *Ernestine Raclin*, former Chairman of the Board, 1st Source Bank and Chairperson of numerous community committees and task forces

- *Rick Rice*, President, Teachers' Credit Union, and resident of Mishawaka, IN

- *Todd Schurz*, Editor and Publisher, *The South Bend Tribune*

Representing Friends of the St. Joseph County Public Library Board

- *Dr. Mark Green*, Dentist in South Bend and Member of SJCPL Friends Board

- *Tony Luber*, Attorney, Public Defender; Vice Pres. of SJCPL Friends board; and member of the library board, SJCPL

- *Christine Pochert*, Educator and Public Relations Administrator, South Bend Community School Corporation

Representing the library board:

- *Julie Annis*, Educator, Union North United School Corporation, and President of the library board (ex officio member of the Long Range Planning Task Force)

- *Dr. Robert M. Sweeney*, Pediatrician, President of the SJCPL board and Member of the library board, SJCPL

- *Christyne M. Woolridge*, Educator, South Bend Community School Corporation, and Secretary of the library board, SJCPL

Representing the library staff:

- *Becky Bahu*, Coordinator of Extension Services (Branches and Special Services)

- *Linda Broyles*, Coordinator of Networking Services

- *Paula Dale*, Branch Librarian, Western Branch

- *Shirley Eger*, Head Clerical, Francis Branch

- *Debra Futa*, Assistant Director, Administration

- *Julia Hill,* Reference Librarian, Main Information and Reference Services

- *Nancy Korpal,* Coordinator of Main Library Public Services

- *Don Napoli,* Director, Administration

Other staff members were very much involved in this planning process. Those who did substantial work in developing the plan included:

For Community Data and Demographic Research:

- *Joyce Hug,* Web Developer Specialist, Networking Resources and Training Services, SJCPL

For the Oakwood Two-Day Planning Retreat (October 21—22, 1999):

The following staff participated in a two-day planning retreat at the Oakwood Inn, Syracuse, Indiana, with the task force members representing the staff (listed above) and facilitator Sharon Wiseman. The aim of this retreat was to work out the goals, measurable objectives, and practical strategies for the library's vision and mission statements that were developed by the task force. These goals, objectives, and strategies constitute a major portion of the new long range plan. These staff members included:

- *Linda Conyers,* Area Branch Librarian, Francis Branch

- *Carole Fowler,* Head Clerical, Centre Township Branch

- *Dave Haslett,* Head of Automated Services

- *Shirleen Martens,* Financial Services Administrator

- *Connie Nicely,* Personnel Services Administrator

- *Joe Sipocz,* Head of Adult Reference and Information Services, Main Library

- *Ralph Takach,* Facilities Manager, SJCPL

The next section of this document will describe what we developed and are proposing to the library board and staff as a working vision and mission statement toward which the library plans to commit its present and future resources and our best energies over the next five years. Your feedback is critical as we try to complete the first full cycle of a continuous long-range planning process. We hope to have your support and approval at the December 13, 1999 library board meeting.

A Vision Statement For the South Bend Community

"Vision comes from the heart, not the head. Our purpose in creating the vision is to clarify what we wish to create, knowing all along that we may never get there."

Peter Block

The SJCPL Long-Range Planning Task Force 2000 needed to identify what kind of future the residents of our community would want and how the library might focus its finite resources on what is most important to these residents. As defined by the planning manual, a vision statement should contain declarations that describe an ideal future. It should consist of six (6) to eight (8) declarative sentences that embody the dreams that the members of the task force, as representatives of all the people of the community, have for the place that they, their children, and the residents of the entire community will inhabit in the future.

Borrowing directly from the PLA *Planning for Results* manual, we have tried to include answers to the following questions in each of the following declarations:

- Who will benefit if the ideal state is achieved?

- What benefit they will receive?

- What will result from the benefit?

All the members of the Long-Range Planning Task Force have agreed to the following "Community Vision Statement":

By achieving the following ideals, the South Bend area will ensure a high quality of life in our community. We seek to achieve these ideals through the following community goals:

Statement #1:

"All residents, at various economic levels, will be able to find a variety of adequate housing that is affordable and will be financially able to own their own homes, if they so desire."

Statement #2:

"Amid continuing cultural and multigenerational diversity, all residents will celebrate each others' differences, eliminating racial prejudice, discord, and violence."

Statement #3:

"Equal employment opportunities will be plentiful and will be accessible at all levels."

Statement #4:

"All residents will share or appreciate strong values and virtues such as mutual respect, fairness, honesty, responsibility, dependability, empathy, compassion, and no resident will be homeless and/or not feel valued."

Statement #5:

"All residents at various economic levels and all businesses will be able to access and compete effectively in the global economy through the Internet and telecommunications and will be financially solvent and prosperous."

Statement #6:

"All residents, at various economic levels, will have access to high quality educational services that are affordable and that will prepare themselves and their children for jobs and career opportunities that meet their future needs."

Statement #7:

"All residents, at various economic levels, will be able to find diverse family cultural activities that meet their needs and expand their knowledge and appreciation of others."

Statement #8:

"All residents, at various economic levels, will be able to find affordable health care that meets their health needs."

The Five Critical Community Needs or Obstacles to the Community Vision Identified by the Task Force

What did the task force identify as the community's most critical needs?

While creating the community vision statement, the task force identified the following community needs:

- Improve K–12 education results.

- Improve transportation at all levels, including local and regional.

- Improve intergovernmental cooperation.

- Change parochial thinking (i.e., white/black tensions, relationships between county/city government, ethnic groups, religions, schools, and police).

- Prepare for global electronic communications.

How can the library, with its resources, meet these community needs to help reach the community's vision?

The task force focused on areas of these community needs that could best be incorporated into a library vision statement. The library's vision statement also had to be compatible with the community's vision statement and the community needs identified by the task force. *Key concepts discussed by the task force included the following:*

340

Education

Education was an issue with the task force. The library supports formal education as well as readiness for formal education. This includes getting the youngest children ready to go to school as well as helping people to continue their education after they finish formal schooling. The real key is lifelong learning and this was an area in which the task force believed very strongly that the library had a definite role. Education breaks down many of the barriers we face as a community.

Partnerships

While partnerships are not a goal in and of themselves, they help us accomplish our goals and are becoming more and more a part of everything we do. While many of our partnerships in the past have had more of a direct benefit on the partnering agency, we may begin to look for equality in our partnerships. The time may come when we seek corporate funding for projects that benefit the community at large (this can help change parochial thinking and improve government communication).

Global Information Access

The library has a large role in direct response to this community need. Even though the manner in which we access information continues to change, we are still the broker or navigator of information needed by the community. Sorting and deciphering information is critical. "Push technology," which would create individualized profiles of what people want to read and what kinds of information they need may be in our future.

The Library as a Gathering Place

Libraries can be destinations in themselves. This concept includes programming, public meetings, and remaking our libraries into "fun" places (an essential concept that went into the building program of the Centre Township Branch). Even though futurists predict people will be afraid to leave their houses and will seek information as well as goods and services through their home computers, there is still the need to interact with other people. Libraries can fill a part of that need.

Training

People need to acquire information literacy in order to access the information in our society. Training in how to use our resources will be important, especially in a rapidly changing technological environment.

Marketing

To use Peter Drucker's words: "Marketing is so basic that it cannot be considered a separate function. It is the whole business seen from the point of view of its final result, that is, from the customer's point of view." Using this definition, everything a patron sees, smells, hears, or touches in a library is marketing. Marketing then becomes a part of every facility, every service, and every employee's job. Over the next five years, the library will make more concentrated efforts to improve our products and services to better meet our customers' needs. We will also pursue increased promotion of library services.

SJCPL's Vision Statement

As the result of the discussions about these key concepts, the task force created the following overall "working" vision statement:

"To be recognized as the best public library, meeting and anticipating the needs and wants of our community."

What makes a library great? Over time, that question has had a variety of answers for libraries. A hundred years ago, it might have been answered by how many works of great literature a library held. Today, our definition of a great library comes through a combination of people, materials, setting, and technology all operating at peak quality.

For SJCPL to be the best it can be for our community, there will need to be a strong combination of high technology and high touch. All of the elements contained in our service responses will flow into a seamless blend of knowledge, courtesy, and friendliness, which will not just meet, but will exceed our customers' expectations. In beginning to redefine library services for the next five years, we'll be working toward the kind of quality that transcends traditional library stereotypes and creates a new image of fully integrated services that go the extra mile and ensure that customers keep coming back. Such integration involves everything we do: from creating imaginative and useful physical spaces to inspiring the smile on the face of the three-year-old with his first library card; from providing whatever the latest technology might be to providing a friendly front desk clerk who understands that people may be intimidated by that very technology; from acquiring the newest bestsellers to employing a dedicated branch staff willing to stay past closing because someone needs to finish a report. These are the images of our future.

In helping inspire dreams, our dream must be that we don't just have a building with books and computers inside. We must create experiences for first time users to make them lifelong users.

"You're going to want a library card when you see what we have!" seemed to be another statement that summed it all up for us.

SJCPL's Mission Statement

From this vision, the task force identified *four major areas* where the library could effectively *respond* to the identified needs of the community and concentrate its energies and resources. The following four statements represent *service responses* that comprise the *Mission Statement* of the St. Joseph County Public Library for the years 2000 through 2004:

I.   INFORMATION LITERACY

"We provide expert training and instruction so that you can use the latest technology to find what you need."

2.   CURRENT TOPICS AND TITLES AND LIFELONG LEARNING

"We provide easy access to the most wanted and needed library materials of all types so you can reach your goals and satisfy your whims."

3.   COMMONS

"We provide a community gathering place to learn, to meet neighbors, to make new friends, and to have fun."

4.   GENERAL INFORMATION

"Whatever information you want, wherever it is, SJCPL, the best public library anywhere, will find it."

From these four service responses, the task force members representing the staff, along with seven other representatives of the staff, went on a two-day retreat to work out the goals and objectives for each of these four service responses. After some discussion of possible strategies under each service response, the staff felt that some of the service responses could easily be combined since they tended to generate the same types of objectives and strategies. The result was to combine the four service responses into three service responses, in the following way:

- Information literacy with information access

- Current topics and titles with lifelong learning

- Commons

SJCPL's Service Response Information Literacy and Information Access

In order for our community to thrive in a future where information is accessed in many ways and technology is increasingly prominent, Information Literacy and Information Access is one of our service responses. This response addresses the need for training and instruction in skills related to locating, evaluating, and using information effectively. Teaching the public to find and evaluate information will be stressed, and we will provide state-of-the-art access to information resources.

Goal I

SJCPL will provide state-of-the-art access to a variety of information resources to meet community needs.

Objective Ia

SJCPL will keep abreast of constantly changing technology by allocating 1 percent of the personnel budget to ongoing staff development.

Sample activity: Mandated debriefing sessions after every major conference (e.g. ALA, PLA), open to all staff.

Objective Ib

By December 2002, SJCPL will provide a range of resources that effectively cover the information needs of the community, and provide state-of-the-art access to these resources.

Sample activity: Establish standing committee to assess current resources and research new ones.

Sample activity: Continue to upgrade one-third of our computer equipment per year.

Objective Ic

By December 2003, patron surveys (via kiosk, oral interviews, focus groups, etc.) will reflect a 90 percent satisfaction rate with our information resources.

Sample activity: Establish base rate of satisfaction during 2000.

Goal II

We will have an information-literate community whose members are skilled in locating, evaluating, and using information effectively.

Objective IIa

By December 2002, no one will be turned away from information literacy training sessions, and the overall program will be comprehensive.

Sample activity: The staff providing information literacy training will include all public service professionals and paraprofessionals.

Objective IIb

By December 2002, SJCPL will develop measures to evaluate and improve patron searching effectiveness.

Sample activity: Contact SLIS at Indiana University for strategies.

Sample activity: Evaluate public catalog search reports and add cross references to increase searching effectiveness.

Objective IIc

By December 2003, the community will know that SJCPL is the place to go for excellent training and instruction in locating, evaluating, and using information effectively.

Sample activity: Have IUSB do an independent survey of users, nonusers, and businesses by Fall of 2000, to establish baseline statistics for "name recognition."

GOAL III

Skilled staff will provide accurate and reliable information and reference service, and public training in the use of information resources.

Objective IIIa

SJCPL will develop a customer service staff orientation/training profile and plan, to be approved by the library board in December 2000 and implemented in 2001–2004.

Sample activity: Mandate regularly scheduled ongoing customer service orientation and training sessions for all staff.

Objective IIIb

SJCPL will develop a staff technology assessment/training profile and plan, to be approved by the library board in December 2000 and implemented in 2001–2004.

Sample activity: Mandate regularly scheduled ongoing technology training and skills assessment for all staff.

SJCPL's Service Response Current Topics and Titles and Lifelong Learning

The Current Topics and Titles service response will help fulfill the community residents' appetite for information about popular culture and social trends and their desire for satisfying recreational experiences.

The Lifelong Learning service response helps address the desire for self-directed personal growth and development opportunities for all community residents. While Lifelong Learning applies to people of all ages, special efforts will be made to encourage specific groups to use library resources to support their formal and informal learning.

GOAL I

The library is a resource that supports the educational/learning efforts of all community members to stimulate their interests, to explore imaginative possibilities, and to pursue their dreams.

Objective Ia

By 2004 the library will serve ____ percent of the population in defined groups, measured by the number of card holders and program attendance.

Sample activity: Determine current library demographics by defined groups. Compare total demographics in age groups in our service area. Consider where the gaps may be. Explore the possibility of using census data to ensure the library is reaching a diverse population.

Objective Ib

User satisfaction by predefined group will increase to 90% by 2004.

Sample activity: We will examine usage statistics and conduct annual focus groups from all predetermined groups, or target one group per year throughout this planning cycle, to determine user satisfaction with library services, collections, and programs.

GOAL II

Community members will have easy access to information in a variety of formats that will enlighten and inform them about current issues and topics and popular culture.

Objective IIa

Patron waiting time (for information, materials, checkout) will be reduced by ____ percent by 2004.

Sample activities: Determine current waiting times as a baseline measurement. Streamline checkout process.

Objective IIb

Increase usage of the SJCPL Hotlist by ___ hits per month by 200___.

Sample activities: Actively promote Hotlist to all users. Establish a "What's New and Current" spot on our Web site.

Objective IIc

Increase circulation of new material by 1 percent each year by 2004.

Sample activities: Determine baseline circulation of new material during 2000. Conduct monthly Readers Advisory staff meetings. Promote NoveList use. Displays will reflect hot/current topics. Develop an Intranet "Current Topics" hotline.

SJCPL's Service Response—Commons

A library that provides a *commons* environment helps address the need of people to meet and interact with others in their community. This includes community participation or attendance at library programs and events, use of meeting rooms by community groups, and the use of the library as a gathering place for enjoyment or fun. We believe that providing a commons environment also includes offering a variety of spaces such as caf s, hands-on children's activity spaces, presentation spaces, videoconferencing or teleconferencing capabilities, and warm and inviting spaces for conversation and discussion.

GOAL I

SJCPL will become a safe community destination to learn, to exchange information, to meet neighbors, to make new friends, and to have fun.

Objective Ia

_____ percent of people using the library will indicate via survey or interview that they use the library as a destination.

Sample activity: Evaluate library surveys for results.

Objective Ib

100% of SJCPL staff will be trained in security and safety procedures within three months of employment.

Sample activity: Develop training program and schedule for training new staff.

Objective Ic

100 percent of SJCPL staff will receive at least one follow-up session per year on security or safety procedures.

Sample activity: Develop a range of programs dealing with security and safety issues and require attendance to at least one program per year.

GOAL II

SJCPL provides a variety of inviting and technologically equipped, accessible meeting room spaces so that community members have a place to gather.

Objective IIa

SJCPL will accept bookings from at least 90 percent of the groups requesting meetings.

Sample activity: Using statistics gathered from Objective Ia, evaluate the percentage of refusals and why groups have been turned down. Revise meeting room policy to provide more flexibility in the library's ability to accommodate groups.

Objective IIb

SJCPL will serve at least _____ people in our service area through their attendance at a public meeting or program.

Objective IIc

SJCPL will increase the number of meetings system-wide by _____ percent.

Sample activity: Promote meeting room space to the community. Develop promotional material to be used for a Chamber of Commerce distribution.

Objective IId

_____ percent of the people attending meetings will indicate that they were satisfied with the rooms and that the space met their needs.

Sample activity: Use comment cards to evaluate meeting rooms for attractiveness, flexibility and usefulness. Wire all meeting rooms to accommodate technology

Goal III

SJCPL provides diverse spaces to facilitate a variety of activities that meet the needs of our community.

Objective IIIa

Through observation conducted annually, SJCPL will determine what and how library spaces are being used.

Sample activity: Hire or train staff to use observation, which will be used to evaluate library facilities for ease of use, general attractiveness and accessibility.

Objective IIIb

Through staff journals and logs, SJCPL will track customer comments concerning library facilities.

Sample activity: Analyze logs for patterns which would aid in redesigning library spaces. Use data to make library spaces more attractive and functional.

Sample activities: Determine baseline circulation of new material during 2000. Displays will reflect hot/current topics.

Appendix 5

Brookfield Public Library Long-Range Plan

Brookfield Public Library Plan 2004–2006

Section 1: Executive Summary and Background

Acknowledgements
Executive Summary
Library Data for Southeastern Wisconsin Libraries of Comparable Size

Section 2: Planning Environment

Community Background
Library Strengths
Library Weaknesses
Challenges
Opportunities
Vision and Mission
Library Values
Public Library Service Roles
Stakeholders

Section 3: Goals and Objectives

Goal One: Administration
Goal Two: Personnel
Goal Three: Automated Services
Goal Four: Collection Development
Goal Five: Programs and Services

Section 4: Demographics, Statistics, Financial

Circulation
Waukesha County Library Standards

State Standards and Brookfield Actual Amounts
Current Budget, Capital Needs, and Multiyear Projections
Equalized Valuation Projections
Section 5: Appendix Materials
HALPR Rating for Brookfield Library

Section 1: Executive Summary & Background

ACKNOWLEDGEMENTS

Library Board

- *Richard Brandt*, Secretary, 185 N. Eastmoor Avenue, Brookfield, WI 53005

- *Ald. Kari A. Clappier*, 16745 Golf Parkway, Brookfield, WI 53005

- *Margaret Courtright*, 15540 Springwood Court, Brookfield, WI 53005

- *Thomas Fotsch*, Treasurer, 20985 Carrington Drive, Brookfield, WI 53045

- *John Grisa*, President, 3580 Chapel Road, Brookfield, WI 53045

- *Susan Hay*, Vice President, 14205 Lindsay Drive, Brookfield, WI 53005

- *Kay Benning*, 19770 Brian Drive, Brookfield, WI 53045

- Denise Hoffman, W230 S4361 Milky Way Road, Waukesha, WI 53189

- *Judy Hughes*, 15525 Apple Valley Court, Brookfield, WI 53005

- *Gordon Miller*, 17815 Colline Vue Court, Brookfield, WI 53045

- *Edell M. Schaefer*, Director

- *Thomas J. Hennen Jr.*, Waukesha County Federated Library System Director

EXECUTIVE SUMMARY

In January of 2003, the library board began meeting with Waukesha County Federated Library System Director Tom Hennen to develop a long-range plan.

The Brookfield Library is a well-supported facility that provides excellent service in a community that demands high standards. The challenge is to maintain that level of excellence even as the community changes and the technological environment changes as well.

The Brookfield Public Library provides excellent service and offers a wide array of materials, services and programs in a community that demands high quality. The challenge will be maintaining that level of excellence as technological advances and the needs of the community evolve.

"We plan to develop the Brookfield Public Library into the premier digital library in the region while continuing to serve the interests of our traditional print users," says board President John Grisa.

Key Objectives for the Plan Period

1. *Provide ease of access and convenience to the user.* Focus on new and innovative ways of serving library patrons, such as better use of the Internet and improved material pick-up and drop-off capabilities.

2. *Maintain collection, hours, and staffing at high current standards levels.* For summary comparison, see Section 4 of main report State Standards and Brookfield.

3. *Create a technology plan.* The board and administration plan to develop a multiyear technology plan by the year 2004. It will include directions for technology. The plan to will investigate the following issues:

a) Develop a plan for wireless capability in the library for library owned laptops, as well as publicly used laptops. Implement plan if appropriate.

b) Establish 24/7 e-mail reference services.

c) Build a computer-training lab using wireless technology.

d) Create a casual cyber cafe atmosphere in commons area with wireless computers for at least ten users.

e) Provide a high tech conference center for business in the meeting room.

f) Establish a media center that allows the public to use the Internet for services such as broadband downloads, printing, and scanning.

4. *Establish a foundation.* Establish Perform research on developing a Library Foundation that can raise funds for library special projects, and programs and materials.

5. *Allow fundraising on the Web.* Investigate feasibility of fundraising on the Web using e-commerce options such as those available from Amazon.com.

Scenarios

At the beginning of the planning process, board members were asked to describe the community context for the library. Board president John Grisa responded with this potential news article for the year 2014.

> Think Milwaukee. Harley-Davidson motorcycles...Miller Beer...the Marquette Golden Eagles. And now a suburb just west of Milwaukee has found its own distinguished place in the metro landscape by becoming the epicenter of digital resources for libraries.
>
> It all started in 2003 when the Brookfield Public Library embarked on a program to be a test bed of emerging digital

technologies. The idea attracted local youth, who began experimenting to improve the application of these technologies to libraries and its visitors.

Fast forward ten years. Those youth have turned their curiosities and passions into three new companies in Brookfield, transforming the local economy.

Trent Ryan was the first to cash in on the digital revolution launched at the library. His invention, the mp3 cell phone, allows book lovers to wirelessly download their favorite books into mobile devices so they can be enjoyed anywhere. Here's how Ryan saw it, "Everyone was getting a cell phone back then, so I thought why not use that technology as a means of getting books to people." The device allows users to log onto the Brookfield Library's Web site, download the text and audio versions of the book, and read or listen to it anytime they have a spare moment.

The young inventor has become one of the area's greatest philanthropists. Thanks in large part to his generosity, the city recently celebrated the opening of a 28,000 square foot addition to the library, which includes a 100-seat lecture amphitheatre and the new home of the Brookfield Young Entrepreneurs Club.

The addition also includes a bistro area for local residents to meet and to enjoy some of their favorite coffees in a relaxed atmosphere. It also features a new parking area configured to make access to the library easier and the drop-off of borrowed materials more convenient. What's Ryan's latest idea? "How about smart books?"

The young inventor dreamed out loud, "I envision books equipped with small chips that will remind library guests when their books are due. People are constantly losing their book receipts. This will replace them. They can be set to beep a day before the book is due. Or display the due date in a little window. And the beauty of this technology is that they can never be lost as they are imbedded on the inside flap."

John Smith, grandson of city councilman Jack Smith, is another youth who saw a new idea and took it to even greater heights. Inspired by the new software the library installed in 2003, he developed a new standard for shared automation library systems that has become the market leader worldwide.

Says Smith, "I took a good idea shared automation and made it better." The local library community seems to agree what began as a couple of libraries on a single system in 2003 has resulted in 100 percent participation by all libraries in the Waukesha Federated Library System.

Worth a reported two billion dollars, his local baseball team, the Milwaukee Brewers, has just won the World Series for the second straight year.

Finally, teenager Jane Pronto said she just wanted a better way of selecting movies to watch with her friends. "They say you shouldn't judge a book by its cover. Well, it's the same with movies. What we wanted was to look on the computer screen at a list of movies and click on the ones we're interested in and get a preview you know, the movie trailer.

I asked my Dad if he thought it was possible and he said, 'Ya.' I told my friends about it and they said 'Wo.' So we fiddled with a few things on our home PC and came up with a few ideas. I got a grant from that John Smith dude, and like *wow*, we developed this cool new module for the library system." That cool new module has now been installed in more than 1,000 libraries throughout the US.

What's next for the Brookfield Library? Board President Bob Garvens says the future is bright. "Our technology intern program is drawing in some of the brightest minds in the world. The annual Library Technology Conference we host each year has allowed us to showcase both our library, as well as the city worldwide. And the new ideas these kids are talking about at the Young Entrepreneur's Club would blow your mind. And to think it all started with adding a few digital resources at the library."

Key Conclusions about Brookfield Library:

1. *Excellence.* The library is well-run and serves its clientele very well. The HAPLR library ratings service (see Section 5) ranked Brookfield in the 94th percentile nationally of nearly 800 libraries in its population category for overall input and output measures. The library was at the 50th

percentile or higher on all fifteen measures and at the 75th percentile or better on nearly all measures.

2. *Shared automation.* The recent move to upgrade the automated service capability by working with Waukesha Public Library was bold and forward-looking. The move has put the library in a position to upgrade and enhance customer services very cost effectively. The challenge for the future will be to ensure that the developing consortium of many libraries in the county serves the needs of Brookfield residents.

3. *Balance books and bytes.* As important as the Internet and electronic data services are, the board and staff remain committed to serving the needs of print users. We will "balance the books and bytes" as we move forward.

4. *Policies are up to date.* The library board reviewed the policies and procedures manual of the library using the state recommended standards inventory and other sources. The policies and procedures are up to date and comprehensive and will be reviewed on a periodic basis. Nevertheless, the library will need to continue to watch policy developments regarding privacy of records, especially electronic records.

5. *Collection size is excellent.* State voluntary standards define four levels of standards: basic, moderate, enhanced, and excellent. The county standards are set at the *basic* or minimum level. Currently the library is at an enhanced or excellent level for most areas of the collection by comparison to library peers statewide. The goal is to get the collection size to stay at these exemplary standards level while aggressively weeding the collection for outdated items. For specific information, see the State Standards portion of Section 4, or the Collection Development goals in Section 3. Staff work to make the quality match the quantity.

6. *Building.* The current 50,000 square foot building built in 1990 serves the community well. Its parking is fully handicapped accessible, but further work may be necessary to make the computer workstations and the electronic

catalog accessible. While parking is limited and somewhat inconvenient at times, the facility It is well stocked and maintained. It has sufficient equipment for the present; the challenge for the future will be to maintain it while upgrading the technological infrastructure. During the plan period, the board and administration will be considering proposals to expand the electronic capabilities of the library both in the meeting room and the main portion of the library.

7. *Staffing.* The library exceeds standards for staffing at present levels. The HAPLR ratings information in Section 5, and the library data for Wisconsin libraries both demonstrate that the level of staffing has been translated into high levels of library use, services, and programs.

8. *Technology.* At present the library has an adequate number of computer workstations, but the workstations are in fixed positions. The installation of wireless capability in the building would add to the flexibility and utility of these stations, but add to the privacy and copyright issues to be addressed. One of the key objectives is to develop a technology plan.

9. *Marketing Plan.* Because of changes in the demographic nature of the community, as well as the rapidly changing technological environment, there is a major need for additional marketing and public relations work. The library needs to develop an ongoing marketing plan.

LIBRARY DATA FOR SOUTHEASTERN WISCONSIN LIBRARIES OF COMPARABLE SIZE

The data below indicate the averages for the twenty Wisconsin libraries of comparable size to Brookfield Public Library.

Comparing the Brookfield Public Library on a per capita basis to its nineteen peer libraries of comparable size, we can proudly say that the overall Library operates efficiently and effectively. The Brookfield Library circulation is 40 percent more than other communities the same size. While the library is well funded with an operating budget almost twice that of comparable communities, the effective mill rate for the library in Brookfield is 20 percent below that of comparable communities. A significant portion of the Brookfield Library's operating budget each year goes directly for new materials. The Library spends 85 percent more than comparable communities on materials to support the high level of circulation.

1. Expenditures on materials are 83 percent higher.

2. The building is 58 percent larger.

3. Users check out 40 percent more materials.

4. Nonresidents borrow 16 percent more materials.

5. User visits are 11 percent higher.

6. County revenues are 11 percent higher.

7. Cost per Full Time Equivalent Staff member is about the same.

8. The tax rate per $1,000 of taxable property (mill rate) is 20 percent lower.

Section 2: Planning Environment

COMMUNITY BACKGROUND

The Brookfield Public Library is a well-supported facility that provides excellent service and offers a wide array of materials, services and programs in a community that demands high standards and high quality. The challenge is to maintain that level of excellence even as the community evolves and the technological environment changes.

The City of Brookfield began as a "bedroom community" of Milwaukee commuters but has grown and evolved into a vibrant and vital discrete community with highly desirable residential properties. The commercial tax base is sufficient to keep residential taxes relatively modest. It also has a well-educated and affluent but aging populace that demands top-notch performance from all municipal services.

Most perceive the school system as excellent. That adds to the pressures for state-of-the-art library resources to augment those of the school system. The community especially emphasizes and prizes business services and children's services.

Excellent municipal leadership in recent years emphasized long-range planning in all areas and at all levels to ensure the continued health and prosperity of Brookfield. The community attempts to balance the services offered to its residents whose homes range in value from approximately low $1,500,000 to over $1 million.

LIBRARY STRENGTHS

The library serves the needs of the community well. The materials, children's programs, adult programs and other services meet the varying needs of the community. The library has a dedicated staff and a community that has been supportive of the library's needs. The newer physical plant facility built in 1990 has helped to the library achieve its mission.

The library rates well by most objective measures of library services. It has has a high level of visits and circulation. In fact, it has one of the best HAPLR ratings in the state (as based on the HAPLR system, which rates public libraries in the United States using the latest data from almost 9,000 U.S. libraries).

LIBRARY WEAKNESSES

While the library has been supportive of the community's needs, there is a lack of connectedness between residents and the library. There is no "community group" supporting or advocating for the library. In addition, the library and its board are struggling with the future vision of the library. It is hard to answer the question, "What will the library be like in twenty years, other than what it is today?" That is one key reason this long-range plan has been created.

The library needs to maintain a positive image as the best reflection and resource of the community. There is a need for more positive publicity and information about programs and services. There is presently no advertising budget, no "flash."

CHALLENGES

The expectations of the well-paid and professional residents are often very high and are likely to remain so. Meanwhile, the community is turning toward redevelopment because portions of the community that were developed sixty and seventy years ago need to be redeveloped and revitalized, which may create new and different needs for the library. At the same time, the funding difficulties at the state level and the likely reductions in funding to the city will make it increasingly difficult to maintain that service level.

Various housing options, including higher density developments in targeted areas with mixed uses such as housing, retail, and office, are in either the planning or development stages. In the future, we expect an aging population and a change of population from strictly single family homes to residential, multifamily, and senior homes, which will mean a more diverse population of young, old, single individuals, and traditional families. Bike paths will provide more connection among neighborhoods within a more clustered development scheme. All of these changes will have an impact on the community's library needs. There will be more groups needing more specific services than the library has offered in the past. The traditional focus of the library on children and single family adults will expand to include an elderly population, as well as more adults without children.

OPPORTUNITIES

There is a continuing community need for with the creation of gathering places with a sense of community feeling an important role for the public library, of course. An effective library foundation can help to fulfill this goal and when libraries help build community, communities repay the favor.

The library must build on its already strong base to keep up with the ever-changing technology. Brookfield residents are even more technologically adept than most.

Renewing the commitment to partnerships with the Park and Recreation Department, the Sharon Lynne Wilson Center for the Arts, public and private schools, and civic organizations will bear fruit in wider use and acceptance of the library and its mission.

VISION AND MISSION

Vision Statement—City of Brookfield (Brookfield Year 2020 Master Plan)

This vision holds that Brookfield's future lies in enhancing the quality of its public and private built and natural environment so as to ensure its competitive advantage well into the twenty-first century. Brookfield will be a city where the parklands and natural landscape provide spaces for recreation, as well as connect safe and attractive neighborhoods; where superior schools, high quality public services, a wide range of employment, and broad-based commercial services all join to create a unique community that is highly desirable to families and business alike.

Mission Statement—City of Brookfield (Brookfield Year 2020 Master Plan)

The mission of the City of Brookfield is to work cooperatively with public and private entities, providing leadership in the pursuit of the development and maintenance of high quality neighborhoods complimented by a strong commercial sector and superior schools. The city is committed to protecting and preserving its parklands, environmentally sensitive lands, and green spaces, and integrating these assets into a system for community-wide benefit. The city needs to provide high quality municipal services in a cost-effective manner. The city must plan and provide for ongoing development and maintenance of the public infrastructure and and provide a safe environment to assure the future attractiveness of the community.

Vision Statement—Brookfield Public Library

The Brookfield Public Library will support the vision and mission of the City of Brookfield by striving to provide the broadest possible spectrum of residents with the information resources to meet their current and future educational, informational, and recreational needs. The Brookfield Public Library envisions a future where all individuals and families are lifelong learners who recognize the value of reading and other forms of gaining knowledge.

Mission Statement—Brookfield Public Library

The Brookfield Public Library is an essential community information service that provides materials and programs in support of lifelong learning, recreational, and educational interests of a diverse and ever-changing community.

LIBRARY VALUES

- The Brookfield Public Library is committed to *quality library service*. Staff is committed to assisting library users in finding, using, and evaluating information sources. They strive to meet the demand for popular materials and to ensure that use of the library facility is a pleasant experience. All users are served fairly and equally.

- The Brookfield Public Library is committed to *intellectual freedom* and the need for the library's collections to represent many different points of view. Individuals are responsible for making their own choices regarding appropriateness of materials, and parents/guardians are responsible for the choices made for their children.

- The Brookfield Public Library is committed to *education*. Staff work to provide service for students, teachers, and independent learners and to provide learning opportunities for all members of the community.

- The Brookfield Public Library is committed to providing *basic library services at no charge.* This includes general access to online resources. Some optional services may carry a fee.

- The Brookfield Public Library respects *intellectual property rights and copyright law.* These legal rights may affect access to resources and remote accessibility.

- The Brookfield Public Library acknowledges that funding controls our ability to fund hardware, collections, formats, and services. Staff strives to support *technological growth* within our tax-supported budget and to expand the funds available through system contributions and donations and other fund sources.

- The Brookfield Public Library views *technology as a means to better library services,* and not an end in itself. Staff is committed to assisting and providing training and educational opportunities.

- The Brookfield Public Library honors *diversity,* and seeks to represent diversity in its collections, programs, services, and other areas.

Public Library Service Roles

The Public Library Association has recommended that libraries consider focusing their activities by choosing some of the thirteen possible "Public Library Service Responses" found in the appendix. In an effort to realize its mission, the library board of trustees has chosen to focus on three major services roles:

1. *Popular materials library*: to feature current, high-demand, high-interest materials in a variety of formats for persons of all ages. For example:

   - Shelving displays to enhance and promote interest

   - Multiple copies of popular materials and best-sellers

- Videos, audio CDs and tapes, books-on-tape, and CD-ROMs

- Reader's advisory services from trained professionals

- Enhanced collections such as fine arts, business, travel

2. *Preschoolers' door to learning:* to encourage children to develop and sustain an interest in reading and learning through services for children, parents and other caregivers. For example:

- Extensive programming that includes story times, school class visits, and other

- Group visits after school, on the weekend, and for holiday events and puppet shows

- Supplemental book lists for parents and caregivers to encourage reading to children

- Cooperative programs with day care providers and schools

- Computerized homework centers and public PCs

- Internet access

3. *Reference library:* to actively provide timely, accurate, and useful information for community residents in their pursuit of job-related and personal interests. For example:

- Enhanced business reference collection and services, "Ready Reference" telephone service, and online electronic resources in-house

- Access to *Badgerlink* and county-provided online resources

- Intemet Internet access

- Study rooms and public PCs

- Skilled and approachable reference staff

- Public instruction on the use of resources in all formats

Stakeholders

It is essential that a variety of key stakeholders interact cooperatively to ensure a responsive, strong, and viable public library within the Brookfield community.

- *Residents of Brookfield and the local service area.* The library's patrons expect a high level of access to a wide variety of materials, services, programs, equipment, and technologies in a cost-effective manner. They require exceptional customer service from qualified and trained staff. Brookfield residents expect to use any of the sixteen WCFLS libraries, and to link with other information providers through state-of-the-art electronic networks.

- *Library staff and volunteers.* Staff and volunteers are essential resources. They are dedicated to quality service and act as an indispensable bridge between the library user and other stakeholders.

- *The Mayor and Common Council.* City administrators expect the library to participate in and adhere to the overall vision and master plan for Brookfield. They expect competent administration of the facility, its staff, and the budget. High-quality, enhanced services, provided in the most cost-effective and efficient manner, are valued.

- *Other City departments.* The Library is one member of the team of internal service departments that administer city services. The Library works closely with the Mayor, Parks and Recreation, Human Resources, Information Services, Information Technology, the City Attorney, and Finance and Accounting.

- *Waukesha County Federated Library System (WCFLS).* The WCFLS is bound by State statute to distribute State aid and County reimbursement dollars to promote resource sharing among its members. As one of sixteen public libraries in Waukesha County, the Brookfield Public Library looks to the WCFLS:

- to facilitate access to programs and materials among System libraries

- to provide continuing education programs

- to provide a timely and functional interlibrary loan system (with van delivery)

- to secure adequate funding to allow the library to provide service to nonresidents without diluting the ability to maintain or improve local services

- to ensure the benefits of collective access to information resources both within and from outside of the county (e.g. *Badgerlink* and other online services)

- to provide guidance and vision for future library services

- *Division for Libraries and Community Learning (DLCL)*. The Division's mission is to provide leadership, consultation, and services to assure that all Wisconsin citizens have access to high quality library services either directly or through cooperative arrangements. The Division coordinates statewide library planning and research, facilitates interlibrary loan and state aid payments, and maintains a library to supplement the resources of other libraries in the state. It develops standards for service, personnel, and facilities and plays a major role in the development and implementation of library legislation.

- *Library Board of Trustees*. Chapter 43 of the Wisconsin Statutes gives control of library funds, property, and expenditures to the board of trustees. The board works cooperatively with the library director and staff to make informed decisions on the strategic direction and focus of administration and operating activities for the facility. Successful team efforts at this level ensure that the policies, services, and programs of the public library are targeted to meet the needs of the community both now and in the future.

Section 3: Goals and Objectives

This section includes the goals and objectives chosen for the library during the planning period. There are five main parts:

1. Administration
2. Personnel
3. Automated services and technology
4. Collection
5. Programs and services

Goal	Obj	Task	Task	2004				2005				2006			
				Q1	Q2	Q3	Q4	Q1	Q2	Q3	Q4	Q1	Q2	Q3	Q4
Goal One: Administration: Administer the library to meet the service requirements and policies established by the library board and funded by the Common Council.															
Adm	A	1	Annually review the library long-range plan and policy manual.		X				X				X		
Adm	A	2	Annually calculate the minimum requirements for meeting county and state standards and the related costs.	X				X				X			
			Communicate resulting budget needs to the council.												
Adm	A	3	Maintain staffing levels at about the same 33 FTE level as at present. This puts the library at the *excellent level* by state standards.				X				X				X
Adm	A	4	Establish and annually implement a program of staff training in emergency procedures such as fire, medical emergencies and related issues. Involve municipal emergency and police officials.				X				X				X
Adm	A	5	At least annually have a meeting between the staff and the library board to discuss public service goals. Communicate the results of the meeting as appropriate.			X				X				X	
Adm	A	6	Perform research on developing a Library Foundation. that can raise funds for library special projects and materials.	X											
Adm	A	7	Establish training and development budget equivalent to 1% *of the entire library-operating budget.*				X				X				X
Objective 1.1: Develop and administer the annual budget consistent with policies approved by the library board, and guidelines provided by the City.															

371

Goal	Obj	Task	Task	2004 Q1	Q2	Q3	Q4	2005 Q1	Q2	Q3	Q4	2006 Q1	Q2	Q3	Q4
Adm	1.1	1	Prepare background information for the next budget cycle. Research all means of cost containment and fiscal flexibility allowable within Statutes and laws. Identify pressure points and service initiatives that require funding or that can be reduced.			X				X				X	
Adm	1.1	2	Prepare capital improvements budget with consideration to the City guidelines, for facilities and automation plans, and other service initiatives.			X				X				X	
Adm	1.1	3	Establish training and development budget equivalent to 1% of the entire library-operating budget.				X				X				X
Objective 1.2: Keep informed of current service needs, interests, and developments in the library, librarianship, and in critical service areas (ex. technology).															
Adm	1.2	1	Prepare plans and policies for library services with the participation, review, and approval of the library board. Implement those plans and policies through the library's contract service providers, other City departments, and appropriate outside sources. Assess effectiveness and revise as necessary.	Continuous activity.											
Adm	1.2	2	Conduct surveys and other measures of library service; prepare reports. Utilize to target and improve internal materials and services.							X					
Adm	1.2	3	Prepare records and reports: monthly quarterly, and annually for Waukesha County Federated Library System (WCFLS)	Continuous activity.											
Adm	1.2	4	Prepare records and reports: monthly quarterly, and annually for State Division for Libraries, Technology, & Community Learning (DLTCL)	Continuous activity.											
Adm	1.2	5	Read professional literature, literature; participate in local, state, and national conferences and workshops to keep abreast of library trends and developments.	As needed and appropriate											

Goal	Obj	Task	Task	2004				2005				2006			
				Q1	Q2	Q3	Q4	Q1	Q2	Q3	Q4	Q1	Q2	Q3	Q4
Adm	1.2	6	Provide opportunities for the members of the Board of Trustees to participate in conferences, workshops, seminars, and visits to other library facilities.	As needed and appropriate											
Adm	1.2	7	Foster involvement and understanding of common issues through reciprocal visits with other library boards members in the Waukesha County system.	As needed and appropriate											
Objective 1.3: Maintain good working relationships with City departments, administrators, and the Common Council.															
Adm	1.3	1	Participate in City initiatives	As needed and appropriate											
Adm	1.3	2	Support other department's objectives to increase citizens' overall awareness of city's programs and services	As needed and appropriate											
Adm	1.3	3	Provide such library services as may be of assistance (ex. literature search, periodicals acquisition, and reference) directly to members of the Council, or other departments.	As needed and appropriate											
Adm	1.3	4	Encourage administrators and council members to utilize the services of the library.	As needed and appropriate											
Adm	1.3	5	Provide information on programs , and services via news-letters, brochures, etc.	As needed and appropriate											
Objective 1.4: Maintain good working relationships with professional peer groups.															
Adm	1.4	13	Participate in the Waukesha County Federated Library System: Attend WCFLS board meetings, participate in Task Force activities, serve as member of WCFLS strategic planning committee, serve on WCFLS special interest committees, participate in Alliance of Public Librarians (APL), serveand serve on APL special interest committees.	As needed and appropriate.											

373

Goal	Obj	Task	Task	2004 Q1	Q2	Q3	Q4	2005 Q1	Q2	Q3	Q4	2006 Q1	Q2	Q3	Q4
Adm	1.4	24	Participate in the Wisconsin Library Association: cooperate with library advocacy promotions, support appropriate State library legislative legislation, workand work on WLA Public Relations Committee, supervisory staff to be encouraged to work on WLA committees.	As needed and appropriate.											
Adm	1.4	35	Actively support the efforts of the American Library Association, Round Tables, and the Library Council of Metropolitan Milwaukee to advocate for and promote legislative library initiatives.	As needed and appropriat											
Adm	1.4	46	Maintain awareness of current library legislative issues, especially at the Federal and State levels. Advocate and endorse legislation that promotes and strengthens interests, services, and funding.	As needed and appropriate.											
Objective 1.5: Be responsive to the information needs of the community.															
Adm	1.5	1	Increase visibility of the library through pro-active working relationships with media.	As needed and appropriate.											
Adm	1.5	2	Library board and staff are encouraged to network within the community, and participate in civic organizations.	As needed and appropriate.											
Adm	1.5	3	Conduct formal planning activities to set objectives; re-examine goals, programs, services; and identify the needs of the community and develop response strategies.			X									
Adm	1.5	4	Monitor library service hours - adjust as needed.	As needed and appropriate.											
Adm	1.5	5	Seek partnerships to support and supplement the provision of library materials services (e.g.: work with the Parks and Recreation Dept. on programs).	As needed and appropriate.											
Objective 1.6: Library facilities will be clean, well maintained, conveniently located and of adequate size.															
Adm	1.6	1	Regularly review library technology needs as they relate to the facility.	As needed and appropriate.											

374

Goal | Obj |Task |Task

Goal Two: Personnel. Provide for a cohesive, qualified, and highly motivated staff to accomplish the service goals of the library. Recognize staff as an important resource.

Objective 2.1: Keep channels of communication open with all levels of staff to promote of procedures and the enforcement of policies.

Goal	Obj	Task	Task	Timeframe
Pers	2.1	1	Conduct regular administrative and department staff meetings.	Continuous activity.
Pers	2.1	2	Provide training (both in-house and from outside sources) to develop and good listening and customer service skills at all levels.	As needed and appropriate.
Pers	2.1	3	Encourage cross-training of staff, and participation in the library planning process. Increase staff awareness of the inter-relationships of all library services.	Continuous activity.
Pers	2.1	4	Keep staff informed of library-related issues and events locally and statewide.	Continuous activity.
Pers	2.1	5	Conduct quarterly meetings with staff and representatives of the library board.	Every quarter.

Objective 2.2: Provide for a positive, creative, and motivational work environment.

Goal	Obj	Task	Task	Timeframe
Pers	2.2	1	Promote pro-active management at the supervisory and administrative levels through appropriate coaching, counseling, team-building, and interpersonal skills.	Continuous activity.
Pers	2.2	2	Provide opportunities for staff training and professional growth within and outside the library.	Continuous activity.
Pers	2.2	3	Set personal employee goals on an annual basis, review progress quarterly. Conduct employee performance planning and evaluation. Provide appropriate and visible recognition.	X (2005)
Pers	2.2	4	Demonstrate respect and trust in staff members by empowering them to perform to the best of their ability with minimal intervention, while maintaining open lines of communication with administrative staff.	Continuous activity.

375

Goal	Obj	Task	Task	2004				2005				2006			
				Q1	Q2	Q3	Q4	Q1	Q2	Q3	Q4	Q1	Q2	Q3	Q4
Pers	2.2	5	Actively encourage staff to look for creative solutions to job challenges, and to develop innovative approaches to library services.	Continuous activity											
Objective 2.3: Provide for staffing levels sufficient to achieve the library's mission. Administer the library union contract.															
Pers	2.3	1	Hire and train qualified staff to meet expected service levels	Continuous activity.											
Pers	2.3	2	Guide, monitor, and evaluate the work of staff. Maintain current job descriptions. Evaluate performance based on both job description and personal goals.	Continuous activity.											
Pers	2.3	3	Continue to develop and expand the use of volunteers, particularly in visible programs such as book discussion groups, and provision of programs. Involve students and interns when at all possible for a mutually beneficial partnership.	Continuous activity.											
Pers	2.3	4	Monitor workloads and continually look for ways to streamline internal operations that will maximize staff productivity.	Continuous activity.											
Pers	2.3	5	Outsource those activities which that can be more efficiently and cost-effectively accomplished from outside the library.	Continuous activity.											
Objective 2.4.: Administer the library union contract. Provide for staffing levels sufficient to achieve the library's mission															
Pers	2.4	1	Follow the provisions of the current contract.	Continuous activity.											
Pers	2.4	2	Encourage dialogue between the management team, the board, and library staff on current concerns.	Continuous activity.											
Pers	2.4	3	Negotiate new contract in conjunction with the City's Human Resource Department.								X				
Goal Three: Automated Services. Utilize appropriate technological alternatives in providing enhanced information and delivery.															
Tech	A	1	Develop plan for wireless capacity capability in the library for library owned laptops, as well as publicly used personal laptops. Implemented plan if appropriate.	X			X								

Goal	Obj	Task	Task	2004 Q1	Q2	Q3	Q4	2005 Q1	Q2	Q3	Q4	2006 Q1	Q2	Q3	Q4
Tech	A	2	Continue to plan for automated services with CAF (Catalog Access For Everyone) consortium.	Continuous activity.											
Tech	A	3	Investigate feasibility of fundraising on the web. using e-commerce options such as those available from Amazon.com.			X			X						
Tech	A	4	Move toward state suggested minimum standards for public access workstations of at least 1 per 35 user visits per day. At present use rate this means at least 25 public access computers.				X				X				X
Tech	A	5	Develop a multi-year technology plan by the year 2004. (Include directions for technology in current facility and suggestions for new building.) Include the investigation of the following issues:			X									
Tech	A	5.1	Wireless in the library. Develop a plan for wireless capacity in the library for library owned laptops, as well as publicly used laptops. Implement plan if appropriate.												
Tech	A	5.2	24/7 e-mail reference services.												
Tech	A	5.3	Computer-training lab using wireless technology.												
Tech	A	5.4	Cyber cafe atmosphere in commons area for at least 10 users in casual atmosphere with wireless computers.												
Tech	A	5.5	High tech conference center for business in the meeting room.												
Tech	A	5.6	Establishing a media center for the public to use Internet for broadband downloads, printing, and scanning and so forth.												
Objective 3.1: To maintain a user-friendly automated system.															
Tech	3.1	1	Review library operating system options with appropriate stakeholders to assure that functional requirements, internal and external user needs, and expectations for a user-friendly system are met.		X				X			X			
Objective 3.2: Provide broad access and service through electronic resources.															
Tech	3.2	1	Utilize resources available through the Waukesha County Federated Library System and the State of Wisconsin.	Continuous activity.											
Tech	3.2	2	Provide public-access workstations for word processing, spreadsheet, database, CD-ROM, and Internet access functions.	Continuous activity.											

377

Goal	Obj	Task	Task	2004 Q1	Q2	Q3	Q4	2005 Q1	Q2	Q3	Q4	2006 Q1	Q2	Q3	Q4
Tech	3.2	3	Provide training sessions for the public on use of electronic resources.		Continuous activity.										
Tech	3.2	4	Develop and maintain a strong library presence on the worldwide web.		Continuous activity.										
Objective 3.3: Provide internal and external expertise to maximize use and efficiency of the computer, network, and online access capabilities.															
Tech	3.3	1	Send staff to continuing education workshops and training sessions.		Continuous activity.										
Tech	3.3	2	Provide in-house training.		Continuous activity.										
Tech	3.3	3	Keep staff up-to-date on changes to the system, software and services.		Continuous activity.										
Objective 3.4: Monitor product development and integrate innovative technologies. Maintain a current Library Technology Plan.															
Tech	3.4	1	Encourage supervisory staff to set up and/ or attend product demonstrations and to contact vendors for information on new products and services.		Continuous activity.										
Tech	3.4	2	Stay informed about new technological developments affecting libraries. Investigate feasibility of implementing new technologies.		Continuous activity.										
Tech	3.4	3	All supervisory staff should participate in the Wislib online bulletin board from the Division for Libraries and Community Learning. The DLTCL web site should be monitored for announcements and direction taking place at the State level.		Continuous activity.										
Tech	3.4	4	Network with colleagues, particularly county and statewide, to maintain an awareness of new technologies and services that are becoming available.		Continuous activity.										
Objective 3.5: Maintain a current Library Technology Plan. Monitor product development and integrate innovative technologies															
Tech	3.5	1	Revise Brookfield's Library Technology Plan following the . guidelines by the Dept. of Public Instruction Division for Libraries and Community Learning.		X				X					X	

Goal	Obj	Task	Task	2004				2005				2006			
				Q1	Q2	Q3	Q4	Q1	Q2	Q3	Q4	Q1	Q2	Q3	Q4
Goal Four: Collection Development. To develop and maintain a diverse and dynamic collection (regardless of format) the library's mission and service roles.															
Objective 4.1: Maintain collection standards and benchmarks.															
Coll	4.1	1	Aim for/Meet or exceed a total collection size at the moderate level by state standards.	X				X				X			
Coll	4.1	2	Maintain the base materials budget at the excellent level by state standards.				X				X				X
Coll	4.1	3	Aim for/Meet or exceed an annual book addition rate of about 11,000 volumes. This is a book replenishment rate allowing for a complete replacement of the collection in just under 13 years.	X				X				X			
Coll	4.1	4	Aim for/Meet or exceed an annual book-weeding rate of 10,000 volumes. This rate would allow for an increase in book collection size of 1,000 volumes per year.	X				X				X			
Coll	4.1	5	Plan to maintain the periodical collection between the enhanced and excellent rate by state standards.	X				X				X			
Coll	4.1	6	Maintain audio collection at between the moderate and enhanced rate by state standards.	X				X				X			
Coll	4.1	7	Maintain video & DVD collection at the moderate to enhanced rate.	X				X				X			
Coll	4.1	8	Evaluate the collection development plan annually based on usage in each Dewey Decimal category.	X				X				X			
Objective 4.2: Conduct regular collection maintenance activities.															
Coll	4.2	1	Analyze collection use reports. Remove outdated materials and replace following established de-selection cycle.	Continuous activity.											
Coll	4.2	2	Adjust calls number/location designations and subject headings to maximize their browse-ability.	Continuous activity.											
Coll	4.2	3	Repair and recondition materials as needed.	Continuous activity.											
Objective 4.3 Track collection use and utilize results to improve the collection.															
Coll	4.3	1	Conduct annual user fill rate survey.	X				X				X			
Coll	4.3	2	Conduct annual reference survey.	X				X				X			
Coll	4.3	3	Conduct annual in-house use survey.	X				X				X			

Goal	Obj	Task	Task	2004				2005				2006			
				Q1	Q2	Q3	Q4	Q1	Q2	Q3	Q4	Q1	Q2	Q3	Q4
Coll	4.3	4	Track collection turnover rates and shifts in material use annually.	X				X				X			
Coll	4.3	5	Establish methods to track use of non-print materials, and resources electronically, either in-house or via the Web site.	X											
Objective 4.4: Purchase new materials and information resources.															
Coll	4.4	1	Hold monthly materials selection meetings.	Continuous activity.											
Coll	4.4	2	Solicit input from the public via inter-library loan requests, purchase consideration forms, public suggestion boxes, and other means.	Continuous activity.											
Coll	4.4	3	Participate in acquisition programs such as Baker and Taylor Leased Book Plan; leased Books plan to maximize quantity and timely availability of popular materials, materials with high numbers of reserves.	Continuous activity.											
Coll	4.4	4	Watch for developing formats (ex.: E-books) and incorporate into collection based on community need and expectation.	Continuous activity.											
Objective 4.5: Effectively promote the collection: Prepare and distribute reading lists and web-site recommendations to integrate new technologies with the traditional.															
Coll	4.5	1	Host programs that will encourage the public to look for supplemental print and electronic resources.	Continuous activity.											
Coll	4.5	2	Package and display materials for ease of use and visibility.	Continuous activity.											
Coll	4.5	3	Provide outreach to organizations and individuals (ex.: library use instruction to school classes, online catalog classes for seniors.)	Continuous activity.											
Coll	4.5	4	Ensure that the layout and display of collections are user-friendly.	Continuous activity.											
Coll	4.5	5	Provide all community organizations that, which use the meeting rooms, with suggestions for areas of the library's material collections that may be of interest to them.	Continuous activity.											

Goal	Obj	Task	Task	2004				2005				2006			
				Q1	Q2	Q3	Q4	Q1	Q2	Q3	Q4	Q1	Q2	Q3	Q4
Goal 5: Programs and Services. Provide programs and services that support the Library's mission and service, service, and that augment the collection.															
Objective 5.1: Periodically assess accessibility and program development.															
Prog	5.1	1	Do periodic assessments for meeting Americans with Disabilities Act requirements for accessibility, especially with regard to use of computer and audio-visual equipment and meeting accessibility.	X				X				X			
Prog	5.1	2	Maintain open hours at between 65 and 67 66 hours per week as compared to the current 66. This puts the library at between the moderate and enhanced level by state standards.	X				X				X			
Prog	5.1	3	Expand book clubs for adult readers. Provide for at least six sessions for discussion groups.	Continuous activity.											
Prog	5.1	4	Establish group meetings and workshops in such areas as Investments, Gardening, etc. Aim forMeet or exceed adult attendance at such meetings at an average of 20 per meeting and aim for at least 10 meetings per year.	Continuous activity.											
Prog	5.1	5	Perform a user survey to evaluate user needs at least once every three years. Report on the results and recommended changes to the board and city council.						X						
Prog	5.1	6	Enhance current web page as time permits. Use it as a tool for communicating information about the library and for receiving public comment on services.	Continuous activity.											
Prog	5.1	7	Provide classes for the public on Internet access, how to use computers, parental supervision of children, children's Internet use, and so forth.	Continuous activity.											
Objective 5.2: Provide programs for children that stimulate their interests and develop an appreciation for reading and learning.															
Prog	5.2	1	Conduct summer reading programs, puppet shows, toddler lap-sits, story hours, book talks, school visits, and special family or seasonal events.	Continuous activity.											
Prog	5.2	2	Prepare special interest displays, handouts, and reading lists.	Continuous activity.											

Goal	Obj	Task	Task	2004 Q1	Q2	Q3	Q4	2005 Q1	Q2	Q3	Q4	2006 Q1	Q2	Q3	Q4
Prog	5.2	3	Publish a monthly newsletter and events calendar.	Continuous activity.											
Prog	5.2	4	Cooperate with schools, caregivers, home school parents, day care centers, and civic organizations to promote library services to children.	Continuous activity.											
Prog	5.2	5	Provide book discussion groups for children.	Continuous activity.											
Objective 5.3: Provide programs for young adults.															
Prog	5.3	1	Provide a book discussion group for youth.	Continuous activity.											
Prog	5.3	2	Encourage participation in special programs (ex:. Jason Project, Milwaukee Bucks Reading Challenge) that reflect the diversity of interests of the young adult population.	Continuous activity.											
Prog	5.3	3	Partner with the schools to identify the needs and interest of teens. Look for creative ways to involve and interest teens in library services.	Continuous activity.											
Objective 5.4: Provide programs for adults.															
Prog	5.4	1	Sponsor book discussion groups.	Continuous activity.											
Prog	5.4	2	Sponsor programs that address community, continuing education, job-related and quality of life issues.	Continuous activity.											
Prog	5.4	3	Partner with the Parks & Recreation Dept. to enhance programs for adults.	Continuous activity.											
Objective 5.5: Provide support services appropriate in a library setting.															
Prog	5.5	1	Provide and maintain functional copiers, public computers, microfilm reader/printers, and other equipment needed to access the library's collections and services.	Continuous activity.											
Prog	5.5	2	Cooperate with other City departments to provide programs, displays, and A/V materials that foster citizen involvement in and awareness of communityl initiatives.	Continuous activity.											
Objective 5.6: Provide accurate and timely reference and reader's advisory services.															
Prog	5.6	1	Adequately staff adult and children's reference desks during open hours.	Continuous activity.											
Prog	5.6	2	Improve reference service by providing ongoing training for staff.	Continuous activity.											
Prog	5.6	3	Develop and implement instructional classes for the public.	Continuous activity.											

Goal	Obj	Task	Task	2004 Q1	Q2	Q3	Q4	2005 Q1	Q2	Q3	Q4	2006 Q1	Q2	Q3	Q4
Prog	5.6	4	Provide booklists, brochures, and other supplemental material that promote usepromote use of the collection, electronic resources, and services.	Continuous activity.											
Prog	5.6	5	Implement online reference service through the web site.								X				
Objective 5.7:			Address Internet and emerging technologies.												
Prog	5.7	1	Review computer hardware and software needs annually.			X				X				X	
Prog	5.7	2	The library will cooperate with the City and the WCFLS in the development of computer based information systems.	Continuous activity.											
Prog	5.7	3	The Library, along with the Information ServicesTechnology Dept., will look tofor acquire, maintain, repair and replace the technological infrastructure infrastructure.	Continuous activity.											
Objective 5.8:			Actively market/promote library materials and services.												
Prog	5.8	1	Develop and annually review a Marketing Plan.	X				X				X			
Prog	5.8	2	Target one major photo opportunity each quarter for newspaper coverage.	Continuous activity.											
Prog	5.8	3	Develop and enhance the library presence on the City Web site.	Continuous activity.											
Prog	5.8	4	Identify non-users and develop strategies to draw them to library services.	Continuous activity.											
Prog	5.8	5	Develop strategies to increase awareness within the community of the depth of library services.	Continuous activity.											
Prog	5.8	6	Host programs in parks and other community locations.	Continuous activity.											
Prog	5.8	7	Be alert to ways to make the library a gathering place for the community.	Continuous activity.											

383

Section 4: Demographics, Statistics, Financial

CIRCULATION

2002 Library Circulation Data for City Residents

Community	Brookfield	Waukesha P.L.	Elm Grove	Other Libraries	Totals
Brookfield	418,085	23,986	22,946	10,218	475,235
Other county nonlibrary communities	51,584	415,211	1,148	404,244	872,187
Other county library communities	77,554	131,058	3,877	227,808	440,297
All other	934	934,197	75,234	3,216,040	2,438,686
Totals	548,157	1,504,452	103,205	3,858,310	4,226,405
Ratio by column					
Brookfield	76.3%	1.6%	22.2%	0.3%	11.2%
Other county nonlibrary communities	9.4%	27.6%	1.1%	10.5%	20.6%
Other county library communities	14.1% s	8.7%	3.8%	5.9%	10.4%
All other	0.2%	62.1%	72.9%	83.4%	57.7%
Totals	100.0%	100.0%	100.0%	100.0%	100.0%
Ratio by row					
Brookfield	88.0%	5.0%	4.8%	2.2%	100.0%
Other county nonlibrary communities	5.9%	47.6%	0.1%	46.3%	100.0%
Other county library communities	17.6%	29.8%	0.9%	51.7%	100.0%
All other	0.0%	38.3%	3.1%	131.9%	100.0%
Totals	13.0%	35.6%	2.4%	91.3%	100.0%

Population density and traffic patterns, as well as state and county policies result in considerable circulation traffic among the communities of Brookfield, Elm Grove, and Waukesha. The "2002 Library Circulation Data for City Residents" chart indicates current use patterns at libraries and by residents.

Ratio By Column: lines 11 to 15 indicate percent of library use at Brookfield, as well as other county residents as a percentages by column. For instance, column B, lines 11 through 14 indicate that Brookfield residents borrowed 76.3% of the items that Brookfield checked out, other county nonlibrary community residents checked out 9.4% of the items, other library community residents (mostly Elm Grove) borrowed 14.1% of the items, and all other residents borrowed just 0.2%. The remaining columns indicate the use rates at nearby libraries and other libraries in the county; thus, the 23,986 items loaned to Brookfield City residents by the Waukesha Public Library in Column C, Row 4 amounted to 1.6% of Waukesha Public Library's circulation.

Ratio By Row: Rows 18 to 22 look at the use ratios across rows rather than down columns. As line 18 indicates, Brookfield residents borrowed 88.0% of their items from the Brookfield library, 5.0% from Waukesha, 4.8% from Elm Grove, and 2.2% from all other libraries in the county.

Circulation

2001 Library Circulation Data for City Residents

Community	Brookfield	Waukesha P.L.	Elm Grove	Other Libraries	Totals
Brookfield	418,085	23,986	22,946	10,218	475,235
Other county non-library communities	51,584	415,211	1,148	404,244	872,187
Other county library communities	77,554	131,058	3,877	227,808	440,297
All other	934	934,197	75,234	3,216,040	2,438,686
Totals	548,157	1,504,452	103,205	3,858,310	4,226,405
Ratio by column					
Brookfield	76.3%	1.6%	22.2%	0.3%	11.2%
Other county non-library communities	9.4%	27.6%	1.1%	10.5%	20.6%
Other county library communities	14.1%	8.7%	3.8%	5.9%	10.4%
All other	0.2%	62.1%	72.9%	83.4%	57.7%
Totals	100.0%	100.0%	100.0%	100.0%	100.0%

Ratio by row					
Brookfield	88.0%	5.0%	4.8%	2.2%	100.0%
Other county non-library communities	5.9%	47.6%	0.1%	46.3%	100.0%
Other county library communities	17.6%	29.8%	0.9%	51.7%	100.0%
All other	0.0%	38.3%	3.1%	131.9%	100.0%
Totals	13.0%	35.6%	2.4%	91.3%	100.0%

Population density and traffic patterns, as well as state and county policies result in considerable circulation traffic among the communities of Brookfield, Elm Grove and Waukesha. Use between libraries has been the source of friction over reimbursement payments.

Population projections: The state library agency annually assigns a portion of the 83,000 county residents without their own library to communities with libraries. The assignment is based on library use. This constitutes the service area.

	City	Service area
Population 2000	38649	44335
Projected 2005	43000	49326
Projected 2020	47000	53915

WAUKESHA COUNTY LIBRARY STANDARDS

See appendix for further information, including definition of the Library Service Effort Ratio (LSER). The county standards are being phased in through 2007, but the Brookfield exceeds all county standards now. The LSER measures whether a library is a crossover lender or borrower that is, whether it lends more materials to other library community residents than it borrows. Brookfield, with a ratio above 100%, is a net lender.

Standard		Minimum	Actual
Materials Spending	Per capita	$4.96	$8.63
Collection Size	Per capita	3.60	4.00
Total Staff	Per 1,000 residents	0.50	0.84
Hours Open	Per week	62	66
Library service Effort Ratio		95%	103%

STATE STANDARDS AND BROOKFIELD ACTUAL AMOUNTS

Brookfield Public Library is above state "basic" levels for all measures. It is close to or exceeds excellent levels for hours, staffing, and materials budget. The other measures are mostly moderate to enhanced. Video and audio holdings are lower than expected. *A long-range plan needs to define the targeted level for each of these and then define a method for change, if needed.*

CURRENT BUDGET, CAPITAL NEEDS AND MULTIYEAR PROJECTIONS

The strategic objectives outlined in this plan call for the development of both marketing and technology plans. While there is a potential for increased costs, there should be a corresponding increase in utilitization.

Library	2002 Actual	2003 Budgeted	2004 Est.
Municipal	1,764,198	2,076,222	2,138,096
County	283,288	297,452	315,299
State	3,619	3,619	3,619
Intersystem	1,452	1,234	1,065
Federal	0	0	0
Other	49,298	52,000	56,000
Revenue Total	**2,101,855**	**2,430,527**	**2,514,079**
Salaries	1,034,561	1,097,205	1,115,605
Benefits	301,761	347,515	377,935
Materials	333,567	346,269	353,769
Other Operating	380,451	285,233	290,787
Operating Expend Total	**2,050,340**	**2,076,222**	**2,138,096**
Debt Retirement	537,883	Not available	Not available
Capital	2,450	0	0
Capital and Debt Retirement	**540,333**	**0**	**0**

EQUALIZED VALUATION PROJECTIONS

Most library support comes from the property tax. Taxes are typically measured as a tax per $1,000 of property value or "mill rate." The library portion of a City of Brookfield 2003 tax bill included $0.35 for every $1000 of property. That means that the owner of a $100,000 home paid $35.00 for library services.

Library planners need to look at what planners call "tax capacity" the amount of property value behind the average tax-payer in a community. The state average for the twenty Wisconsin communities in Brookfield's population category was $58,246. Brookfield's tax capacity was more than twice that amount at $124,460. What that means is that the same mill rate generates twice as much money in Brookfield as it would in most other Wisconsin communities.

The tax base has been growing at a high rate and the "2002 Library Circulation Data for City Residents" chart projects continued, though lower, rates of growth.

Section 5: Appendix Materials HAPLR Rating and Census Data

HAPLR RATING FOR BROOKFIELD LIBRARY

Focus Group Response Summary—Brookfield Public Library Board

Imagine that you have been selected to write the encyclopedia article for Brookfield. Give the past, present, and future prospects of the service community.

Forty years ago, Brookfield was almost a rural area in comparison to today. There has been growth in business, churches, homes and the library. The future holds continued growth in the above areas. (The forty years I have lived in the community.)

Brookfield began as a bedroom community of Milwaukee, but has grown and evolved into a vibrant and vital discrete community with highly desirable residential properties, but with a commercial tax base sufficient to allow relatively modest residential taxes charged to a well-educated and affluent populace which demands top-notch performance from all municipal services. A school system commonly perceived as excellent adds to the pressures for state-of-the-art library resources to augment those of the school system. Business services and children's services are especially emphasized and prized by the community. Excellent municipal leadership in recent years emphasized long-range planning in all areas and at all levels to insure the continued health and prosperity of Brookfield.

Brookfield is a great community of wonderful friendly people and great resources, filled with natural beauty, parks, and more.

Brookfield is a growing, middle-class community. People generally move here because of the good reputation of the school system, closeness to downtown, and good affordable housing. The prospects are good. The future challenge for the city will be to maintain the current level of services while tax revenue and bond interest decline. This may affect library funding in the future.

Community of all ages. Growth of technology. Past: "just books." Present: books, technology, networking. Teaching tools. Summer programs, etc. Future: community changing. Growth, usage of library according to finances and usage keeping up with technology advancements. Programs. Teaching.

Brookfield was a rural community with an agricultural base that grew into a suburban community as Milwaukee expanded. Over the past 20 years, the community has developed most of its available land and has drawn many businesses into its area. The community attempts to balance the services offered to its residents who range in home values from low $100,000 to well over $1 million. As a result of having many residents who are well employed and professionals, the expectations of the residents are often high. The future of the community is turning toward redevelopment. Portions of the community that were developed 60 and 70 years ago need to be redeveloped and revitalized.

Past: more rural, single-family residential areas. Present: evolving into a more urban area. Currently in planning and/or implementation process for various housing options, higher density in targeted areas with mixed uses (i.e. housing, retail, office), bike paths, creating developments and areas of our community with gathering places and a sense of community feeling. Future: aging population and change of population from strictly single family home residential. We will have senior housing and multifamily dwellings, which will mean a population of young, old, single individuals, and traditional families. We will have more clustered development and the bike paths will provide more connection among neighborhoods.

What is good about the Brookfield Public Library?

I interviewed three grandchildren for these questions. Always open. Read in quiet, like it quiet. Do not pay. Good arrangement of books. Computers. Librarian answers children's questions. Good children's area and good variety of books.

The Brookfield Public Library is characterized by a commitment to excellence, a dedication on all levels to fulfilling that commitment, the employment of staff with the ability to carry out the commitment and the traditional support of the mayor and the common council in the pursuit of excellence. There exists what I would call "technological vigilance," a perceived need and desire for the library to be as state-of-the-art as budget constraints will allow. We are assisted in the endeavors by the nature of our clientele, which provides additional impetus to pushing technological frontiers and maintaining enhanced services. The school system and business community, likewise, have the expectation of optimum performance.

BPL has excellent resources and materials. BPL has a friendly staff. BPL is an inviting place. BPL has a good variety of programs.

The library has a good collection, good staff, is open adequate hours and is centrally located in the community. The administrative staff is enthusiastic and open to new ideas.

Provides information and learning tools for enjoyment. Supported by tax dollars. Access to all ages. Clean, comfortable, safe place.

The library serves the needs of the community well. The materials, children's programs, adult programs and other services meet the varying needs of the community. The library has a strong staff and a community that has been supportive of the library's needs. The physical plant has been helpful to the library's mission in serving the community.

Have a very nice facility, excellent staff, facility is centrally located in the city and is in the civic area, offer a good variety of various materials, provides meeting facilities to our community,

beautiful courtyard, offer a variety of programs, have created partnerships with Park and Rec, Wilson Center, and other libraries.

What is bad about the Brookfield Public Library?

Same children interviewed: Can't think of anything. No food.
More e-books for children. (Youngest one) "Always hush, hush."

Sorry, but I've been on this board for 16 years and have the
implicit belief that anything "bad" would have been identified and
corrected as it occurred, to the extent of our ability to do so.

BPL needs to maintain a positive image as the best reflection and resource of the community. As much positive publicity
and info circulated about programs and services. No advertising
budget. No flash. Need to work with public schools, share
resources, good PR.

There is nothing "bad." But the things that can be improved
include: more available staff, friendlier and more helpful. Better
video and DVD collection. Improved atmosphere: signage, fire-
place, make things easier to find, take ideas from Schaumberg.
Better hours. Drive through drop off, ideally pick up too. Better
system (coming soon). Union employees can make changes difficult. The board has quite a few liaison positions. As such, these
people cannot hold office. That leaves about half the board members to serve in leadership.

Political—takes time. Need to be accountable about the
usage. Example: cards good for three years. Possibly behind in
technology due to politics.

While the library has been supportive of the community's
needs, there is a lack of connectedness between residents and the
library. There is no "community group" supporting or advocating
for the library. In addition, the library and its board are struggling
with the future vision of the library. It is hard to answer the question, "What will the library be like in 20 years, other than what it
is today."

People aren't always aware of the materials and programs
we offer. Facility is land locked. Limited weekend hours. Still
know people who stereotype libraries as not being fun or friendly.

Where should the Brookfield Public Library be going? Include information on how WCFLS can and should help.

Continue to promote a unified system, but keep reflecting each community's unique personality.

Try to envision what a library will look like and act like at various points in the future, and strive to provide the services and technology to realize the vision. Strive for technological excellence, though not to the detriment of traditional library products of books, serials, tapes, etc. Market vigorously to enhance user base and increase circulation. Continue to provide an attractive and congenial physical plant and service-oriented staff. Maintain our commitment to providing optimum library services to all county residents, regardless of neighborhood library affiliation. WCFLS as an essential role in fostering this goal among all member libraries.

WCFLS can help by providing guidelines and ideas to help us be the best that we can be.

The library should take advantage of technology. The library needs to keep up with the needs of the community, as it changes and grows. I'm not sure how WCFLS can help.

Keep up on technology. Use tax dollars effectively, based on users. Continue teaching, summer programs. Keep current on books and materials. Linking libraries due to community. Survey, assessment on how libraries are doing, and accountability.

That is *the* question! WCFLS can help by attempting to give us a picture of the future. What types of services will be needed/provided? What will funding models look like? What type of physical space will be needed? We need to understand the impact of the Internet, and the expectations of residents in the socioeconomic class similar to Brookfield.

Continue to strive to be a gathering place for our community. Continue to try to keep up with the ever-changing technology. Continue to provide materials and programs to the changing demographics of our community. Continue to create and build on partnerships with Park and Rec, Wilson Center, public and private schools, civic organizations, etc. Tap into other civic events happening at the civic center concerts in the park, etc. Create a Friends group or foundation.

Census Data—Narrative

- At 2.8 percent, the unemployment rate in the 2000 Census was considerably lower than U.S. or state rates.

- The commuting time for a Brookfield resident is a lower than county, state, or national rates, but almost everyone commutes by private vehicle rather than by public transportation, bike, or foot.

- The 51 percent rate for management and professional employment was higher than county, state, and national rates.

- With 55 percent of household incomes at $75,000 or higher, Brookfield residents have much greater income than state or national averages, and do marginally better than even most county residents. At over $100,000, median income is twice the state average.

- Brookfield residents have a high level of educational attainment 49 percent have a bachelor's degree or higher, nearly twice the national average; 94 percent have a high school diploma compared to 80 percent nationally.

- Disability rates at every age level are lower in Brookfield than in the county, state, or nation.

- People in Brookfield tend to stay put by the 2000 census 64 percent were in the same home as in 1995 compared to 54 percent nationally.

- Nearly 9 percent of Brookfield residents speak a language other than English in the home. That is lower than the national average, but higher than found on average in the county or state.

BROOKFIELD PUBLIC LIBRARY
March 20, 2004

Number of Libraries in this Population Category:	911
HALPR Score for this Library	797
Rank of Libraries in this population category	49
Percentile	94.7%

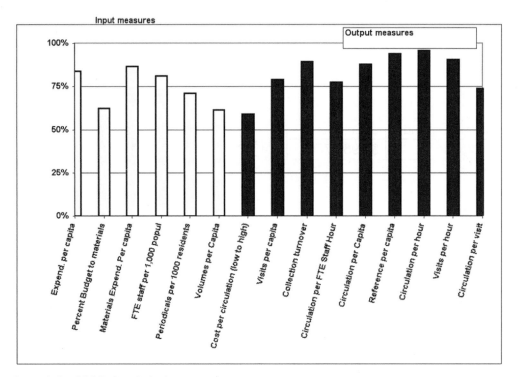

Copyright 2003: haplr-index.com
Permission to reprint with this notice included.

Table 1. Data, Rank and Percentile

Number of Libraries in this Population Category:	911
HALPR Score for this Library	797
Rank of Libraries in this population category	49
Percentile	95%

Name of Library   **BROOKFIELD PUBLIC LIBRARY**

Address   1900 N. CALHOUN RD.

City   BROOKFIELD

State   WI

Zip   53005

Population	44,273
FTE Staff	32.6
Collection Expend.	$320,680
Total Expend.	$1,959,760
Book Volumes	137,057
Periodical Subscr	382
Hours of service	3,427
Visits	295,125
Reference	90,350
Circulation	551,707

Note that population used is the **service area population** assigned by the Federal State Cooperative Service (U.S. Department of Education) not the census data population of the community.

Factor	Amount	Rank	Percentile	
Expend. per capita	$44.27	146	84%	Input Data
Percent Budget to materials	16.4%	343	62%	
Materials Expend. Per capita	7.24	123	86%	
FTE staff per 1,000 popul	0.74	173	81%	
Periodicals per 1000 residents	8.6	264	71%	
Volumes per Capita	3.1	353	61%	
Cost per circulation (low to high)	$3.55	373	59%	Output Data
Visits per capita	6.7	190	79%	
Collection turnover	4.0	96	89%	
Circulation per FTE Staff Hour	8.1	205	77%	
Circulation per Capita	12.5	110	88%	
Reference per capita	2.0	55	94%	
Circulation per hour	161.0	39	96%	
Visits per hour	86.1	85	91%	
Circulation per visit	1.9	237	74%	

Table 2. Percentile Comparisons for Input and Output Measures

Number of Libraries in this Population Category: 911

Measurement Category	HALPR Weight	BROOKFIELD PUBLIC LIBRARY	75th Percentile	50th Percentile	25th Percentile
Expend. per capita	3	$44.27	$35.41	$23.03	$13.56
Percent Budget to materials	2	16.4%	18.0%	14.9%	12.2%
Materials Expend. Per capita	2	$7.24	$5.43	$3.41	$1.88
FTE staff per 1,000 popul	2	0.74	0.67	0.45	0.31
Periodicals per 1000 residents	1	8.63	9.21	6.33	3.79
Volumes per Capita	1	3.10	3.59	2.66	1.85
Cost/circulation (low to high!)	3	$3.55	2.91	4.00	5.54
Visits per capita	3	6.67	5.98	4.15	2.44
Collection turnover	2	4.03	3.11	2.14	1.43
Circulation per FTE Staff Hour	2	8.14	7.84	5.96	4.37
Circulation per Capita	2	12.46	9.09	5.80	3.12
Reference per capita	2	2.04	1.00	0.51	0.26
Circulation per hour	2	160.99	81.37	47.56	25.12
Visits per hour	1	86.12	57.23	36.95	17.33
Circulation per visit	1	1.87	1.90	1.43	1.08

The HAPLR Index adds the scores for each library within a population category to develop a weighted score. The population categories change at **500,000; 250,000; 100,000; 50,000; 25,000; 10,000; 5,000; 2,500** and **1,000**. The HAPLR Index is similar to an ACT or SAT score with a theoretical minimum of 1 and a maximum of 1,000, although most libraries score between 260 and 730. The index includes data for print services, book checkouts, reference service, funding and staffing. It excludes audio and video data, as well as Internet access and other electronic measurement.

Number of Libraries in this Population Category: 911

NATIONAL Comparisons	BROOKFIELD PUBLIC LIBRARY	ROWLETT PUBLIC LIBRARY	BELLEVUE PUBLIC LIBRARY	SISKIYOU COUNTY FREE LIBRARY	WINDHAM CO. READS	SEGUIN GUADALUPE COUNTY PUBLIC LIBRARY
City	BROOKFIELD	ROWLETT	BELLEVUE	YREKA	WEST BRATTLE-BORO	SEGUIN
State	WI	TX	NE	CA	VT	TX
Zip	53005	75088	68005	96097	05303	78155
Population	44,273	44,503	44,382	44,300	44,216	44,161
HAPLR Rating	797	305	538	369	195	473
Overall Percentile Rank	49	740	407	655	863	507
Expend. per capita	$44.27	$15.05	$17.97	$20.54	$24.76	$8.20
Percent Budget to materials	16.4%	16.5%	13.7%	6.6%	0.5%	22.5%
Materials Expend. Per capita	$7.24	$2.48	$2.46	$1.35	$0.12	$1.85
FTE staff per 1,000 popul	0.74	0.27	0.36	0.35	0.03	0.18
Periodicals per 1000 residents	8.63	2.88	4.55	5.76	0.14	2.72
Volumes per Capita	3.10	1.18	2.53	3.32	0.08	1.37
Cost per circulation (low to high)	$3.55	$5.88	$2.57	$3.94	$122.66	$2.11
Visits per capita	6.67	1.99	4.18	2.71	0.14	3.19
Collection turnover	4.03	2.17	2.77	1.57	2.56	2.83
Circulation per FTE Staff Hour	8.14	4.56	9.27	7.17	3.67	10.33
Circulation per Capita	12.46	2.56	7.00	5.21	0.20	3.89
Reference per capita	2.04	0.15	0.26	0.46	0.79	0.50
Circulation per hour	160.99	52.50	86.53	18.47	20.66	53.63
Visits per hour	86.12	40.92	51.70	9.60	14.77	43.97
Circulation per visit	1.87	1.28	1.67	1.92	1.40	1.22

Note that population used is the service area population assigned by the Federal State Cooperative Service (U.S. Department of Education) not the census data population of the community. The FSCS web site is at: http://nces.ed.gov/surveys/public.html#contents.

Number of Libraries in this Population Category: 911

STATE Comparisons	BROOKFIELD PUBLIC LIBRARY	WAUWATOSA PUBLIC LIBRARY	BELOIT PUBLIC LIBRARY	MARINETTE COUNTY CONSOLIDATED PUBLIC LIBRARY	SUPERIOR PUBLIC LIBRARY	SHAWANO CITY-COUNTY
City	BROOKFIELD	WAUWATOSA	BELOIT	MARINETTE	SUPERIOR	SHAWANO
State	WI	WI	WI	WI	WI	WI
Zip	53005	53213	53511	54143	54880	54166
Population	44,273	47,221	44,783	43,589	43,506	40,901
HAPLR Rating	797	818	662	469	592	535
Overall Percentile Rank	49	28	208	511	330	412
Expend. per capita	$44.27	$35.11	$34.79	$16.04	$28.01	$16.20
Percent Budget to materials	16.4%	13.6%	12.0%	17.8%	10.2%	16.9%
Materials Expend. Per capita	$7.24	$4.79	$4.17	$2.86	$2.85	$2.73
FTE staff per 1,000 popul	0.7	0.6	0.6	0.3	0.5	0.4
Periodicals per 1000 residents	8.6	6.5	7.1	15.7	6.6	3.7
Volumes per Capita	3.1	3.7	3.0	3.6	2.7	3.1
Cost per circulation (low to high)	$3.55	$2.12	$4.08	$3.93	$3.40	$2.23
Visits per capita	6.7	7.4	5.8	7.4	5.5	4.4
Collection turnover	4.0	4.5	2.9	1.1	3.0	2.3
Circulation per FTE Staff Hour	8.1	13.2	6.8	5.7	7.5	9.2
Circulation per Capita	12.5	16.6	8.5	4.1	8.2	7.3
Reference per capita	2.0	5.0	2.4	0.8	0.4	0.6
Circulation per hour	161.0	230.7	123.3	17.6	107.4	28.5
Visits per hour	86.1	102.5	84.2	32.1	72.0	17.2
Circulation per visit	1.9	2.3	1.5	0.5	1.5	1.7

Note that population used is the service area population assigned by the Federal State Cooperative Service (U.S. Department of Education) not the census data population of the community. The FSCS web site is at: http://nces.ed.gov/surveys/public.html#contents.

Bibliography

Contents

General

Hayes, Robert M., and Virginia A. Walter. 1996. *Strategic Management for Public Libraries: A Handbook.* Westport, CT: Greenwood Press. A comprehensive but very technical treatment that will probably be used by only larger libraries engaged in planning.

Larson, Jeanette, and Herman Totten. 1998. *Model Policies for Small and Medium Public Libraries.* New York: Neal-Schuman.

McCabe, Ronald B. 2001. *Civic Librarianship: Renewing the Social Mission of the Public Library.* Metuchen, NJ: Scarecrow Press. When libraries build community, communities return the favor. This book looks at the communitarian movement and urges libraries to plan to be integral parts of their community. A useful item for planners and policy makers.

Molz, Redmond Kathleen, and Phyllis Dain. 1999. *Civic Space/Cyberspace: The American Public Library in the Information Age.* Cambridge: MIT Press. An excellent overall description of the place of the history and prospects of libraries as an American institution.

———. 1990. *Library Planning and Policymaking: The Legacy of the Public and Private Sectors.* Metuchen, NJ: Scarecrow Press. Provides an excellent overview of the types of planning literature and techniques developed for the public and business sectors and how these trends have influenced the development of library planning in the U.S.

Walter, Virginia A. 1992. *Output Measures for Public Library Service to Children: A Manual of Standardized Procedures.* Chicago: American Library Association.

Zweizig, Douglas, et al. 1993. *Evaluating Library Programs and Services: TELL IT!* Madison, WI: UW School of Library and Information Studies.

———. *The Tell It! Manual: The Complete Program for Evaluating Library Performance.* Chicago: American Library Association, 1996. These two items are the result of a grant by the U.S. Office of Education to the University of Wisconsin library school. They are based on a series of workshops by the participants and provide a useful way of talking about what libraries do for their communities.

Governance and Administration

Hayes, Robert M. 2001. *Models for Library Management, Decision-Making, and Planning* (with CD-ROM). San Diego: Academic Press.

Kuntz, Jerry. "LibraryLand Index to Resources for Librarians." LibraryLand. Available: http://sunsite.berkeley.edu/Library Land/admin/policy.htm. This site contains links to sample public library policies on the Web.

Mason, Mailyn Gell. 1999. *Strategic Management for Today's Libraries*. Chicago: American Library Association.

Minow, Mary, and Tomas Lipinski. 2003. *The Library's Legal Answer Book*. Chicago: American Library Association.

Nelson, Sandra, and June Garcia. 2003. *Creating Policies for Results: From Chaos to Clarity*. Chicago: American Library Association.

Nelson, Sandra, Ellen Altman, and Diane Mayo. 2000. *Managing for Results: Effective Resource Allocation for Public Libraries*. Chicago: American Library Association. This book, produced for the Public Library Association, is the third in a series. The first two in the series are *Planning for Results* and *Wired for the Future*. It contains lots of data forms and samples, and the work forms on staffing are particularly useful. It has a sparse index and no bibliographic citations.

Sager, Donald J. 2000. *Small Libraries: Organization and Operation*. 3rd ed. Fort Atkinson, WI: Highsmith Press.

Weingand, Darlene E. 2001. *Administration of the Small Public Library*, 4th ed. Chicago: American Library Association.

Budgeting and Financial Administration

American Library Association. "Library Operating Expenditures: A Selected Annotated Bibliography." *ALA Library Fact Sheet Number 4*. Available: www.ala.org/library/fact4.html. This bibliography was prepared to describe sources of information on library operating expenditures. It covers public, academic, and school libraries.

Hamon, Peter, Darlene E. Weingand, and Al Zimmerman. 1992. *Budgeting and the Political Process in Libraries: Simulation Games.* Englewood, CO: Libraries Unlimited. Library budgeting is, of course a very serious game. The authors use game theory to help library planners improve their game.

Smith, G. Stevenson. 1999. *Accounting for Libraries and Other Not-for-Profit Organizations.* 2nd ed. Chicago: American Library Association. This book helps deal with audits and fund accounting. A companion volume, *Managerial Accounting for Libraries and Other Not-for-Profit Organizations,* covers issue relating to cost analysis of proj ects and other managerial accounting issues.

————. 2002. *Managerial Accounting for Libraries and Other Not-for-Profit Organizations.* 2nd ed. Chicago: American Library Association.

Trumpter, Margo C. 1985. *Basic Budgeting Practices for Librarians.* Chicago: American Library Association. This older volume provides very basic and accessible information on library budgets. It includes information on line item and zero-based budgeting, but not on program budgets, which did not come into vogue until after the book was published.

Turock, Betty J., and Andrea Pedolsky. 1992. *Creating a Financial Plan: A How-To-Do-It Manual for Librarians.* New York: Neal-Schuman. Written by the editor of *The Bottom Line* magazine, this book deals with financial planning as opposed to simply budgeting. It recommends strategies for setting objectives tied to a multiyear financial plan.

Fund Raising

American Library Association. *Library Fund Raising: A Selected Annotated Bibliography.* ALA Library Fact Sheet Number 24. American Library Association. Available: www.ala.org/library/fact24.html.

American Library Association, and Taft Group. 2002. *The Big Book of Library Grant Money, 2002–2003: Profiles of Private and Corporate Foundations and Direct Corporate Givers*

Receptive to Library Grant Proposals. Chicago: American Library Association.

Corson-Finnerty, Adam. 1998. *Fundraising and Friend-raising on the Web.* Chicago: American Library Association.

Geever, Jane C. 2004. *The Foundation Center's Guide to Proposal Writing.* 4th ed. New York: The Foundation Center. Available: http://fdncenter.org/learn/shortcourse/prop1.html.

Reed, Sally Gardner. 2001. *Making the Case for Your Library: A How-To-Do-It Manual.* New York: Neal-Schuman.

Sherman-Smith, Amy. 2000. *Legacies for Libraries: A Practical Guide to Planned Giving.* Chicago: American Library Association.

Steele, Victoria. 2000. *Becoming a Fundraiser: The Principles and Practice of Library Development.* Chicago: American Library Association.

Swan, James. 2002. *Fundraising for Libraries: 25 Proven Ways to Get More Money for Your Library.* New York: Neal-Schuman.

Public Relations

Baker, Sharon L., and Karen L. Wallace. 2002. *The Responsive Public Library: How to Develop and Market a Winning Collection.* Englewood, CO: Libraries Unlimited.

Jones, Patrick. 2002. *Running a Successful Library Card Campaign: A How-To-Do-It-Manual.* New York: Neal-Schuman.

Karp, Rashelle S. 2002. *Powerful Public Relations: A How-To Guide for Libraries.* Chicago: American Library Association. This useful volume includes information on Web-based PR, news releases, desktop publishing, and more.

Walters, Suzanne. 2003. *Marketing: A How-To-Do-It Manual for Librarians.* New York: Neal-Schuman.

Staffing

Hayes, Robert M. 2001. *Models for Library Management, Decision-making, and Planning.* San Diego: Academic Press.

Metz, Ruth F. 2002. *Coaching in the Library: A Management Strategy for Achieving Excellence.* Chicago: American Library Association.

Rubin, Richard E. 1993. *Hiring Library Employees: A How-to-Do-It Manual.* New York: Neal-Schuman. Dated, but still contains relevant information.

Collection and Resources

American Library Association. 2002. *ALA's Guide to Best Reading in 2002.* Chicago: American Library Association. This is a good checklist source for most libraries interested in evaluation of the quality and usability of their selections and selection process.

———. 1996. *Intellectual Freedom Manual.* 5th ed. Compiled by the Office for Intellectual Freedom of the American Library Association. Chicago: American Library Association. It would be a mistake to devise a collection development policy or long range plans on collections without reference to this work, or at least the principles it delineates.

Baker, Sharon L. 2002. *The Responsive Public Library: How to Develop and Market a Winning Collection.* Englewood, CO: Libraries Unlimited.

Boon, Belinda. 1995. *The Crew Method: Expanded Guidelines for Collection Evaluation and Weeding for Small and Medium-Sized Public Libraries.* Revision for the Texas State Library of the 1976 CREW manual by Joseph P. Segal. Chicago: American Library Association. This classic work has helped many, many libraries to get through the often diffi cult process of weeding the collection down to manageable and useful size.

Cassell, Kay Ann. 1999. *Developing Reference Collections and Services in an Electronic Age: A How-To-Do-It Manual for Librarians.* New York: Neal-Schuman.

Gregory, Vicki L. 2000. *Selecting and Managing Electronic Resources: A How-To-Do-It Manual for Librarians.* New York: Neal-Schuman. This very useful item should be consulted by those seeking to navigate the turbulent waters of data base and other electronic resources. Great information on pricing, copyright and licensing issues are provided for library planners.

Saricks, Joyce G. 2001. *The Readers' Advisory Guide to Genre Fiction* Chicago: American Library Association.

Saricks, Joyce, and Nancy Brown. 1997. *Reader's Advisory Service in the Public Library.* Chicago: American Library Association.

Slote, Stanley J. 1982. *Weeding Library Collections II.* 2nd rev. ed. Littleton, CO: Libraries Unlimited.

Sweetland, James H. 2001. *Fundamental Reference Sources.* 3rd ed. Chicago: American Library Association.

Wynar, Bohdan, ed. 2002. *Recommended Reference Books for Small and Medium-sized Libraries and Media Centers, 2002.* Greenwood Village, CO: Libraries Unlimited.

Services to Special Populations

American Library Association. 1992. *Library Standards for Adult Correctional Facilities, 1992.* Prepared by the Association of Specialized and Cooperative Library Agencies, a division of the American Library Association. Chicago: American Library Association.

———. 1999. *Library Standards for Juvenile Correctional Facilities.* Prepared by the Association of Specialized and Cooperative Library Agencies, a division of the American Library Association. Chicago: American Library Association.

Cirillo, Susan E., and Robert E. Danford. 1996. *Library Buildings and the ADA: Compliance Issues and Solutions.* Chicago: American Library Association. This is the publication of the proceedings of a Library Administration and Management Association conference on Americans with Disabilities Act requirements as they apply to public libraries. It contains very specific and useful specifications regarding a variety of ADA requirements as they affect libraries.

McCook, Kathleen de La Pe a. 2000. *A Place at the Table: Participating in Community Building.* Chicago: American Library Association. Beautifully written and important, this book will inspire planners to assure that every type of user does, indeed, have a place at the library table.

405

Quezada, Shelley. 1996. *Developing Literacy Programs in Small and Medium-Sized Libraries.* LAMA Small Libraries Publications Series. Chicago: American Library Association.

Access and Facilities

Brawner, Lee B., and Donald K. Beck, Jr. 1996. *Determining Your Public Library's Future Size: A Needs Assessment and Planning Model.* Chicago: American Library Association.

Dahlgren, Anders. 1996. *Planning the Small Public Library Building.* 2nd ed. LAMA Small Libraries Publications Series. Chicago: American Library Association.

———. 1998. *Public Library Space Needs: A Planning Outline.* Madison, WI: Department of Public Instruction. Available: www.dpi.state.wi.us/dltcl/pld/plspace.html. This very useful guide to space needs assessment is also reprinted on the CD accompanying this volume.

Dancik, Deborah, and Emelie J. Shroder, eds. 1995. *Building Blocks for Library Space: Functional Guidelines 1995.* Chicago: Library Administration and Management Association.

Hagloch, Susan B. 1994. *Tips for Survival.* Englewood, CO: Libraries Unlimited. This is a useful assessment of how to get through a building project from a library director who has been there and done that.

Kahn, Miriam B. 2002. *Disaster Response and Planning for Libraries.* 2nd ed. Chicago: American Library Association. This guide for writing a disaster plan has been completely revised and updated from the 1998 original. New information has been added since 9/11 recovery.

Koontz, Christine M. 1997. *Library Facilities Siting and Location Handbook.* Westport, CT: Greenwood Press.

Sannwald, William W. 1996. *Checklist of Library Building Design Considerations.* 3rd ed. Chicago: American Library Association.

Internet and Automation Technology

Bertot, John Carlo, Charles R. McClure, and Joe Ryan. 2001. *Statistics and Performance Measures for Public Library Networked Services.* Chicago: American Library Association.

Bocher, Robert. 1999. *Library Technology Planning: An Outline of the Process*. Madison, WI: Department of Public Instruction. Available: www.dpi.state.wi.us/dltcl/pld/planout.html.

Jones, Barbara M. 1999. *Libraries, Access, and Intellectual Freedom: Developing Policies for Public and Academic Libraries*. Chicago: American Library Association. Compare this to the Smith volume below. This book takes the ALA Intellectual Freedom position on the subject.

Mayo, Diane, and Sandra Nelson. 1999. *Wired for the Future: Developing Your Library Technology Plan*. Chicago: American Library Association.

Pew Internet and American Life Project. An Initiative of the Pew Research Center, a project of the Tides Center, and fully funded by the Pew Charitable Trust. Available: www.pewinternet.org.

Schneider, Karen G. 1997. *A Practical Guide to Internet Filters*. New York: Neal Schuman. The former "Internet Librarian" at *American Libraries* magazine and current head of the Librarian's Index to the Internet led a team of librarians in developing this useful critique of filters. Although the fil ters have changed and the Web has changed since its publication, there is still much here for library planners to consider about Internet filtering.

Smith, Mark. 1999. *Internet Policy Handbook for Libraries*. New York: Neal-Schuman. The author acknowledges that at times libraries may end up restricting access and allows for the development of such policies in a professional and careful manner. Compare to Jones volume above, which sticks more closely to the ALA Intellectual Freedom positions on the issues.

Trustee Manuals on the Web

Alabama Public Library Trustee Manual. Available: www.apls.state.al.us/webpages/pubs/TrusteeManual.pdf.

Connecticut Public Library Trustee Handbook. Available: www.aclb.org/TrusteesHandbook.pdf.

Illinois Fact File: Available: www.cyberdriveillinois.com/library/isl/ref/readyref/pdf/trustee/ILA_Trustee.pdf.

Indiana. IN The Public Trust. Available: www.statelib.lib.in.us/ WWW/LDO/TMAppdx.html.

Iowa Public Library Trustee Handbook, 1998. Available: www.ilsa .lib.ia.us/trustees.htm.

Kansas Public Library Trustee Handbook. Available: http://sky ways.lib.ks.us/KSL/development/trustee.html.

Kentucky Public Library Trustee Manual. Available: www.kdla .state.ky.us/libserv/trustees/trusteemanual.pdf.

Maine Library Association Public Library Standards. Available: www.mainelibraries.org/standards/mla_chap1.htm.

Minnesota Public Library Trustee Handbook. Available: http://cfl .state.mn.us/library/trustees.html.

Michigan Public Library Trustee Manual 1998 edition. Available: http://persephone.libofmich.lib.mi.us/publications/trustee98 _1.html.

Montana Public Library Trustee Manual. Available: http://msl .state.mt.us/slr/trustee.pdf

Nebraska Trustee Handbook. Available: www.nlc.state.ne.us/ libdev/trustee/preface.html.

New Hampshire Library Trustees. Available: www.state.nh.us/ nhlta/manual.htm.

New York State Library Trustees Handbook. Available: www .nysalb.org/Handbook.pdf.

Rhode Island Public Library Trustee Handbook, 1999. Available: www.lori.state.ri.us/trustees/default.htm.

Utah Library Trustee Roles and Responsibilities. Available: www .state.lib.ut.us/trustee2.html#Effective.

Virginia Public Library Trustee Handbook, 1999. Available: www .lva.lib.va.us/ldnd/trustee/trustee.htm.

Washington Public Library Trustee Manual. Available: http://wlo .statelib.wa.gov/services/trustee_manual/trustees.htm.

Wisconsin Library Trustee Resource Page: Tools and Resources for Wisconsin Public Library Board Members (Trustees). Available: www.dpi.state.wi.us/dpi/dltcl/pld/trustee.html.

Outcome Based Measures

Durrance, Joan C., and Karen E. Fisher. "Determining How Libraries and Librarians Help." *Library Trends* 51, no. 4:

305–334. Available: www.ischool.washington.edu/fisher/pubs/library.trends.2003.pdf.

Durrance, Joan C., and Karen Pettigrew-Fisher. "Putting Outcome Evaluation in Context: A Toolkit." School of Information, University of Michigan. Available: www.si.umich.edu/libhelp. An online Outcome-Based Evaluation Toolkit launched by researchers in the School of Information at the University of Michigan and the Information School at the University of Washington.

Holt, Glen E., Donald Elliott, and Amonia Moore. "Placing a Value on Public Library Services." St. Louis Public Library. Available: www.slpl.lib.mo.us/libsrc/restoc.htm.

Lance, Keith Curry, et al. "Counting on Results." Library Research Service. Available: www.lrs.org/Pub_Res.htm. The Counting on Results (CoR) study is a nationwide examination of the impact of public library services on individual patrons. Volunteer libraries throughout the U.S. participated in the project.

ALA's Planning Process Series

American Library Association, Public Library Association. 1979. *The Public Library Mission Statement and Its Imperatives for Service.* Chicago: American Library Association. While this volume is not technically part of the Planning Process series, it is one of the pivotal documents in the change from standards to output based standards. It looks at the need for locally defined mission statements and fol lows the then-prevailing atmosphere for public enterprise planning.

Himmel, Ethel, and William James Wilson. 1998. *Planning for Results: A Public Library Transformation Process.* Chicago: American Library Association. Third in the series. Roles were described as "service responses," and the book was divided into two separate volumes with one including the work forms and the other including descriptive materials.

McClure, Charles R., et al. 1987. *Planning and Role Setting for Public Libraries.* Chicago: American Library Association. As the title implies, this book focused on both the planning process and the roles indicated in the previous item in the series. In addition to focusing on out put (see the output

409

measures volume by Van House, et al.) it concentrated on defining distinct roles for libraries.

Nelson, Sandra, for the Public Library Association. 2001. *The New Planning for Results: A Streamlined Approach.* Chicago: American Library Association. This volume marked the fourth in the series, just three years after the previous in the Planning Process series. It continues the strong stress on role definitions and the assertion that excellence must be defined locally by the library with less emphasis on comparisons to other similar libraries.

Palmour, Vernon E., and Marcia C. Bellassai. 1977. *To Satisfy Demand: A Study Plan for Public Library Service in Baltimore County.* Arlington, VA: Center for Naval Analyses, Public Research Institute. While this volume is not techni cally part of the Planning Process series, it set the stage for the move from quantitative standards to a planning process that emphasized role setting, output measures, and locally determined goals and objectives.

Palmour, Vernon E., Marcia C. Bellassai, and Nancy V. DeWath. 1980. *A Planning Process for Public Libraries.* Chicago: American Library Association. This volume marked the aban donment of standards in favor of planning for outputs.

Van House, Nancy A., et al. 1987. *Output Measures for Public Libraries: A Manual of Standardized Procedures,* 2nd ed. Chicago: American Library Association.

Van House, Nancy A., and Thomas A. Childers. 1993. *The Public Library Effectiveness Study.* Chicago: American Library Association.

Outcome Assessment

STANDARDS AND PLANNING—MONOGRAPHS

American Library Association, Public Libraries Division. 1956. *Public Library Service.* Chicago: American Library Association.

American Library Association, Public Libraries Division. 1966. *Minimum Standards for Public Library System* Chicago: American Library Association.

Berelson, Bernard. 1949. *The Library's Public: A Report of the Public Library Inquiry.* New York: Columbia University Press.

Geiske, Joan. 1998. *Scenario Planning for Libraries.* Chicago: American Library Association.

Joeckel, Carleton B. *The Government of the American Public Library.* Chicago: University of Chicago Press, 1935.

Joeckel, Carleton B., and Amy Winslow. 1948. *A National Plan for Public Library Service.* Chicago: American Library Association.

Junion-Metz, Gail, and Derrek L. Metz. 2001. *Instant Web Forms and Surveys for Public Libraries.* New York: Neal-Schuman.

Leigh, Robert D. 1950. *The Public Library in the United States.* New York: Columbia University Press. The Inquiry was funded with a $200,000 grant to the American Library Association from the Carnegie Foundation. ALA contracted with the Social Science Research Council at the University of Michigan to conduct the study, which resulted in at least ten volumes published between 1949 and 1952.

Shera, Jesse. 1949. *Foundations of the Public Library: The Origins of the Public Library Movement in New England, 1629–1855.* Chicago: University of Chicago Press. This classic work is still worth considering more than a half century after its publication for its insights into the roots and prospects of the American public library experiment.

U.S. National Commission on Libraries and Information Science. 1975. *Toward a National Program for Library and Information Services: Goals for Action.* Washington, DC: U.S. Government Printing Office.

STANDARDS AND PLANNING—PERIODICAL, ARTICLES AND REPORTS

DeProspo, Ernest R. 1971. *Measurement of Effectiveness of Public Library Service Study. A Report on Phases I and II.* Bureau of Libraries and Educational Technology (Deparment of Health, Education, and Welfare/Department of Education, Washington, DC). Public Library Association: Chicago.

411

Hennen, Thomas J., Jr. 2000. "Why We Should Establish a National System of Standards." *American Libraries* (March): 43–45.

Moorman, John. 1997. "Standards for Public Libraries: A Study in Quantitative Measures of Library Performance as Found in State Public Library Documents." *Public Libraries* 36, no.1 (January/February): 32–39.

O'Connor, Daniel O. 1982. "Evaluating Public Libraries Using Standard Scores: The Library Quotient." *Library Research.* 4, no. 1 (Spring): 51–70.

Owen, Amy. 1992. "Current Issues and Patterns in State Standards for Public Library Service." *Public Libraries* 31, no. 4 (July/August): 213–22.

———. 1991. "Public Library Standards: The Quest for Excellence." White House Conference on Library and Information Services. Paper prepared for the White House Conference on Library and Information Services (Washington, DC, July 9–13).

Van House, Nancy A., and Thomas Childers. 1990. "Dimensions of Public Library Effectiveness II: Library Performance." *Library and Information Science Research* 12, no. 2 (April-June): 131–153.

Weech, Terry L. 1989. "National Accreditation of Public Libraries: A Historical Perspective." *Public Libraries* 28, no. 2 (March/April): 119–125.

Wheeler, Joseph L. 1970. "What Good Are Public Library Standards?" *Library Journal* 95, no. 3 (February 1): 455–462.

Author's Publications

2002. "Are Wider Library Units Wiser?" *American Libraries,* June/July: 65–70.

1986. "Attacking the Myths of Small Libraries." *American Libraries* 17, no. 11 (December): 830–834.

1999. "Building Benchmarks to Craft a Better Library Future." *Australasian Public Libraries and Information Services* 12, no. 2 (June): 52–59. Available: www.haplr-index.com/APLIS HAPLR99.pdf.

2000. "Catalog as Community: A Metadata Meditation." *Library Computing* (Formerly *Library Software Review*) 18, nos. 1/2 (March/June).

1981. "Catalog Stores, Smoky the Bear, Stone Soup and Libraries." *Occasional Papers of the Minnesota Library Association.* 1–6.

1999. "Celebrating the Best Ranked HAPLR Index Libraries in Ohio." OCLC Press release. December 9, 1999. Available: www.haplrindex.com/OCLCPressRelease12Dec99.htm.

2001. "Do You Know the Real Value of Your Library?" *Library Journal* 126, no. 11 (June 15): 48–50.

1982. "The Effect of Publisher's Book Promotions on Interlibrary Loan," in *Research and Reality: Library Services to Rural Populations*, edited by J. Houlahan, 48–57. Chicago: American Library Association.

1980–1986. "Farming and Rural Materials" (quarterly book review column). *Booklist.*

1999. "Go Ahead, Name Them: America s Best Public Libraries." *American Libraries* 30, no. 1 (January): 72–76. Available: www.ala.org/alonline/archive/hennen.pdf.

2000. "Great American Public Libraries: HAPLR Ratings, 2000." *American Libraries* 31, no. 10 (November): 50–54.

2002. "Great American Public Libraries: The 2002 HAPLR Rankings." *American Libraries* 33, no. 9 (October): 64–68.

2003. "Great American Public Libraries: The 2003 HAPLR Rankings." *American Libraries* 34, no. 9 (October): 44–48. Available: www.ala.org/Content/ContentGroups/American_Libraries1/ALOnline_Home_Page_Content/hennen2003.pdf.

1999. "Great American Public Libraries: HAPLR Ratings, Round Two." *American Libraries* 30, no. 8 (September): 64–68.

1999– . "Hennen's American Public Library Rating Index (HAPLR)." Available since January 1999 on the World Wide Web: www.haplr-index.com.

1999. "Index Rates Wisconsin Libraries Highly." *Communique* (a publication of the Wisconsin Library Association) (Spring): 5.

1996. "Invited Introductory Testimony to the Wisconsin Legislative Study Committee on Libraries." October 3, 1996. Available: www.haplr-index.com/LEGCOU96 FINAL.htm.

1977. "Let There Be Peace in Children's Literature." *Language Arts* 54, no. 1 (January): 66–70.

1981. "Library Services to Farmers." *American Library Trustee's Association Publication Number 3.* Chicago: American Library Association. 6-page pamphlet.

1988. "Invitational Conference on the Future of the Public Library: Public Librarians Take Cool View of Future." *American Libraries* 19 (May): 390–92.

2003. "Performing Triage on Budgets in the Red." *American Libraries* 34, no. 3 (March): 36–39.

1981. "Popular Farm Magazines." *Serials Review* 7, no. 3 (July/September): 12–14.

1980. "Publicity for Rural Areas." *Library P.R. News* 13, no. 6 (November/December).

1986. "Rural Libraries Seen as Centers for Hope and Learning." *American Libraries* 17, no. 5 (May): 323.

1981. "Seeds of Power." Self-published pamphlet. (Sold to over 3,000 libraries in 50 states and 6 Canadian provinces.)

1978. "Serving the Last Minority." *Library Journal Special Report*, Number 6: 46–50.

1980. "Using the Minnesota Statutes, Code of Agency Rules, and State Register." *Minnesota Libraries* (Spring): 48–56.

2000. "Why We Should Establish a National System of Standards." *American Libraries* 31, no. 3 (March): 43–45. Available: www.haplr-index.com/LibraryStandardsArticle.htm.

Index

About the Author

Thomas J. Hennen Jr. has over 30 years of library experience. He is presently the Director of Waukesha County Federated Library System in Wisconsin. He previously directed library systems elsewhere in Wisconsin and Minnesota.

He is the author of more than forty articles on topics ranging from children's literature to rural library service to library futures, standards, and accounting that have been published in library periodicals such as *Library Journal, American Libraries,* and *Australian Library and Information Science Journal.*

He has addressed professional library associations in 15 U.S. states and in several Canadian provinces.